THE
HOLY LAND

THE
HOLY LAND

TEXT
FABIO BOURBON
ENRICO LAVAGNO

DESIGN
CLARA ZANOTTI

ENGLISH TRANSLATION
RICHARD PIERCE

CONTENTS

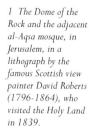

1 The Dome of the Rock and the adjacent al-Aqsa mosque, in Jerusalem, in a lithograph by the famous Scottish view painter David Roberts (1796-1864), who visited the Holy Land in 1839.

2-3 In this magnificent aerial view of the Old City of Jerusalem seen from the East, the Haram es-Sharif esplanade stands out in the foreground. At left is the grey al-Aqsa mosque and, in the middle, the dazzling Dome of the Rock. The square opposite the Western Wall can be seen at left, while the dome of the Holy Sepulchre is in the upper central part of the photograph.

© 2003 White Star S.r.l.
Via Candido Sassone, 22-24
13100 Vercelli, Italy
www.whitestar.it

ISBN 88-8095-920-4
REPRINTS:
1 2 3 4 5 6   07 06 05 04 03
Printed by C&C Offset Printing Co. LTD, China

MEDITERRANEAN
SEA

Baram
Safed
Monfort
Korazim
Acre
Capernaum
Qasrin
Sepphoris
Tabga
Gamla
Bet She'arim
Kursi
Tiberias
Dor
Hammat Gader
Megiddo
Belvoir
Cesarea
Bet Shean
Pella
Taanach
Bet Alpha
Nazareth
Gerasa
Jericho
Qumran
AMMAN
Ashdod
JERUSALEM
Bethlehem
Madaba
Ashqelon
Herodium
Mar Saba
Bet Guvrin
En Gedi
DEAD SEA
Arad
Masada
Beer Sheba
al-Karak

ISRAEL

Shivta
Mamshit

Avdat

ash-Shawbak

Petra

Timna

SINAI
PENINSULA

JORDAN

GULF OF SUEZ

GULF OF AQABA

St. Catherine

INTRODUCTION

What immediately strikes one about the Holy Land is the relatively small size of a region whose history and culture are almost beyond comparison. The fields of human activity that rose up and developed in the territory ranging from Egypt in the south to the plateaus of Iraq in the east–the so-called 'Fertile Crescent' of which Palestine is the central-southern section–are amazingly more numerous and important than any other place in the world. It was in this crucial area of historic geography that, at the end of the Stone Age, the human race took the first steps in the development of agriculture, metallurgy, urban and social-political organization, trade, and–an innovation of crucial importance–in the total mastery of the art of writing, from ideographic-cuneiform script to the alphabet we know today. The essential key to unveiling the fascination of these ancient lands and following their evolution–which is the theme of this guide–is naturally the archaeological research which for over one hundred years has brought to light mighty fortified cities 7,000 years old; immense palaces and other monuments decorated with exquisitely beautiful mosaics; ports and quays that have witnessed the passage of goods such as the purple dye, gold and lapis lazuli of the Egyptian pharaohs and spices from the East, as well as the arrival of the Sea Peoples, Philistines, Romans, Crusaders and others who, attracted by its resources and history, have gone to Palestine. Though the surface area is small, the field of research is vast. Using the Dead Sea as an ideal center, this volume takes in over 50 localities scattered throughout the territory: from the luxuriant slopes of Mount Hermon, sacred to the woodland divinities, to the mines at Timna, the most ancient in the world, and from the slopes of Mount Carmel facing the Mediterranean and already inhabited in very ancient times, to the incomparable ruins of Petra and the Nabataean cities. Thus readers will follow the trade routes used by merchants, bandits and armies from the Neolithic era to the present. They will cross over the thresholds of the megalithic gates and house doors of the first cities built by Man, and admire the mosaics that decorated the luxurious palaces of Herod the Great as well as the basilicas, synagogues, Crusader churches and mosques that are a testament to a sequence of cultures that is perhaps unique in the entire world. However, the ancientness and wealth of archaeological and cultural marvels are not the only fascinating features of Palestine, as is demonstrated by the simple fact that this land has been called 'Holy' to underscore its other fundamental characteristic, a factor that is truly unique: the presence of the divine as revealed by the testimony of the Patriarchs, brought to light from the depths of time after being hidden in the Dead Sea Scrolls at Qumran, and by the teachings of Jesus, which in the cultural history of the Holy Land introduced an urgent appeal for peace and brotherhood, the first and certainly the only such message in the course of many centuries. The singular sequence and superimposition of events that caused the sacred Promised Land of the Jews to become equally holy for Christians and, to a large extent, for Muslims as well, can be seen in many of the sites described in this guide–such as Nazareth, Capernaum and Tiberias, names that are familiar to all of us–but above all in Jerusalem, the magnificent epitome of the Holy City (indeed, the thrice holy city), rich in sites that are worshipped either spiritually or physically by millions of persons throughout the world. This guide therefore proposes a journey through thick layers of the archaeological past and equally important and unique strata of the spiritual past and present. However, readers will notice that, besides the historic and artistic uniqueness, because of their position as a sort of crossroad of spheres of influence of great and warlike civilizations, the sites in the Holy Land are often marked by a history of centuries-old conflicts that unfortunately are still very much alive. From this point of view, delving into the history and traditions of this region of the world can also offer an opportunity to appreciate fully the need for peace and to disseminate the hope that the religions that have risen here can finally move in the direction of tolerance and understanding.

HISTORIC SURVEY

FROM THE STONE AGE TO THE IRON AGE

6 This marble griffo—carved in the Seleucid period (311-65 BC) and kept in the Israel Museum, Jerusalem—depicts Nemesis, the implacable goddess of divine retribution. The overbearing fiscal and religious policy of the Seleucid rulers in Palestine provoked the Maccabean revolt.

7 left A cow's head decorates this bone tool produced by an artisan who lived around the 9th millennium BC, during the period of the Natufian culture.

7 right A bronze crown found at Nahal Mishmar, in the Judaean desert. It dates from the Chalcolithic age and may depict the two entrances to a temple.

Prehistoric man inhabited Palestine in very ancient times: in fact, the oldest human remains date from around 1,400,000 years ago, at the dawn of the Stone Age, and belong to the *Homo erectus* species, the first hominid who began moving from central-eastern Africa about two million years ago to begin the human colonization of the Earth. At that time humans hunted and gathered wild fruit. They lived, primarily, along the rivers, which, because of the significantly more humid climate, were larger and more numerous than today, especially in those areas that are now deserts such as the Sahara, Sinai and the Mesopotamian plains.

In order to note the first signs of progress from the most ancient settlements we must go back thousands and thousands of years: the slopes of Mount Carmel, Wadi el-Amud and Gebel Qafzeh are three sites in Palestine that have left traces of *Homo sapiens neanderthalensis*, who settled between the coast south of Haifa and the shores of the Sea of Galilee between 100,000 and 45,000 years ago. Much more similar to us than was thought in the past, Neanderthal men in the Middle East worked stone with consummate skill, probably developed a rudimentary language, and began to manifest the first signs of religion, as can be seen in the tombs ornamented with flowers that received their dead.

From that time on humans made rapid progress, almost certainly because of the more favorable climatic and living conditions in general and also thanks to a more complete and steady diet. Around 10,000 BC the Natufian culture, characterized by the first cave dwellings, began to grow stronger, and in the course of two thousand years human civilization here took giant leaps toward the establishment of more well-defined cultures. The birth of agriculture,

8 right Egyptian influence was quite strong in Palestine during the entire Bronze Age (4th-2nd millenia). This gilded pendant found at Tel el-Ajjul depicts Astarte (Ashtoreth), the goddess of fertility related to the Egyptian goddess Hathor.

which took place around the 9th millennium BC, also brought about the rise of urban civilization, which spread throughout the Middle East from Palestine, and more precisely, from Jericho, the oldest city in the world. A sign of the great strides made in Jericho is the plan of the houses found in the city; they were no longer round, but rectangular, as is the case with the great majority of houses built today. If, as some authoritative scholars believe, it is true that it was the farmers themselves rather than agriculture that spread, we could surmise that one of the most powerful stimuli for human progress in the nine millennia before the birth of Christ is to be attributed precisely to the ancient Palestinians.

Between 4500 and 3200 BC further development marked the end of the Stone Age and the beginning of the Chalcolithic period, that is to say, the 'stone and copper' era, which coincided with the exploitation of the rich copper mines at Timna which the members of the Tell el-Husn culture soon alloyed with tin to produce bronze. The tools, ornaments and weapons produced in what were most probably considerable quantities already in very ancient times, was a decisive boost in the development of commerce. In the Early Bronze Age, between 3300 and 3200 BC, the names of the various cultures that succeeded one another in Palestine during the preceding millennia were finally replaced by the name of a distinct ethnic group, the Canaanites, indefatigable builders of fortified cities with megalithic walls that protected the already ancient trade routes that linked Egypt with Syria and the Mesopotamian plains with the Mediterranean.

The rise of city-states in Mesopotamia and of a unified monarchy in Egypt posed a threat to security of the Canaanite settlements, caught between the two leading powers of the time. Around 2200 BC the Proto-Palestinian people disappeared temporarily, or perhaps declined, either because of disastrous drought or an unknown invasion. Hazor, the leading Canaanite city, and the other towns declined and a more primitive population of livestock-raising nomads settled in Palestine for a couple of centuries, after which the former city-states flourished once again.

The two millennia of the Bronze Age gave rise to other major innovations in industry and agriculture, such as the introduction of the potter's wheel and the cultivation of grapes and olives. Already in the 20th century BC the power of the Canaanite cities began to worry Egypt, as is documented in the list of the cities that were 'damned' because they were unfaithful to the pharaohs, the so-called 'execration texts' (12th dynasty: 1991-1786 BC). Four centuries later their wealth led Tuthmosis III to conquer Canaan, which became a vast Egyptian province. The Canaanite cities remained Egyptian tributaries up to the beginning of a turbulent period that drove two peoples to Palestine in search of new places to settle. A date somewhere between myth and

9 left The coils of serpents that decorate this cultic vessel, which may have been used in fertility rites, were made in the Iron Age (13th-6th century BC), which corresponds to the 'heroic' period of the Jewish Patriarchs.

9 right A seated woman reacting to the movements of the child still in her womb. This beautiful Syrian-Phoenician style terracotta statuette, with its essential form and eloquent gesture, was found in the port of Achzib and dates from the 6th century BC

history, from the 21st to the 18th century BC, coincided with the arrival of the Israelites led by Abraham from Ur, one of the great city-states along the lower course of the Euphrates River. Five centuries later it was the turn of the Philistines, expert sailors of Aegean origin who settled in the territory around Gaza and immediately manifested their hostility toward the Israelites.

While from an industrial standpoint the Iron Age–that is, the biblical age of the Judges and Patriarchs–led to the major innovation of the exploitation of this metal, which may have begun with the bellicose Hittites, from a strictly historical viewpoint this age marked the decline of Canaanite power and the rise of an interminable struggle between the five Philistine cities (Gaza, Ashqelon, Ashdod, Ekron and Gath) and the tribes of Israel, which gradually wrested all the key localities from the Canaanites. For the future history of Palestine and, in the long run, of the world, the more important of these two invading peoples were undoubtedly the Israelites: these nomadic shepherds were in fact the ancestors of Saul, David and Solomon, the first kings of the Hebrews, and what is more important, their oral traditions would give rise to the most famous and widespread literary work in the world, the Old Testament. Saul, the first monarch of the rapidly developing kingdom of Israel, conquered the powerful strongholds of Edom, Moab and Ammon and died around 1015 while fighting against the Philistines. He was succeeded by his son David (1004 ca.-965 BC), who took Jerusalem and extended his now stable dominion over most of Palestine, leaving only the strongholds on the southern coast to the Philistines. After David's death, Solomon (965-928 BC) consolidated the unity of his reign, founded the First Temple in Jerusalem and fortified some major cities, such as Hazor, Megiddo and Gezer. But when he died his two sons shared royal power, thus initiating the so-called 'Divided Monarchy,' consisting of the kingdom of Israel to the north and the kingdom of Judah to the south. This division led to great instability and the kingdoms suffered a series of defeats, as the Old Testament tells

us, which began with the Egyptian conquest of Judah on the part of the Libyan pharaoh Sheshonq in 923 BC Two centuries later Samaria (Israel) was taken by the Assyrians led by Sargon II, who scattered the ten northern Tribes of Israel, and in 701 BC Judah was again conquered, this time by the Neo-Assyrian ruler Sennacherib. However, the collapse of the vast Assyrian Empire in 611 did not signal freedom for the two subject kingdoms of Israel and Judah, but merely a change in foreign masters: in three successive invasions (605, 597 and 587 BC) the Babylonians conquered Jerusalem, destroyed Solomon's Temple and deported almost the entire population of Judah to Babylonia.

THE PERSIAN PERIOD
(538-332 BC)

THE HELLENISTIC PERIOD *(332-37 BC)*

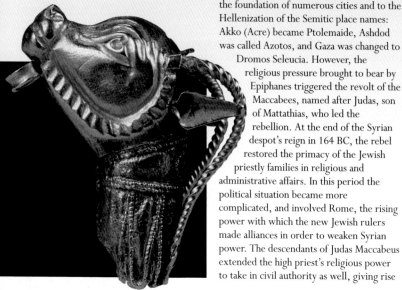

Less than fifty years after the beginning of the Babylonian Captivity, the unstable political situation in the Near East changed once again when great Babylonia succumbed to the rising power of the Persians. The victorious 'king of kings' Cyrus the Great conquered the Mesopotamian city in 539 BC and, with an act of clemency that would have been unthinkable on the part of the ruthless Assyrian-Babylonian rulers, let the captive Jews free to return to Jerusalem to rebuild their Temple. However, the return to Palestine, which in the meantime had become a satrapy of the Persian Empire, was disrupted by the misunderstanding between the exiles and the people who had inhabited their land during the "Captivity", a mixed population consisting of the Jews who had escaped deportation and the colonists Nebuchadnezzar had sent to occupy the newly conquered territory.

During the Persian dominion important material and cultural progress was made. The rebuilding of the Temple was finished around 516 BC under the supervision of the prophets Haggai and Zechariah, and the reconstruction of the walls of Jerusalem on the part of Nehemiah was effected in the middle of the following century. Ezra and Nehemiah saw the codification of the Old Testament and laws were passed to avoid further ethnic mixing between Jews and foreigners.

The new power that disrupted the established order in Palestine arrived from the west in 332 BC. After laying siege to Gaza, dominating the rebellious Samaritans and conquering the Persian Empire, Alexander the Great became master of the satrapy of Palestine as well. However, his empire, though vast, was short-lived. After the great Macedonian leader's premature death, the conquered territories were divided among his generals and administrators, the *diadochoi*. As a result, Palestine was assigned to the Ptolemies as part of the province of Syria and Phoenicia, while Judaea and Jerusalem were granted an autonomous status under the leadership of the high priest of the Temple. In the Near East the period from the 4th to the 1st century BC was characterized by the cultural growth as well as the political instability of the Hellenistic kingdoms. In 198 BC Ptolemy V Epiphanes had to cede the provinces outside Egypt to the Seleucid king Antiochus III, and the latter's successor Antiochus IV put an end to Judaean autonomy, violated the Temple and tried to Hellenize the religious administration. The heavy-handed Seleucid cultural policy led to the foundation of numerous cities and to the Hellenization of the Semitic place names: Akko (Acre) became Ptolemaide, Ashdod was called Azotos, and Gaza was changed to Dromos Seleucia. However, the religious pressure brought to bear by Epiphanes triggered the revolt of the Maccabees, named after Judas, son of Mattathias, who led the rebellion. At the end of the Syrian despot's reign in 164 BC, the rebel restored the primacy of the Jewish priestly families in religious and administrative affairs. In this period the political situation became more complicated, and involved Rome, the rising power with which the new Jewish rulers made alliances in order to weaken Syrian power. The descendants of Judas Maccabeus extended the high priest's religious power to take in civil authority as well, giving rise to the Hasmonean dynasty, which soon made important territorial conquests. In 142-141 BC Jerusalem fell under the complete control of the Jews and was guaranteed direct access to the sea, and in the 70 years that followed the Hasmoneans gradually took over Galilee, Transjordan, Negev and the Gaza coastline. The civil war in 67 BC over the succession to the Hasmonean throne provoked the direct intervention of the Romans, who in 63 BC declared the end of Seleucid power and created the province of Syria, extending their power over most of the land of the ruling dynasty and over its members. Not having secured total control over Palestine, the Romans found it convenient to have the descendants of the Idumaean Herod Antipater, father of Herod the Great, govern in their stead who proved to be precious allied for several decades. In 40 BC the Parthians launched an attack against the Hasmonean kingdom, forcing the king, John Hyrcanus II, into exile in Babylonia and Herod to flee to Rome, where he was appointed king of Judaea. Strengthened by the support of Rome, in 37 BC Herod reconquered his country, Samaria and Galilee, captured Jerusalem and had the last Hasmonean king, Mattathias Antigonus, put to death. The ascent to power of a local king who was, however, a faithful ally of Rome, virtually ensured the latter's total dominion of the Palestinian region.

10 bottom A golden earring with a ram's head brought to light at Ashdod but probably made by a Persian goldsmith. The Achaemenid period in Palestine was relatively peaceful.

10 top The silent roar of this panther found at Advat, a Nabataean city in the Negev desert, was immortalized in bronze in the 1st century BC, at the beginning of the Roman conquest of Palestine.

11 top A lily on a Yehud coin (an Aramaic word indicating an administrative district) that was struck during the period of Persian dominion.

11 bottom This bust found during the digs at Scythopolis (Bet Shean) portrays Hadrian, the industrious Roman emperor who founded the pagan city of Aelia Capitolina over the ruins of Jerusalem.

THE ROMAN PERIOD *(37 BC-324 AD)*

Although the majority of the people he ruled never fully accepted him, the fact is that in the nine centuries from the division of the Israelite kingdom, Herod the Great was the only non-foreign monarch able to unite the Jews under one crown in Palestine. What is more, he was a skillful politician, and for at least two decades guaranteed peace and stability, building new ports and grandiose architectural works, the most important of which was the new Temple in Jerusalem, the most majestic and the last one in which the Jews were able to worship.

However, the unification of Judaea was not destined to outlast Herod, as his three sons divided the kingdom after his death. However, relations between Archelaus and Augustus were not as good as those between the Roman emperor and Herod the Great had been, so the ethnarch of Samaria, Edom and Judaea was exiled, leaving Judaea under direct Roman rule, which at first was represented by prefects and then by procurators. This period of ferment and crisis witnessed the ministry of Jesus, who was born during Augustus's rule and condemned to crucifixion by the procurator Pontius Pilate, an official of the emperor Tiberius.

From 37 to 41 AD Palestine was temporarily united under the favorite of Caligula and his successor Claudius, Herod Agrippa, who in the last three years of his reign wisely governed a territory that was equal in size to the one ruled by his grandfather, Herod the Great. Despite Agrippa's rather pro-Jewish stance, the situation in Judaea had been deteriorating for years, as the people not only had to bear the oppressive fiscal and cultural policy of the Romans, but suffered from the lack of a homogeneous social fabric in their society. The Jews were divided into factions that never managed to find a common and effective course of action (the name of one of the religious sects of this period, Sicarii–'hired killers' in Latin–is eloquent proof of the violence of these internecine conflicts) and were therefore destined to suffer a series of terrible setbacks.

In 66 AD the imprudent policy of the Roman procurators and the social tension ended by triggering an insurrection in the provincial capital, Caeserea, which rapidly spread to the rest of Palestine. After a number of initial successes on the part of the rebellious Jews–including major victories such as the conquest of the Herodian fortress of Masada by the Zealots–the Romans began to bring their overwhelming strategic superiority to bear, and in the year 70, after the fall of Jerusalem, the Jewish population paid an enormous price for the First Jewish War: those who were not massacred became slaves; the Herodian Temple was razed to the ground; and, at least formally, Jews were barred from Jerusalem. The Zealots who had occupied Masada resisted for three more years, but only to write the final, tragic page of the epic of this war: in 73 AD the dream of Jewish independence came to an abrupt halt with the collective suicide of the inhabitants of the fortress.

After this abortive revolt, Roman control over Jerusalem and Judaea became tighter, and the population dwindled. Yet, though the Jews had failed to gain their political objectives, their culture survived. Indeed, it flourished in the outlying towns of the Holy Land, in the synagogues and in the new religious schools headed by famous rabbis. During Hadrian's reign matters got worse. The emperor's determination to Romanize Palestine thoroughly, epitomized by the construction of the colony of Aelia Capitolina over the ruins of Jerusalem, reached its height in 132 AD with his decree that prohibited circumcision. This move virtually sparked the Second Jewish War, which was shorter than the first one but equally dramatic for the rebels. After three years of fighting the Jewish spiritual leaders were executed, hundreds of villages were destroyed and the Jewish population in the Holy Land decreased even more, leaving room for other populations and religions.

During the 3rd and 4th century it was Rome that had to resist an invasion from Judea, albeit a cultural one: in two centuries Christianity had struck such deep roots that the Roman emperors themselves supported the new religion, and Palestine was no longer considered a minor province, as it became the Holy Land under Constantine the Great.

THE BYZANTINE
PERIOD *(324-640 AD)*

Whether or not it was sincere, the Roman emperor's veneration of the sacred sites of Christianity took on concrete form in the construction of many basilicas, monasteries and chapels, and gave rise to the peaceful invasion of the pilgrims, one of the major features of the Byzantine period in the Holy Land. During the 4th and 5th centuries, which were much more peaceful than the two preceding ones, the Christian popoulation was free to settle in Palestine and grew in size, so much so that in the early 6th century it was larger than the pagan and Jewish populations. Although limited to the outlying localities, under Byzantine rule there were numerous Jewish communities that survived and were relatively free to follow their religious practices, despite the increasing hostility on the part of the Christian empire. The anti-Jewish restrictions imposed by the Byzantine rulers between the late 4th and early 7th century, which were even more widespread and severe than those of the ancient Romans, provoked three revolts. The first involved the Jews and was quickly suppressed; the other two, begun by the Samaritans, were equally unsuccessful. However, these last two insurrections, which broke out in 485 and 529, were particular in that they also involved the future conquerors of the Holy Land, the Persians, who in 614 put an end to Byzantine dominion and destroyed a great number of sacred sites and towns. The brutal rule of the Persian shah Khosru II was short-lived, but so was the Byzantine reconquest of Jerusalem carried out by the emperor Heraclius in 627.

THE EARLY ARAB
PERIOD *(640-1099 AD)*

Immediately after the death of the greatest prophet of Allah, Mohammed, the first two caliphs who succeeded him, and then the Omayyad caliphs, undertook a policy of conquest of vital space for the new religion of Islam. They headed north and west of their home base, the Arabian peninsula south of the line that connects Elat on the Gulf of Aqaba and Bassora, at the mouth of the great Mesopotamian rivers. The Byzantine cities fell rapidly one after the other and the Arabs colonized the newly conquered territory equally rapidly in order to prevent the Byzantine rulers from regaining their domain. In 641 all the Holy Land was under Islamic dominion, and this initial invasion was characterized by a spirit of tolerance that was never again to be seen. The caliph Omar was obviously a pious and rational person, as he carefully avoided any destruction or profanation and granted a certain degree of autonomy to the Christian inhabitants and the few Jewish communities that had survived persecution and the Diaspora.

During this period the third great monotheistic religion—which has just risen up in the desert and was a mixture of Bedouin, Semitic and Jewish traditions—penetrated the Holy Land. At the beginning of the 8th century the Omayyad dynasty set up its administrative center in the new city of Ramla, but already at the end of the 10th century the relative stability and tolerance so characteristic of their rule were overturned by a series of invasions effected alternatively by the Shiite Fatimid caliphs, the Ismaili Qarmathians and the Byzantines. The moderation manifested by the Arab conquerors disappeared during the caliphate of Hakim (1009-1013), when many churches and synagogues were destroyed and heavy restrictions were imposed on non-Muslims. Sixty years later the condition of these 'infidels' worsened greatly with the arrival of the Seljuks, and the violent reaction from Europe was not late in coming: the end of the 11th century witnessed the first of the many attempts—from eight to ten according to various interpretations, almost all of which were unsuccessful—to restore Christian dominion in the Holy Land.

12 left and right
Similar in form and
ritual use, these oil-
lamps are distinguished
by the shape of their
handles, one being a
menorah and the
other a cross. Both
lamps date back to the
4th century AD, when
Christianity was
consolidaing its
position in the Holy
Land.

12-13 This Persian
copy (1553)
reproduces the map
drawn four centuries
earlier by the great
Arab geographer
Edrisi, who, in
keeping with Muslim
tradition, oriented his
work southward
instead of to the
north. The two round
green forms in the
middle represent the

Sea of Galilee and
the Dead Sea, while
the elongated shapes
represent the
mountain chains.

13 A Gothic crucifix
made in the 12th
century, when the
Crusader dream of
reconquering the
Holy Land seemed to
be realizable.

THE CRUSADER PERIOD (1099-1291 AD)

The Crusaders' conquest of Jerusalem, with the colors of Godfrey of Bouillon, occurred on July 15, 1099 and was marked by the terrible massacre of Jews and Muslims alike and the deportation of the few survivors into slavery. Once they had gained control of the key positions in the land, on Christmas day of the year 1100, the victors set about reproducing the social-political organization of their native countries, creating various principalities under the dominion—often merely nominally—of Jerusalem, the holy capital of th Latin Kingdom.

Threatened by the Seljuk Turks, who in 1144 reconquered the northern Crusader county of Edessa, the unstable Crusader rule imposed on the Holy Land suffered a severe setback during the Second Crusade, which failed to conquer Damascus. However, the land under the Latin rulers remained essentially intact only until July 1187, when at Hattin, near the Sea of Galilee, the Islamic hero Saladin inflicted a humiliating defeat on the European knights, who in October

were forced to abandon Jerusalem and much of the former Crusader territory.

Despite the rather obscure end of the emperor 'Red-Beard' Frederick, who drowned in Cilicia before setting foot in the Holy Land, and the consequent withdrawal of the strong German army from the Third Crusade, in 1191 the remaining Christian forces managed to take Acre. Saladin proved to be a rather wise ruler, because he chose to negotiate the right of partial access to Jerusalem with the Crusaders. But the Holy City (except for the Temple Mount), Nazareth and Bethlehem returned to Crusader dominion only in 1228-1229, strangely enough without bloodshed, since the Sixth Crusade ended with a diplomatic agreement. Thus, despite the later defeats due to the weakening of the Crusaders in Palestine—who were engaged in bitter fratricidal struggles (much like their respective native countries) and were helpless against the attacks of the Egyptians, who recaptured Jerusalem in 1244—the Christians managed to remain in the Holy Land until 1291, when the fall of Acre and of Atlit, the last Crusader stronghold, signalled the end of the Crusader period.

Although the two centuries of Christian expeditions against the rising power of Islam led only to rather unstable

conquest, the Fourth Crusade produced important, long-lasting results: in 1202-1204, instead of attempting to reconquer Jerusalem, with shameful, unbridled and opportunistic vengeance the Christian armies attacked Byzantium and declared the end of the Empire, ending this inglorious crusade with a horrifying massacre of Greek Christians.

THE MAMLUK PERIOD

(1291-1517 AD)

Baybars, the sultan of Egypt who won the last war against the Crusaders, was a descendant of the Turkish-Slav soldiers recruited by the Ayyubids as slaves who then took power in Egypt. The Mamluks, the new lords of Palestine, faithful to their origin as mercenaries, kept the country under strict military control and paid little attention to its development. Thus the situation was worse than it was during the first period of Arab dominion, when local commerce had virtually come to a halt in favor of agriculture and livestock raising. During the Mamluk period the economy suffered under the management of viceroys appointed by the sultans of Egypt, persons who were often brutal and corrupt and who levied extremely heavy taxes on the Christians and Jews, who also had to bear a good deal of injustice.

Now that the ports that for centuries had been used by pilgrims and Crusaders

14 top The Mamluks combined military skill and fine craftsmanship, as can be seen in the blade of this battle-axe, decorated in the middle with a sultan's blazon.

14 center The naïve vivacity compensates for the lack of refinement in this cover of an Arab lamp depicting a dog chasing a cat.

14 bottom Probably a part of the sacred furnishings of al-Aqsa, this bronze candlestick reminds one of the shape of the Dome of the Rock.

had either been destroyed or were buried in sand, the non-Muslim communities in the Holy Land found themselves isolated. Although they enjoyed limited religious freedom, they fell into poverty and were subject to heavy taxation. However, like the Omayyads and their Muslim successors, the Mamluks left fine civil and religious architecture in Jerusalem, Ramla, Nablus, Lydda and the other towns in the Holy Land. In the early 16th century the solidity of the dynasty began to deteriorate, so much so that the Mamluk sultans' rule in the Holy Land ended with a dreadful famine, a plague of locusts, and a catastrophic earthquake.

THE OTTOMAN PERIOD
(1517-1917 AD)
AND THE MODERN AGE

15 A 17th-century Ottoman miniature depicting Mohammed and Abu Bekr, his first successor. Ottoman *dominion in the Holy Land began with great promise in the 16th century, but declined qualitatively for four centuries.*

The new power at the northern borders of the Mamluk sultanate, the Ottoman Empire, had risen from the ashes of Byzantium and the short-lived Christian and Seljuk dominions, and was rapidly expanding to the west in the Balkans and to the east towards Mesopotamia, ruled by the Mamluks. In 1516 the two powers clashed on the borderline of northern Syria, and the Mamluks were forced to cede the Holy Land to the Ottomans.

The successor of the victorious Ottoman sultan Selim I, Suleiman the Magnificent, from 1520 to 1566 initiated a period of great prosperity in the country by concentrating on economic development, which, as we have seen, his predecessors had virtually ignored. Futhermore, the stability of his reign was a guarantee of security to both his government and its citizens, something that had been dramatically lacking during the Mamluk period. Besides prosperity and religious tolerance for Jews and Christians, Suleiman's 'golden age' boasted the construction of the walls of Jerusalem, which are those we see today, as well as of a great many exceptional architectural works.

But this lasted only 50 years. In the following decades, and particularly in the 17th century, the successors of this enlightened ruler were unable to adminstrate the territory and keep it under control, weakened and divided Ottoman power, caused the economy to collapse once again, and resumed the persecution of non-Muslim minorities just when they were fully developing. However, through special agreements and the payment of heavy, arbitrary taxes, it was possible for European Christians to be granted franchises that allowed them to extend their influence. Thus, without the Crusader swords and

shields, the monastic orders replaced the knights of the past and began to compete for control of the various holy sites in Jerusalem and Bethlehem.

At the time when the Western world was entering the modern age, at the end of the Enlightenment, Ottoman power wallowed in corruption and decline. Relations with Europe–which was now regarding the Near East with an interest

based more on power politics, strategy and economics, rather than religion–became more direct in 1799, when Ahmed Pasha, known as Jazzar (or 'Butcher'), succeeded in warding off Napoleon's troops during the siege of Acre, forcing them to return to Egypt, where the future emperor had suffered a humiliating naval defeat a year earlier at Abukir. Thanks to the privileges the pasha of Egypt, Mohammed Ali, had granted to foreign consulates and scholars and explorers of the time, by the mid 19th century Western penetration into

Palestine could gain a foothold in diplomatic terms, so that the nations involved–mainly Russia, Germany and France–were able to offer protection to the various ethnic and religious minorities. Given the ineluctable decline of the Ottoman Empire, the race for European supremacy in the Near East soon turned into a sort of semi-colonialism, and in 1869 the inauguration of the Suez Canal served to accelerate this process, creating even keener competition among the European nations.

World War One marked the end of the empire of the Sublime Porte. The British gained control of Palestine, occupying Jerusalem in 1917 and then obtaining the Mandate in 1918 to govern the country, which expired thirty years later after the end of World War Two. The activities of the Zionist organizations, which already in the 19th century had called for the creation of a free, independent Jewish state in the Holy Land, led to the purchase of land from 1901 on. By the time the British Mandate expired, these lots had become a vast territory already owned and colonized (or about to be so) by thousands of Jewish pioneers who had come from all over the world to create what in 1948 became the state of Israel. As we all know, the price paid for the development of the new nation was quite high for Jews and Muslims alike: the Arab-Israeli wars, terrorism, and the state of tension that persists to this day. In the eyes of outside observers, the very sacredness of the Holy Land seems to be in jeopardy because of the violent reactions of the two contenders in this dispute. However, this harsh reality cannot conceal the wonder and beauty of the fact that the dream a people had nurtured for twenty centuries has finally come true in a land that, for this very reason, can be considered holy above and beyond any religious connotations.

JERUSALEM
TOPOGRAPHY OF THE CITY

Rugged hills, deep valleys, land wrenched from Nature's grasp and–by means of grand irrigation works–provided with the water needed for tillage and subsistence: Jerusalem is a city similar to other great ancient Mediterranean capitals such as Athens, Rome and Byzantium. Its topographical features are as complex as its long history and vast culture, which created this great city's social and architectural configuration in the space of at least forty centuries. Again, as is the case with other famous and mighty cities of the past, the place names found in a map of Jerusalem stir universally known memories. But here such evocations transcend the fascination of ancient history, because they attract the followers of three religions that are inspired by the same God and have such closely related tenets, yet are all too often so drastically opposed in the realization of their principles.

The peculiarity of Jerusalem is quite obvious: it is perhaps the only city in the world that is considered holy by three different religions. The present-day urban area lies on a group of hills that on an average are 2,624 feet high. These form a ring around the most ancient nucleus, the Old City, which is delimited to the east by Kidron Valley (also known as the Valley of Jehoshaphat) and the Mount of Olives, where the domes of the Orthodox Church of St. Mary Magdalene shine so brightly, and to the south and west by the Valley of

16 top Detail of the Madaba mosaic map of the 'Holy City' during the Byzantine age. The horizontal line in the middle is the cardo maximus, recognizable by the parallel rows of columns of the arcades lining the Roman street.

16-17 From all angles, the splendor of Jerusalem is highlighted in the dazzling fine gold casing of the Dome of the Rock, which in this photograph is viewed from the west.

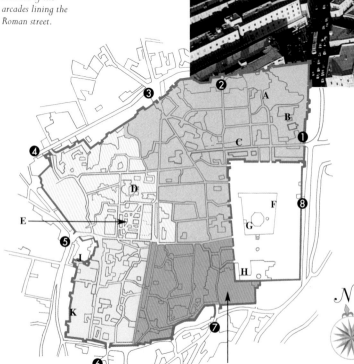

Gehenna (or Valley of Hinnom). The Old City is entirely surrounded by walls and is divided longitudinally by a depression, the Tyropaeion Valley, which runs northward from the Damascus Gate along the Western Wall, passes the Maghreb (or Dung) Gate and descends toward the Pool of Siloam, where it finally merges with the Gehenna and Kidron valleys, thus splitting ancient Jerusalem more or less in half. Mount Zion (2,526 feet), situated southwest of the walls, between the Gehenna and Tyropaeion valleys, is crowned by the Church of the Dormition, while the Gareb hill is the highest one within the city walls (2,578 feet), situated to the northwest in the area of the Christian quarter of Jerusalem, between the Jaffa, New and Damascus gates. Between the Tryopaeion and Kidron valleys stand the rock of Ophel, Mount Moriah and the Bethesda rise. The Ophel ridge is the site where the original nucleus of Jerusalem rose up; in the past it was separated by a hollow in Mount Moriah (2,427 feet), which is now concealed by the Temple Mount esplanade. Lastly, not far from Mount Moriah is the Bethesda rise (2,411 feet), whose original configuration has been altered by the accumulation of rubble over the centuries. This is where the Muslim quarter of the Old City lies.

Modern Jerusalem lies in urban development areas that are separated from one another by wooded rises and barren valleys, extending from the high plain of Judaea toward Bethlehem to the south, Ramallah to the north, Ein Kerem to the west, and Jericho to the east.

THE OLD CITY: THE WALLS AND GATES

The present-day walls of the Old City were built by Suleiman the Magnificent in 1536-42 over the fortification works erected by the Roman emperor Hadrian. Over the centuries, the walls were changed several times, being extended or contracted according to the surface area of the city itself. The walls that protected the original city founded by the Jebusites date back to the 18th-14th century BC. They were rebuilt by King David around the Ophel ridge in the early 12th century BC, and a short time later, the Mount Moriah area, where King Solomon had decided to build the Temple to house the Ark of the Convenant, was enclosed inside a wall. In the following centuries new walls were built around the city, once again being adapted to its expansion and contraction. For example, in the second half of the 8th century BC, many dwellings were built west of the walls in order to take in the numerous Jewish refugees after the Assyrian invasion. But when Sennacherib became a serious threat to the city in 701 BC, the walls were extended to surround the entire inhabited area, thus increasing their length four-fold. However, these new

walls were destroyed in 586 BC during the Babylonian invasion under Nebuchadnezzar.

They remained in ruins until after the end of the Babylonian captivity, because the Jews, who were liberated by the Persian emperor Cyrus in 539, were not allowed to rebuild them until Nehemiah's age (445-443 BC), and even then the reconstruction was only partial. After another ruinous invasion on the part of Antiochus IV Epiphanes in 167 BC, Jerusalem passed through a period of revival under the Hasmonean kings, expanding to the west and north, and was surrounded by a defensive wall that remained the same for several decades.

Not even an indefatigable builder such as Herod the Great, who conquered Jerusalem in 37 BC, altered the wall, although Flavius Josephus claimed that they were extended, a 'third wall' being laid out to the north by Herod Agrippa. Around 70 AD Titus destroyed the fortification works, sparing only the Phasael, Hippicus and Mariamne towers, as well as the western section of the wall in order to defend the Roman garrison. Sixty-five years later, Hadrian completed the destruction of the city wall so systematically that the rebuilt city he founded, Aelia Capitolina, which was quite small and forbidden to the Jews, had no defensive fortification whatsoever.

Jerusalem started to grow again after 313 AD, when the Edict of Milan

granted religious freedom to Christians and pilgrims began to travel to the city in ever growing numbers. In the mid 5th century, the empress Eudocia had a wall built around Mount Zion and the original City of David, and during the 6th century Christian Jerusalem went through a long period of prosperity. This golden age began to wane in the early 7th century due to the destruction wrought by the Persian conquest, which was followed by a brief period of Byzantine rule that ended in 638, when the city was occupied by the Muslim caliph Omar. Since the Muslims also considered Jerusalem a holy city, its holy sites continued to be frequented by pilgrims. However, the city population gradually decreased, so much so that when the Fatimid caliph al-Aziz (975-996) realized that the Byzantine emperor John Tzimisces was about to take the city, he simply abandoned the area surrounded by walls and established a bridgehead in the

northern sector of the city.

In this period the Old City took on what are more or less its present dimensions. Walls were built around it, being destroyed and rebuilt many a time up to the reign of Suleiman the Magnificent (1520-66), who, as we have seen, had the present-day walls built and, according to chronicles, even took part in the manual labor himself. In 1537 the sultan began construction of the walls, starting from the north section and, in the next three years, proceeding eastward and westward. The south section was finished in 1540, as it seems there was a singular dispute over whether Mount Zion–where the Franciscans' Room of the Last Supper (Cenacle) stood–should be enclosed within the new wall. The astute Muslim architects asked the Christian cenobites to pay for the construction of this extra section of the wall; when the friars refused, Mount Zion was left outside the walls. Now since Suleiman had wanted to ensure equal protection for all religions, when he learned that this Christian holy site had been excluded, he had the

architects executed on the spot.

The city wall, sections of which can be walked on, are two and one-half miles long and are interrupted by the six original gates that Suleiman built: Jaffa Gate, Zion Gate, Dung Gate, St. Stephen's Gate, Herod's Gate and Damascus Gate. There are also the Golden Gate, which is sealed off, and the New Gate, which was opened in 1887-89 to facilitate entrance to the Christian quarter. The Ottoman ruler had all the city gates designed in the same shape: a tall arch interrupted by a straight or slightly curved lintel and decorated with an Arab inscription, as well as L-shaped entries for defensive purposes that have remained intact only in some cases. Suleiman also named each gate; over the centuries, the different religious communities added other ones, so that the same gate may have as many as eight names.

Jaffa Gate was opened by Suleiman in 1538-39 over the site of a Roman gate. In Arabic it is called 'Bab al-Khalil,' the 'Gate of the Friend,' referring to the city of Hebron (in whose direction the gate

faces): in fact, the Arabic name of Hebron derives from 'Abraham,' or 'friend of God.' This gate has two distinct entrances. The original, L-shaped one is for pedestrians, while the straight one, for vehicles, was made in 1898 on occasion of the visit of the German Kaiser Wilhelm II in order to allow the imperial coach to enter the Holy City. Moreover, this structure contains the tombs of the two above-mentioned architects who had not enclosed Mount Zion and the Room of the Last Supper within the city wall. From 1948, when war broke out after the foundation of Israel, to 1967, when Jerusalem was unified under Israeli control, Jaffa Gate was a much-contested passageway that marked the border between Israel and Jordan.

Along the southern side of the wall is Zion Gate, built in 1540-41 west of the Roman gate that marked the end of the *cardo maximus*. The section of wall in which the gate is incorporated still has signs of the furious battles waged in 1948 between Jordanians and Israelis, when the latter tried to conquer the Muslim quarter.

20 bottom left The Golden Gate—also called the 'Beautiful' and the 'Gate of Mercy'—has preserved its original Herodian structure more than any other gate of Jerusalem.

20 top left The Golden Gate was bricked up by Saladin because it was traditionally believed that the Messiah would pass through it to liberate Jerusalem.

20 top right Another tradition says that Jesus passed through Herod's Gate, which gives access to the Muslim quarter, when he was taken before this monarch.

Dung Gate was also built during the reign of Suleiman in the southern section of the wall, probably to act as a service accessway: in fact, since it is narrower than the other gates, it was widened by the Jordanians, who used it for vehicle traffic from 1947 to 1967, when Jaffa Gate, situated on the border, could not be used. The gate's strange name derives from the dump that once lay in this part of the city, while its Arabic name, 'Bab al-Maghariba,' or 'Maghreb Gate,' comes from the quarter of the North African immigrants who settled in the outskirts in

the 12th century.

A short distance away, along the wall of the Temple Mount esplanade, one can still see three gates that Suleiman bricked up: the Double Gate, the Triple Gate, and the Simple Gate, respectively with two arches, three arches and one arch. The Golden Gate, also bricked up, lies on the eastern side, along the Temple Mount esplanade. It was built over a Herodian epoch foundation, acquired its present aspect in the 7th century during Omayyad dominion, and was closed when access to the esplanade was prohibited to non-

20 bottom right The elegant Maghreb Gate owes its name to the North African community that settled near it in the 12th century.

21 left Known as 'Lions' Gate' because of its animal decoration, this monument is called 'St. Stephen's Gate' by the Christians.

21 right Damascus Gate is considered the most beautiful in the Holy City. It is also the largest, and when the nearby market is open it is also the most animated.

Muslims in the 8th century. During the Crusader occupation of Jerusalem it was opened twice a year, on Palm Sunday and during the Exaltation of the Cross feast, but after the Muslims reconquered the city the gate was never used again. The two names of 'Gate of Mercy' and 'Gate of Penitence' used for the two flanking fornices, derive from the traditional Hebrew and Muslim belief that the Golden Gate will be crossed by the righteous on Judgement Day, while the word 'golden' came from a mistaken interpretation of the Greek word *horaia*, or 'beautiful,' which was confused with the Latin *aurea* (golden).

St. Stephen's Gate, on the east side of the city wall, was built in 1538-39 by Suleiman, who named it Bab al-Ghor (Jordan Gate), a name that never became popular. In fact, the Christians called it St. Stephen's Gate, the same name of an older gate that once stood nearby. The other commonly used name, Lions' Gate, refers to the feral heraldic emblems the Mamluk sultan Baybars (1260-77) had carved on the sides of the entrance. Its original L-shaped entry was straightened by the English during the British Mandate so that vehicles could have easy access to the Austrian hospital.

Known as 'Bab-ez-Zahr,' or 'Flowery Gate,' in Arabic, Herod's Gate is the northernmost one and took on this name in the 16th-17th century because the

pilgrims believed they had found Herod Antipas' palace in an adjacent Mamluk house. This name is connected to the traditional belief that Jesus passed through this gate when he was brought before Herod. The Crusaders built their first bridgehead here during their conquest of Jerusalem (July 15, 1099).

Also on the northern side of the city wall is Damascus Gate, the largest and most beautiful in Jerusalem, which was built on the site of the previous gate constructed by Herod Agrippa (41-44 AD) and then rebuilt by Hadrian (135 AD) as the main entrance to his newly founded city of Aelia Capitolina.

Damascus Gate is flanked by two square towers and gives access to what in the past were the two main streets in

Jerusalem, the present-day Tariq el-Wad and Suq Khan ez-Zeit. In Arabic it is called 'Bab al-Amud,' or 'Gate of the Column,' a name deriving from the column in St. Stephen's church, which lies about 650 feet outside the city wall. A vast archaeological site was discovered under the present-day street and one can still see the remains of Hadrian's gate there.

At the western end of the north side of the wall is the New Gate ('Bab el-Jadid' in Arabic), which was opened in 1887 by the Ottoman sultan Abdul Hamid II as an accessway to the Christian quarter. It is interesting to note that the present-day Old City is smaller than the area enclosed within the Herodian walls, which at that time perhaps had a larger–though certainly not more composite–population.

THE CITADEL

Owing to its key strategic position, over the centuries the site of the Citadel of Jerusalem was fortified several times. The present-day aspect of the fortress that towers over the starting point of the road connecting Jerusalem and the Mediterranean, Jaffa Gate, dates back to 1635; but as early as the 7th century BC the area now occupied by the fortified complex was an Israelite settlement surrounded by a defensive wall in the 2nd century BC,

in 66 AD during the first Jewish War, while in 70 AD it was spared by the emperor Titus, who did not touch the three towers and used the fortification complex as a camp for his *X Legio Fretensis*. For 200 years the Roman troops had been stationed in the Citadel and the adjacent area south of the walls (now the Armenian quarter), where the largest section of Herod the Great's palace also stood. The towers were finally destroyed by Hadrian in 135 AD and the ruins became the home of the Christian hermits. The Byzantines then identified the remains of the Herodian Citadel as the site of King David's palace, so the ruins were christened 'David's Tower,' a name that in the 19th century was also given to the minaret on the southwest corner of the walls.

At the end of Roman dominion a round tower was added to the fortress, which was again used as a defensive bulwark in the 8th century during the Arab conquest. Between 1128 and 1187 it became the residence of the Crusader rulers, who enlarged it to the west, but in the 13th century the Mamluks destroyed the Crusader

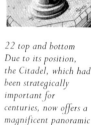

22 top and bottom Due to its position, the Citadel, which had been strategically important for centuries, now offers a magnificent panoramic view of Jerusalem.

22 center David's Tower is really a minaret built in 1635 that was the last addition to the fortress.

22-23 The Citadel, as we see it today, was built by Suleiman the Magnificent, but the complex has traces of Hasmonean, Herodian and Crusader architecture.

during the period of the Maccabean and Hasmonean dynasties. The historian Josephus Flavius mentions a Hasmonean wall in his description of the three towers Herod the Great built to reinforce the citadel: the Tower of Hippicus, dedicated to a friend; the Tower of Phasael, built in honor of his brother; and the Tower of Mariamne, named after his wife.

The Citadel was attacked and burned

fortress and later built new fortifications in successive stages. Suleiman the Magnificent had the entire complex restored and also built the present-day entranceway. The minaret was added in 1635.

At present the Citadel houses the Museum of the History of Jerusalem, a lively exhibition that covers all the complex history of the city by means of films, plans and maps, and reconstruction models. The 1:500 scale zinc model of Jerusalem is especially interesting. It was made by the Hungarian Stefan Illes for the 1873

23 bottom The oldest section of the Citadel lies around the Tower of Phasael, the largest one, which can be seen in the middle of this photograph, flanked by a section of the Hasmonean wall. To the left of the fortress is Jaffa Gate.

World Fair held in Vienna and is now kept in the cavity of the cistern situated under the northwest tower.

In the inner courtyard of the Citadel archaeologists have brought to light many finds that testify to the many changes and frequent rebuilding work carried out over the centuries. Now the strategic position of this very ancient fortress can be best appreciated from an aesthetic and scenic standpoint, because its towers and ramparts afford a splendid panoramic view of Jerusalem and all the surrounding area.

THE ARMENIAN QUARTER

This quarter in the southwestern sector of the Old City is much smaller than it was in the past. It has a population of about 2,000, consisting of priests, monks and laymen of Armenian extraction. The Armenians probably arrived in Jerusalem already in the first century BC, when the Romans conquered Palestine. They were the first ethnic group to adopt Christianity officially, in 301 AD, and soon afterward they began pilgrimages throughout the Holy Land: three centuries later there were no fewer than seventy Armenian Church monasteries in the territory. In 491 the Armenian Church split off from the Roman Catholic Church, but six centuries later the Armenian kingdom established close relations with the Crusaders' Latin Kingdom, and there was even intermarriage between the two communities.

The Armenians were the only Christians allowed to stay in Jerusalem after Saladin's conquest; what is more, they were even granted new privileges and property. But with time their economic lot worsened to such a degree that from 1717 to 1721 the Armenian Patriarch of Jerusalem was forced to beg for alms in front of the Holy Mother of God church in Istanbul in order to pay the debts his community had incurred. This ill-fated religious leader went down in history as the 'chain bearer' because of the iron chain, now a relic in St. James Cathedral, which he wore as a token of expiation. The cathedral lies in the heart of the Armenian

pearl, and carved wood furnishings. A striking feature are the votive crosses, called 'khatchkars,' which are carved in relief in the shape of the tree of life and are set within larger crosses, thus creating the so-called 'Jerusalem cross.' There are about twenty of these (the oldest of which dates from 1161), each one different, set at the entrance of the cathedral and in the courtyard of the tombs of the partriarchs.

The Edward and Helen Mardigian Museum, inaugurated in 1979, is housed in a building constructed in 1843 that was originally meant to be a seminary. The building has two storys, with the monks' cells and common rooms articulated around a rectangular peristyle courtyard. The museum takes up both floors. The ground floor is given over to the history of the Armenian people, from their origins to the terrible genocide of 1915, while the first floor features archaeological finds unearthed in the Armenian quarter, as well as religious objects and the precious gifts that pilgrims donated to the monastery.

By continuing southwards, near Zion Gate you will see an early 14th-century chapel in classical Armenian style that reputedly lies on the site of the house of the high priest Annas, who was chiefly responsible for the condemnation of Jesus. He was a member of the most powerful rabbinic family in Jerusalem during the Herodian and Roman periods.

quarter, flanked by the Mardigian Museum, the Gulbenkian library, the seminary and the residential area.

The streets in the quarter form an intricate structure that is defensive in nature: the houses lining the streetfronts are characterized by their high-set windows, which are often protected with iron grilles, and the anonymous entrance doors are accessible only via inner courtyards. This fortress-like look is more than justified by the long and terrible history of massacres the Armenians suffered at the hands of the Turks. In fact, just like the Jews, for centuries the Armenians were subject to discrimination and persecution that culminated in the late 19th and early 20th centuries, when they were systematically exterminated by the Ottoman Empire, with an estimated two million victims.

St. James Cathedral was dedicated to two saints: St. James the Greater (one of the Apostles), and the so-called 'St. James the Less.' It was built on the area originally occupied by a chapel dedicated to St. James the Greater (420 AD), to which was added another votive chapel dedicated to the Egyptian martyr St. Menas (444). The present-day cathedral dates from the Crusader occupation of Jerusalem. It was modeled after the church at Haghbat, in Armenia, but later on several changes were made, the most important of which was the construction of the narthex in the 17th century, which entailed moving the main entrance. The interior is divided into two side aisles and the square nave with four piers under the dome; it is adorned with canvases, Turkish and Spanish majolica decoration, carpets, inlaid mother-of-

24-25 The decoration in the Armenian cathedral is almost exaggerated and is best appreciated by observing its individual components, from the paintings to the carpets.

24 bottom The name of St. James, to whom the cathedral was dedicated, is written on the entrance in Armenian, Arabic and Latin characters.

25 top In the cathedral complex there are about twenty Jerusalem crosses in different shapes.

25 bottom left The austere, intricate streets in the Armenian quarter remind one of a fortress.

25 right center and bottom The priest and the tabernacle seen here are the repositories of the religion the Armenians have been professing for 17 centuries.

THE JEWISH QUARTER

This quarter, which lies in the southeastern sector of the Old City, was almost entirely rebuilt in fairly recent times, because during the wars of 1948 and 1967 it was the theatre of such furious battles that, by the time the Israelis finally managed to occupy it, almost all the buildings had been reduced to heaps of rubble. Before reconstruction began, however, Israeli archaeologists made a very careful survey of the quarter, and the new buildings were constructed in such a way as to leave the ancient finds beneath them exposed to view. Thus, in the modern buildings, the city's past, clearly visible under the street level, co-exists with the present, which lies at a higher level.

Digs have revealed that this area was inhabited from the time of King Hezekiah (700 BC), was destroyed in 586 BC by the Babylonians, and was then revived in the 2nd-1st centuries BC, during Maccabean and Hasmonean dominion, as is demonstrated by the remains of the Hasmonean walls brought to light in the quarter, as well as by the ruins of Herod Antipas' palace.

A tour of the Jewish quarter could well begin from the *cardo maximus*, the main artery that traversed Jerusalem from north to south during the Byzantine period, partly following the route of the shorter *cardo* that Hadrian had built. The section of this street brought to light, which was forty-one feet wide—only half the original width—has a slight rise in the middle and is flanked by gutters that allowed rainwater to drain on either side. The *cardo* also has remains of the arcade that in ancient times lay on both sides and housed shops and workshops under its columns with Corinthian capitals. In the 12th century the Crusaders covered the northern part of the *cardo* with a continuous vault, and turned the ancient street into a roofed market, which is still active. At the small rotunda at the entrance of this section of the *cardo*, there is a copy of part of the Madaba Map—the magnificent 6th-century mosaic that represents the Holy Land in detail and is kept in the Jordanian city—that reproduces the map of Byzantine Jerusalem.

In a large square east of the *cardo* are the Ramban synagogue and the arch indicating the place where the Hurva synagogue stood before it was destroyed by Jordanian troops in 1948. The name of the former is an abbreviated version of the name of the medieval scholar Rabbi Moshe Ben Nachmanides, a Kabalist of Spanish origin who fled from religious persecution in his country, went to the Holy Land, and arrived in Jerusalem in 1267. Here he found only two surviving Jews, both dyers, and decided to devote his life to reviving a Jewish community in Jerusalem. His synagogue, the

26 top left The essential architecture in most of the Jewish *quarter, rebuilt after 1967, seems to be modeled after formal Classical canons.* *26 top right Along the western border of the Jewish quarter archaeologists found* *the Byzantine cardo maximus, the main street crossing the city from north to south.* *26 center The Byzantine-age cardo maximus was built by following and extending* *the corresponding street built by Hadrian and was lined with shops and storehouses.*

oldest in Jerusalem, was originally built on Mount Zion in the early 15th century and was later moved to its present site, over the ruins of a Crusader church. It was then destroyed in 1474 by the Muslims and was immediately rebuilt, becoming the only Jewish temple in Jerusalem, frequented by a small Sephardic community and by the 'Marrani,' Jews of Spanish and Portuguese origin. However, in 1586 the Ottoman Turks closed it and for centuries the synagogue was used as a shop. The building was badly damaged during the 1948 conflict and was partly restored after 1967, when it finally resumed its original religious function.

26-27 A few steps from the cardo stands the slender arch of the Hurva synagogue, opposite the 15th-century Jami Sidi Umar minaret. *27 bottom left The Crusaders built vaults along the northern section of the cardo, turning the Roman-* *Byzantine street into a covered marketplace that is still virtually intact in its original appearance and function.* *27 bottom right The Ramban—destroyed, rebuilt and then transformed into a workshop—has once again become a synagogue.*

Near this synagogue is the only minaret in the Jewish quarter, the Jami Sidi Umar, built in 1397.

The Hurva synagogue has an intriguing history connected to the vicissitudes of a group of 500 Ashkenazim from Eastern Europe ('Ashkenazi' means 'Germany' in Yiddish) who settled in Jerusalem in the early 18th century with Rabbi Yehuda Hassid. They chose the area next to the Ramban synagogue as a good place to build their own place of worship, and in 1701 began to build a synagogue there, but never managed to finish it: first their rabbi died, then the Arab population was hostile to the construction, and lastly, they were in financial straits, so much so that they had to give the lot back to its former Muslim owners. Thus, the building slowly deteriorated, as its name Hurva (ruin) indicates.

But this is not all. In 1838 Ibrahim Pasha gave the synagogue back to the Ashkenazi community, which finally built its synagogue in twenty years, only to see it utterly destroyed during the 1948 war. Today, the sole testimony of this complicated story is a thin solitary arch, 43 feet high, standing over the ruins of the synagogue. It was one of the four arches that, according to the original plan, was to have supported the dome.

HYPOTHETICAL RECONSTRUCTION OF THE ASHKENAZI HURVA SYNAGOGUE

28-29 The Hurva synagogue, whose only complete arch is to be seen at right, was built by German Jews, or Ashkenazim.

29 top Besides the pulpit and the two decorative menorahs, the west end of the Central (Emtza'i) Synagogue houses the holy ark.

29 bottom left The four Sephardic synagogues form a complex that is the religious heart of the quarter.

29 bottom right The word 'Sephardi' derives from the biblical name for Spain, 'Sepharadh.' Here we see the interior of the synagogue dedicated to the Spanish rabbi Johannan Ben Zakkai.

A short distance south of the arch and the Ramban synagogue are the four synagogues that are the religious hub of the Jewish quarter, the spiritual center of the Sephardic Jews since the 17th century. This complex was damaged during the 1948 war but fortunately was not totally destroyed; thanks to restoration work effected in 1964, it is now perfectly intact.

The Johannan Ben Zakkai synagogue was finished in 1610 and immediately became the main temple after which the entire complex was named. Originally called El Kahal Grande, the Great Congregation, it included the women's section, which was replaced in 1702-20 by the Central (Emtza'i) Synagogue, the smallest of the four.

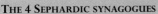

THE 4 SEPHARDIC SYNAGOGUES

1 ISTAMBULI SYNAGOGUE
2 EMTZA'I SYNAGOGUE
3 PROPHET ELIJAH SYNAGOGUE
4 JOHANNAN BEN ZAKKAI SYNAGOGUE
5 HOLY ARCH

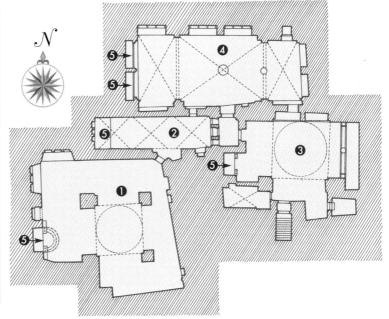

The third temple is known as the Prophet Elijah Synagogue. It was conceived as a study center in 1625 but then became a synagogue as well in 1702. The 16th-century holy ark housed there comes from Livorno, Italy. The fourth synagogue, founded in 1740 and named Istambuli, also contains works made in Italy: a 17th-century holy ark from Ancona, and a four-column *tovah* or podium from Pesaro that dates from the same period.

Continuing along Tiferet Yisrael Street, one comes upon the ruins of two synagogues: Tiferet Yisrael, or 'Glory of Israel,' built in the second half of the 19th century, and Karaites, named after a sect that settled in Jerusalem in the 9th century. Proceeding to the corner of Plugat Hakotel Street, visitors will see the traces of the so-called King Hezekiah's Wall (701 BC) and, close by, in Shonei Halachot Street, are the digs of the so-called Israelite Tower, which was one of the defensive parts of the First Temple.

The 'Burnt House,' also on Tiferet Yisrael Street, is an interesting example of a dwelling in the residential quarter of the upper city, which was razed to the ground by the Romans in 70 AD, a short time after the destruction of the Temple and the lower city. Excavations carried out here have brought to light a stone weight with an inscription found in one

30 left The simple decoration of the easternmost Sephardic synagogue, named after the prophet

Elijah, is enriched by a holy ark made in Italy during the Renaissance, seen at left of the lectern.

30 bottom left and right The Istambuli Synagogue also houses fine Italian furniture: at left is an 18th-century holy Ark, while at right is the tovah, a massive platform supported by four wooden columns with Ionic capitals.

three-apse 12th-century church, and of its annexes, which included a hospital and a hospice for pilgrims that were first run by the order of the Knights of the Hospital of St. John and then by the Teutonic Knights.

Near the city wall there once stood the grandiose Byzantine Nea ('new') Basilica, which can be recognized in the Madaba Map. This church, which Justinian had built around 540, now lies in ruins, but the sheer size of the apse and its walls shows how important it was in the past, lying in the middle of a religious complex that was linked to other secondary buildings.

of the rooms, thus allowing archaeologists to identify one of these houses as belonging to a certain Bar Kathros, a member of a family of the priestly caste. The seven rooms in this house had many finds, which are now on display: among the most interesting objects, besides the pottery and glass articles, are a grindstone for minting coins and several coins, the most ancient of which dates from 69 AD.

On the south side of Ha-Karaim Road, at the point where the road merges with Hurva Square, is the Wohl Archaeological Museum, the ancient complex that lies under the modern Yeshiva Hakotel. This museum is rather special in that it exhibits the artifacts found in situ during the digs carried out from the late 1970s to 1983: objects dating from the 8th and 7th century BC, as well as from the Hasmonean and Herodian periods. Another part of the museum consists of the so-called Herodian quarter, which is made up of the foundations and floors–in some cases laid out with mosaics– of six houses built during Herod the Great's reign that now lie about ten feet under the present-day street level. These houses originally consisted of two or three storys articulated around a central courtyard; they had many rooms, including the ritual baths (*mikveh*) of varying sizes and shapes that were fed by rainwater. The splendid Palatial Mansion is the largest house, measuring about 6,500 square feet, with five ritual baths.

On Misgav Ladach Street are the remains of St. Mary of the Germans, a

THE TEMPLE MOUNT

One of the few places in the world that plays a central role for the three monotheistic religions, the Temple Mount (or Mount Moriah) combines overwhelming religious importance and equally extraordinary historical interest due to its very ancientness as a holy site. Indeed, this locality is first mentioned in the Biblical story of the sacrifice of Isaac, that is, in a still mythical period, twelve centuries prior to the first historic documentation regarding the holy buildings that stood on the Mount in the 10th century BC, when the First Temple was built there. The Holy Scriptures relate that, after the unification of Palestine around 1000 BC, King David planned to build, at the site of the 'stone of Isaac's sacrifice' (the Sacred Stone of Abraham), a worthy shrine for the holiest object in Judaism, the Ark of the Covenant, the testimony of the divine

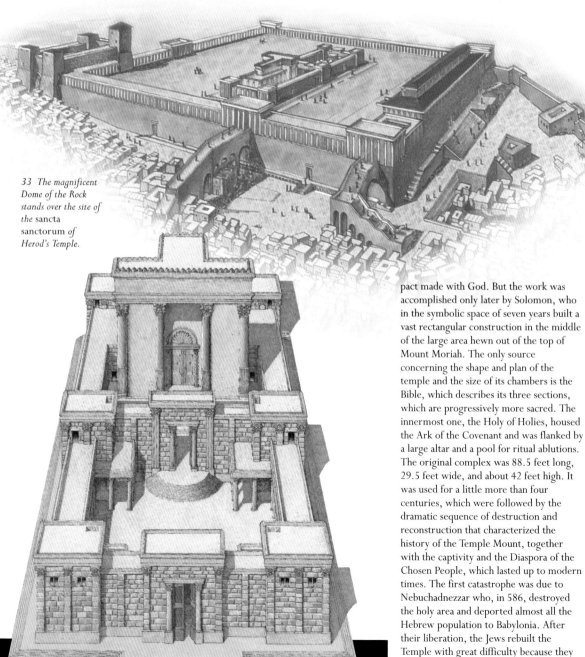

33 The magnificent Dome of the Rock stands over the site of the sancta sanctorum *of Herod's Temple.*

pact made with God. But the work was accomplished only later by Solomon, who in the symbolic space of seven years built a vast rectangular construction in the middle of the large area hewn out of the top of Mount Moriah. The only source concerning the shape and plan of the temple and the size of its chambers is the Bible, which describes its three sections, which are progressively more sacred. The innermost one, the Holy of Holies, housed the Ark of the Covenant and was flanked by a large altar and a pool for ritual ablutions. The original complex was 88.5 feet long, 29.5 feet wide, and about 42 feet high. It was used for a little more than four centuries, which were followed by the dramatic sequence of destruction and reconstruction that characterized the history of the Temple Mount, together with the captivity and the Diaspora of the Chosen People, which lasted up to modern times. The first catastrophe was due to Nebuchadnezzar who, in 586, destroyed the holy area and deported almost all the Hebrew population to Babylonia. After their liberation, the Jews rebuilt the Temple with great difficulty because they

lived in poverty. What is more, they no longer had the very *raison d'être* of the First Temple, that is, the Ark, which had disappeared after the Babylonian invasion. The new Temple resisted time and devastation until Herod the Great's age. Among his many grandiose architectural works, around 20 BC the ambitious conquerer of Jerusalem initiated restoration of the Temple. This work was effected on such a large scale that it continued to the mid 1st century AD, when the Temple achieved its maximum splendor, and the massive trapezoidal shape of the esplanade he envisaged has lasted to this day. However, less than a century after the beginning of the work, Herod's former allies, the Romans, brought about the destruction of the second Temple, and it was never again rebuilt.

During the following six centuries the area occupied by Herod the Great's magnificent Temple and the remains of the Second Temple was first consecrated by the emperor Hadrian to the cult of Jupiter; it then became a site holy to the Muslims led by the caliph Omar, second successor of the Prophet Mohammed and new

conqueror of Jerusalem (638 AD), because they believed that the Prophet went there during his mystical night visit to Jerusalem and then ascended to heaven. In the period bridging the 7th and 8th centuries the most important Islamic buidlings were constructed on the esplanade: the Dome of the Rock and the al-Aqsa Mosque. In the late 11th century the Temple Mount was taken temporarily by the Crusaders. The new conquerers transformed some of the mosques and annexes into places of worship to honor the faith that had brought them to the Holy Land to reconquer the Holy Sepulchre, while other edifices were used as the residence of the Christian kings of Jerusalem–thereby creating a stronghold to defend Christianity and Christians in the heart of the Islamic world. When Saladin conquered Palestine less than a century later, the temple esplanade of the kings of Jerusalem, the Haram es-Sharif, the 'Noble Sanctuary' of the Muslims since the time of Omar's conquest, was restored to its original status as an Islamic mosque, this time for good. The Temple Mount was then administered by the various Islamic

dynasties that governed the Holy City, who gradually added minor buildings and changed it until the 16th century, when Suleiman the Magnificent built the wall on the east and west sides of the esplanade. The edifices built prior to the ones we see today have disappeared completely. The only exceptions are: the massive structure of the esplanade itself, the Herodian retaining walls, the nine gates to the Noble Sanctuary, only two of which, Dung Gate and the Gate of the Chain, can be used by visitors and Muslim worshippers alike, and, lastly, some traces of architecture from the Crusader period .

The Temple Mount is prohibited to orthodox Jews because they consider it a profaned holy place and also because at some unknown point in the esplanade there once lay the Holy of Holies, which only the high priest could (and still can) enter; it is accessible to Christians only if they obey very strict regulations. The area equally sacred for the three religions that have followed one another here in the course of four millennia, is now the third most important Muslim holy site and boasts some of the oldest and most beautiful creations of Islamic art and architecture.

THE AL-AQSA MOSQUE

Al-Aqsa, the largest mosque in Jerusalem, was built in the first two decades of the 8th century at the southern end of Haram es-Sharif, perhaps on the site of the first sacred edifice built in the 7th century by Omar, who utilized the naves of a Byzantine basilica, which in turn had been built over Herodian ruins. The history of the most sacred building in Islam among those in the Noble Sanctuary, is also the story of destruction caused by four earthquakes and of much rebuilding and restoration. In 780 caliph al-Mahdi added fifteen aisles to the mosque, which were reduced to the present-day number of seven in 1033 by caliph az-Zahir, who rebuilt the mosque as we see it today, with the characteristic black dome (which is really a brilliant silver when it is cleaned) that faces the huge golden-hued Dome of the Rock.

The Crusaders occupied the Temple Mount in 1099, converting all the buildings in the esplanade and using the al-Aqsa mosque as the residence of the kings of the Latin Kingdom. They then turned it over to the Knights Templars, the last Catholic rulers of the Temple

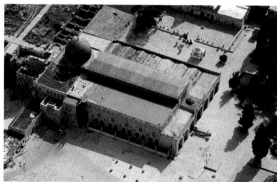

Mount, who enlarged the former mosque, adding three central bays to the porch and surrounding it with new buildings. In 1187 Saladin reconquered Haram es-Sharif and then proceeded to reinstate al-Aqsa as a mosque, decorating it with marble and mosaics, especially the *mihrab*, as well as with a finely carved wooden pulpit. The great conqueror also converted the Templars' Zacharias oratory, a rose window of which has survived, into what is now known as the 'Zakariyeh' *mihrab*. Saladin decided to

34 top Al-Aqsa, the largest mosque in Jerusalem, incorporates the interior of a Byzantine basilica that had been built over Herodian ruins.

34-35 The simple, elegant dome of al-Aqsa remained intact even when the mosque became a Crusader church.

34 center The mosque is divided into seven aisles that end in portals dating back to Saladin's time.

34 bottom The dome of al-Aqsa is almost black from oxidation, but its original color is bright silver.

35 Next to one of the arcades called 'scales' on the Dome of the Rock platform, is the 14th-century Burhan ed-Din pulpit, where the imam led prayer for rain.

tear down the buildings the Templars had placed west of the mosque and used the building material to make other structures in the Haram es-Sharif and inside the al-Aqsa mosque itself: the fruit of this demolition and rebuilding is the large mihrab in the mosque. Saladin did not touch the Knights Templars' refectory, which ran along the south wall; this building is now partly occupied by the two naves of the Women's Mosque, and partly by the Islamic Museum.

From 1249 on, the Mamluks, who were responsible for most of the loveliest architectural works in Muslim Jerusalem, did rebuilding work on two sides of the mosque, adding the bays along the sides of the Crusader porch (1345-50). During the Ottoman period, above all under Suleiman the Magnificent in the first half of the 16th century, restoration work was done on the mosaics that decorate the dome, which was designed by Saladin, and by the beginning of World War Two the ceilings were redecorated and

substantial changes were made. In particular, in 1938 the original columns in the mosque were replaced by white Carrara marble ones that were donated by Mussolini, and some Crusader period windows were enlarged to allow more light into the sanctuary. The French Gothic façade consists of a large open porch with seven arches and the same number of Fatimid entrances to the sanctuary. The interior is 295 x 197 feet and can hold up to 5,000 worshippers in the seven aisles supported by columns and stone pillars dating from different epochs, from the Omayyid period to the pre-World War Two marble columns with Corinthian capitals that support the arches in the central aisle, which is covered with gilded coffering. Opposite the main entrance, a sixteen-step stairway goes down to the underground area of the mosque, which is usually closed, where there were the large halls known as 'Solomon's Stables' used to house the worshippers when the

sanctuary was filled during the chief religious holidays. A long passageway leads to the Double Gate (now bricked up), the ancient southern entrance to Herod's Temple. Just opposite this you can still see the vestibule, which was the entrance to the last Temple, with two large domes supported by a column. Between al-Aqsa and the Dome of the Rock is the el-Kas fountain, the 'bowl,' built in 1336 to be used by the faithful for their ablutions before prayer. In ancient times its water came from a spring near Hebron.

THE DOME
OF THE ROCK

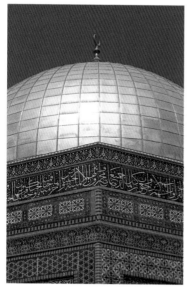

conceals part of the magnificence of the Dome of the Rock, which was gilded by King Hussein of Jordan.

36 center left The Dome of the Ascension dates from Saladin's time and indicates the spot where Mohammed ascended to heaven on his steed.

36 bottom The Dome of the Rock rises up majestically on a platform that covers the top of Mount Moriah.

37 In order to prevent the sun from damaging the vault decoration, the dome consists of two concentric cupolas with a cavity wall between them.

36 top left The simple luxuriousness of the gold contrasts with the elaborate patterns of the majolica tiles that decorate the Dome of the Rock exterior.

36 top right The minaret of the Ashrafiyya madrasa

The middle of Haram es-Sharif is dominated by the Dome of the Rock, also erroneously known as Omar's Mosque to honor the memory of a smaller mosque built by this caliph in 638, six years after the death of Mohammed the Prophet. An incomparable example of early Islamic religious architecture, Qubbet es-Sakhra (the Arabic name for the mosque) was built in the last decade of the 7th century at the behest of caliph Abd el-Malik, who chose to use Roman and Byzantine building material and Greek-Syrian craftsmen and laborers. The caliph's singular decision to entrust non-Muslims with the task of building the mosque was probably due to the lack of building experience among the locals, nomads who had just left their desert tents to lead a sedentary life. In the brief period of Christian dominion the mosque became the *Templum Domini*, hence the name of the Knights Templars order, but already in 1187 it was again used as a mosque under Saladin, who had it richly decorated with marble and mosaics. Later on, restoration work and further decoration continued for centuries, until the last important change, when King Hussein of Jordan had the dome gilded in 1994.

Unlike al-Aqsa mosque, which in all respects is a traditional place of worship and prayer, the Dome of the Rock is a true pilgrimage site, sacred to the commemoration of the Prophet. It also has symbolic importance for all of Jerusalem, the Holy City over which the golden dome shines like a blazon that is respected and venerated by followers of the three monotheistic religions.

The holiness of this mosque is in fact linked to the rock over which the dome lies: it is the site of the mystical night visit of Mohammed, whose horse left a hoof-print there, but above all it is reputedly the place where Isaac was to have been sacrificed, and is thus directly connected to the very origin of monotheism.

With its elegant proportions, this octagonal edifice surmounted by the gilded dome rises up on an elevated trapezoidal platform in the center of the Haram es-Sharif which presumably follows the alignment of Herod's Temple. This elevated area is connected to the esplanade by stairways crowned by graceful arcades

longitudinally: there is a lower part in white marble, and an upper register ornamented by splendid multicolored majolica tiles that form floral and geometric mosaic patterns; the upper margin of the second register bears an inscription that runs continuously along the entire perimeter of the mosque. Very similar to the upper register are the two decorative bands with verses from the *Koran* that line the outer circumference of the drum, which include

built at different times, from the 10th to the 15th century: the arcades are called 'scales,' because according to tradition the pans on which the souls of the dead will be placed on Judgement Day will hang from them. An eschatological meaning is also attached to the Well of Souls, the cave under the rock, where there are two small altars where David, Solomon, Elijah and Mohammed supposedly prayed; this is also believed to be the place where the souls of the dead will gather while awaiting the Last Judgement.

Behind the 'scales' are the portals of the entrances to the mosque, which face the four cardinal points. Each of the eight sides of the lower section of the edifice has seven blind arches, and each of these has one of the 56 magnificent stained glass windows that illuminate the interior. The decoration of the exterior is divided

polychrome majolica tiling and the stained glass windows that illuminate the inside of the drum.

The dome itself consists of two concentric, superposed cupolas supported by wooden ribs and separated by a cavity wall filled with cork to insulate the sumptuous decoration on the vault from potential damage caused by the great differences in temperature in Jerusalem.

Once inside the Qubbet es-Sakhra, you find yourself in the first concentric ambulatory, which symbolically indicates the secular world. This is bordered toward the interior by a colonnade that follows the octagonal plan of the building: it consists of sixteen wonderful marble columns and eight piers aligned with the vertexes of the perimeter. The arches above the rectilinear lintel that is supported by this first colonnade, are

38 top Corinthian capitals frame the modern Khazan majolica tiles, as well as Greek and Italian polychrome and white marble.

38 center Although the decorative tiles of the 56 windows of the

lower section of the edifice are modern, the pattern dates back to the 7th century.

38-39 The stylistic and decorative purity and simplicity of the Dome of the Rock date from the early Islamic period.

magnificently decorated with mosaics with glass tesserae dating back to the original construction of the mosque. Just inside the second concentric circle, which symbolically indicates the intermediate stage between the secular and holy worlds, there is a wooden reliquary which according to popular tradition contains hairs from the Prophet's beard.

The rock in the middle of the mosque, which represents the zenith of holiness and is traditionally considered the center of the world by Muslims, is surrounded by another, circular colonnade consisting of twelve columns with capitals in different styles that come

39 top Rigor, stylistic austerity and lively colors are quite evident in all aspects of the construction.

39 bottom left and right Islam perfected calligraphic art in order to reproduce the will of Allah as expressed through the words of the Prophet, which appear in the exquisitely wrought bands of tiles that decorate the Dome of the Rock.

from more ancient buildings (including Christian ones, as can be seen by the crosses on some of them). The Sacred Rock of Abraham is therefore the hub of the building, standing about six feet above the pavement in an enclosure with an irregular perimeter that is crowned by the tall cylindrical drum of the dome with sixteen stained glass windows that illuminate the interior of the dome (which, for that matter, seems to be illuminated by its own brilliance).

This sublime achievement of early Islamic art has undergone restoration work many times over the centuries, but the original Omayyad conception has always been respected. The mosaics of green, red and white tesserae against the gold background depict Byzantine-style floral patterns with ears of wheat and bunches of grapes that cover the entire surface of the dome drum, which is separated from the vault of the dome itself by an elegant arcade of arabesqued arches. The vault is also dominated by the splendid gold of the Hellenistic inspired motifs in the rich mosaic decoration, which is topped by another circular band with inscriptions.

Over the centuries the Dome of the Rock has remained virtually unaltered and

has maintained its extraordinary harmony of proportions between plan and elevation that make it one of the finest examples of Arab architecture.

Once outside the mosque, we discover that the entire platform on which the Qubbet es-Sakhra lies is studded with extremely interesting minor buildings. Right next to the mosque is the octagonal Dome of the Ascension (Qubbet el-Miraj), built on the spot where Mohammed prayed before ascending to heaven astride his magic steed. During the Crusader occupation, this building was used as a baptistery and then as a church. Beside the arcade at the end of the stairway at the northwestern corner of the platform, are the eight marble columns of the Dome of the Winds (or Spirits), which was probably built in the 16th century. Behind the south arcade, the marble *minbar*, or pulpit, of judge Burhan ed-Din, erected in 1388 with Byzantine and Crusader architectural elements from other buildings, was used by the *imam* for solemn holidays and, in particular, on days dedicated to prayers for rain.

In the eastern part of the platform lies the Dome of the Chain (Qubbet es-Silisleh), a small building supported by columns built by caliph Abd el-Malik. Legend has it that Solomon hung a chain from the top of the vault here, and those who swore falsely while holding it were struck by lightning. Among the other

41 top Islamic law considers the reproduction of the human body in sacred places as conducive to idolatry, hence the refined floral, geometric and calligraphic decoration in the mosques.

40 The inside of the dome rivals the exterior in brilliance, since the beautiful, radiant vault serves to enhance the Sacred Rock of Abraham.

40-41 What strikes one in the second of the three concentric ambulatories is the sophisticated play of geometric patterns created by the Byzantine archiects and Arab craftsmen.

N

41 bottom left The details of the friezes and the style of the mosaics inside the drum of the dome reveal classical and Byzantine influences.

edifices in the Haram es-Sharif, mention must be made of the theological schools, the *madrasas*. The oldest one, the Uthmaniyya, built for a noblewoman in 1437 along the western side of the sacred precinct, was followed in 1482 by the Ashrafiyya, which is considered one of the gems of Mamluk architecture in Jerusalem.

The Fountain of Sultan Qaytbay (Sabil Qaytbay) was built in 1487 by Egyptian artisans and workmen, as was the above-mentioned Ashrafiyya *madrasa*. This fountain is truly singular. Since the Egyptian artisans, led by a Christian master builder, were experts in funerary architecture, they imparted a monumental spirit to it that was usually reserved for important tombs. Thus, the four outer sides are decorated with verses from the *Koran* in gold inscription, while the inner sides are decorated with star patterns which clearly betray the Egyptian tradition that inspired this work.

ALONG THE TEMPLE MOUNT ESPLANADE

42-43 The foot of the Western Wall, better known as the Wailing Wall, represents the holiest aspect of Jewish religious life, from individual prayer to such ceremonies as the bar-mitzvah, during which 13 year-old boys attain adulthood.

At the foot of the Temple Mount esplanade are two sites that are extremely interesting from a historic and archaeological standpoint: the area of Hakotel Hama'aravi, or Western Wall, also known as the Wall of Prayer and Wailing Wall; and the zone which goes from the southwestern end of the wall itself to a point south of the wall and then to the Double and Triple gates, which is known as the Ophel Archaeological Garden.

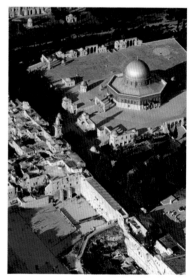

The square opposite Hakotel is the heart of world Judaism. It is here that Jews venerate the memory of their most sacred site, the Temple, so often destroyed and rebuilt and then destined never to rise up again in 70 A.D., a tragic date that is commemorated every year on the ninth day in the month of Av (July-August). This sad and nostalgic recurrence gave birth to the name Wailing Wall, which was coined in the Middle Ages by Christians and is still commonly used to designate this historic spot. The Hakotel Hama'aravi is really the brief stretch of the west retaining wall that

42 left The wall revered by Jews is dominated by the Dome of the Rock, built on the site of the Temple, the destruction of which is lamented by the faithful.

42 right In the past the square opposite the Western Wall was occupied by a Muslim quarter that was destroyed in 1967.

43 At the Western Wall religious feeling often becomes grief, yet the Scriptures offer hope: the two tefillin (boxes) attached to the forehead and left hand of the worshippers speak of the liberation of Israel.

Herod the Great built to reinforce, and then enlarge, the esplanade, on which he then built the Temple. The history of this place as regards Judaism began immediately after the destruction of the Temple and continued for centuries, with an alternation of permission to pray there and prohibition from doing so—depending on those who ruled the Holy City. This state of affairs finally ended in 1967 when the Israeli troops occupied the area and definitively reinstated it as a place of worship for Jews. Afterwards, during the renovation of the

Jewish quarter, all the buildings in the so-called Maghreb quarter (the area opposite the wall), which stood as close as thirteen feet to the wall, were demolished, creating the present-day square. The holy character of this site stems from the fact that the Western Wall is the spot accessible to Jews that is closest to the place where the Holy of Holies in the Temple was located. This makes the area in front of the wall a sort of outdoor synagogue that is used by practising Jews from Jerusalem as well as pilgrims from all parts of the world, who consider its massive stones the most concrete symbol of the Diaspora. Although there are many people there every day, the Western Wall area is particularly crowded on Friday evening and Saturday and, as is the case with all synagogues, it is accessible only to worshippers with their heads covered; what is more, there are separate areas for men and women: the former in the northern section of the plaza, to the left facing the wall, and the latter in the

southern section.

The enormous Herodian-age blocks of stone that make up the wall are also the setting for the *bar mitzvah*, the ceremony for adolescents, who at the age of thirteen (twelve for girls) assume full religious responsibility and join the religious community. The cyclopean blocks in the lower part of the wall, in the cracks of which the faithful put notes with prayers and vows, are surmounted by a section of smaller stone blocks that were placed there during the restoration work effected in the Mamluk and Ottoman periods.

The Western Wall is delimited to the north (the left-hand end) by a building at the foundation of which lies the corridor known as Wilson's Arch, now used as a synagogue, which is the only surviving element of the large viaduct that once connected the Temple Mount esplanade and the West Hill. To the south, the wall ends at the Ophel Archaeological Garden, a vast area around the base of the southwestern corner of the city wall that continues to have surprises in store for archaeologists. Digs have shown that this elevated area was originally a cemetery that was incorporated into the city walls in the late 8th century BC, when the tombs were used for a different purpose, cisterns and baths being built in the area to provide water for the dwellings. Among the twenty-one

44 top The Ophel Garden contains 21 archaeological strata.

44 below At the foot of al-Aqsa, to the south, is the first urban settlement.

44-45 Barely protruding over the Herodian bastion, the back of Robinson's Arch supported a stairway leading to the Temple Mount.

45 bottom left The main staircase of the Temple, seen at right, still exudes its ancient majesty.

45 bottom right A stairway-ramp also went over Wilson's Arch, now a synagogue.

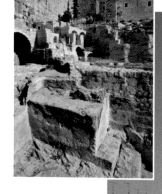

archaeological strata in the Ophel Garden, the richest one dates from twelve centuries later, when the Byzantines renovated the zone, building houses and cisterns that in the 8th century AD, during the Omayyad period, were replaced by three large buildings, the only remains of which are some parts of the masonry at the base of the southwest corner of the esplanade.

Between the southern end of the Western Wall and the southwest corner of the city wall, there are traces of the so-called Robinson's Arch, which is what is left of the supporting structure of the large stairway that went from the royal *stoa* (esplanade) down to the street that skirts the base of the wall. About forty-three feet west of the remains of this arch, archaeologists brought to light the other pier that supported the stairs, built with blocks about the same size as those used

in the construction of the retaining wall; four niches in the ruins of this structure have been interpreted as rooms of workshops that lined the large slabs of the Herodian pavement. At the access ramp, still in the area around the southwest corner of the city wall, archaeologists found the ruins of a rectangular Byzantine pool, covered with an Omayyad-period pavement, but further digs also brought to light a part of the Herodian pavement, which was about six feet under the Byzantine one.

Heading further east, you will see the remains of a large Omayyad palace consisting of long rectangular rooms looking onto a courtyard. A few steps lead to a tower set against the south wall, a Crusader-epoch construction that was rebuilt by Saladin in 1191 and again in the 15th century. Behind the tower you can catch a glimpse of the Double Gate. A

nearby stairway leads to the remains of a Byzantine building that still has its original pavement mosaics, and to a large Herodian cistern. Further east are the impressive ruins of the broad Herodian staircase that goes up to the Double Gate, which is now bricked up. However, you can see the gate from the other side by taking the underground passageway of the al-Aqsa Mosque, which leads to the gate vestibule. A short distance away is the Triple Gate, which was bricked up in the 11th century. Its present aspect dates from the Omayyad period. Excavations carried out in front of the three blind fornices have unearthed the remains of a large Byzantine house whose three storys fit in perfectly with the sloping land and are still connected by the original stairway, which may have belonged to the palace of empress Eudocia, or perhaps to a hospice built under her patronage. Near

these ruins archaeologists found the remains of ritual baths (*mikveh*) that were used by the faithful for purification before entering the Temple, as well as some rock-cut rooms. Further eastward is the Single Gate, a secondary entranceway that dates back to the Knights Templars period and that was sealed off by Saladin in 1187. The wall at the base of this entrance bears traces of the arches that supported the Herodian street. The Byzantine street leads to an open area with the foundations of an Omayyad building. This is an ideal spot for observing the ruins of two structures that are partly hidden from view by the modern street: a Herodian-age palace, perhaps the residence of Queen Helen of Adiabene, to the east, and Byzantine houses to the west.

THE MUSLIM QUARTER

Situated in the northeastern sector of the Old City, that is, along the north and west sides of the Temple Mount esplanade, the Muslim Quarter distinguishes itself in Jerusalem for its size and population. Naturally, these features go hand in hand with the vivaciousness typical of Islamic communities, the life of which usually revolves around the markets–the bazaars and souks–given the eminently commercial nature of Muslim society.

The ancient nucleus of the quarter grew up next to the walls of Haram es-Sharif at the end of the 7th century, when el-Quds, the Muslims' 'Holy Jerusalem,' was born. The Mamluk period marked the height of its growth, and it was then that most of the most important architectural works we see today were built. The main accessways to the Muslim quarter pass through the Ottoman walls: the Bab Sittia Maryam ('Gate of the Virgin Mary,' or 'St. Stephen's Gate') lies in the eastern stretch of the walls, while the Bab ez-Zahira (the 'Gate of Flowers' or Herod's Gate), and the Bab el-Amud ('Gate of the Column' or Damascus Gate) are located on the north side. Bab el-Amud, the most lively gate in the Old City, has an animated market and marks the beginning of Tariq el-Wad, one of the main streets in the Muslim quarter. This street bounds the medieval area at the west side of Haram es-Sharif, the most interesting in this quarter, and also crosses Tariq Bab es-Silsileh, the 'Street of the Gate of the Chain,' which marks the 'border' with the Jewish quarter near the

46 top The Muslim quarter was the first ethnic area to develop north and west of Haram es-Sharif; most of it dates back to the Mamluk period.

46 bottom left El-Qattanim souk, the former cotton merchants' market, begins on the west side of the Haram es-Sharif, in line with the Dome of the Rock.

Western Wall. Many of the buildings jammed into the labyrinth of alleys that rose up from the second half of the 13th century to the end of the 14th century, were religious structures, such as the *madrasas* (theological schools) and the *turbas* (tombs), or a combination of the two. Then there were the hospices for the many pilgrims who flocked to Jerusalem

from all parts of the Islamic world and ended up settling in the Holy City. With time, however, exactly because of overpopulation, the *madrasas*, *turbas* and hospices were not only rebuilt, but were converted, becoming private houses, a development that occurred in most of the quarter.

The cross streets going westward from the walls of the Haram es-Sharif have the same name as the accessways on which they begin. Proceeding from the south, you will find yourself on the already-mentioned Tariq Bab el-Silsileh Street, with the Tankiziyya *madrasa*, built in 1328, which is a characteristic example of refined Mamluk architecture, as well as a series of *turbas*. The Turba Sadiyya (1311) boasts a striking portal with multicolored marble decoration, as does the nearby Turba Turkan Khatun, which was built in 1352 and has geometric and floral motif decoration. Along the stretch of road now used as a market lies the Kilaniyya, another distinguished *turba* (1352) that has a monochrome façade with a group of double windows. A little further down the street is the Barka Khan, a tomb built in 1264-80 and renovated in 1390, when the original arches were sealed off and the present doors and windows were inserted. In 1900 this funerary monument was turned into a

reading room of the Khalidiya Library, which boasts a collection of 12,000 works between books and manuscripts. On the same side of the street is the Tashtimuriyya, a madrasa-turba built in 1382. Its main features are the large door flanked by two windows decorated with an inscription with a blazon, and an elegant balcony on the first floor. Lastly, there is the Khan es-Sultan (1386), a Crusader inn which under the Mamluks retained part of its original function, becoming a caravanserai.

By heading north you will see the roofed street with the cotton merchants' market, the Suq el-Qattanim. This souk became active in the first half of the 14th century. Two beautiful Turkish baths (hammam), el-Ayn and el-Shifa, were added to the souk, which was restored in 1974.

To the north of the Bab el-Hadid, or 'Iron Gate,' is the street of the same name, which has some lovely 13th-15th-century Mamluk buildings. The most interesting are the Ribat Kurt al-Mansuri (1293) and the adjacent Jawhariyya madrasa (1440), and, across the street, the Arghuniyya and Muzhiriyya madrasas (1358 and 1480 respectively). The Ribat Kurt al-Mansuri is a hospice with only one story and a small entrance; however, it has a peculiar feature: on its roof lies part of

the Jawhariyya madrasa, which was built there so that it would touch the wall of the Haram es-Sharif, a surprising and singular expedient that we find in many other Islamic buildings. The Arghuniyya madrasa houses the tomb of the 'Master of the Robes,' Arghun el-Kamili–as a coat of arms on the portal indicates–the founder of the school who died before it was completed. Here again, the roof of this building supports a part of the Muzhiriyya madrasa, in order to 'touch' the Haram.

The lovely Mamluk portion of the Muslim quarter ends with Tariq Bab el-Naazir, or Street of the Inspector's Gate (after the name of the gate of the Haram es-Sharif, also known as 'Gate of the Prison'). On this street are the Manjaakiyya madrasa, built in 1361, rebuilt in 1923 and now used as an office building, and two hospices for pilgrims that are among the oldest Mamluk constructions in Jerusalem: the Ribat Ala ed-Din (1267) and the Ribat el-Masuri (1282). After the junction with el-Wad, Tariq Bab el-Naazir becomes Aqabat et-Takiya. Here lies the Ribat Bayram Jawish hospice, built in 1540 in the late Mamluk period, and the Serai es-Sitt Tunshuq, which was built around 1390 and in 1552 was incorporated into

the imaret–the hospice for Ottoman pilgrims–of the sultan Khassefi, a large complex consisting of a cookhouse for the poor, a convent for Sufi mystics and a caravanserai. In the 19th century the imaret became the residence of the Egyptian governor of Jerusalem and was later converted into an orphanage. Opposite the Imaret is the Turba es-Sitt Tunshuq, or 'Tomb of the Lady,' referring to the owner of the caravanserai, who was perhaps a slave of Turkish extraction who had lived in the building until her death in 1398.

THE CURCH OF ST. ANNE
AND THE POOL OF BETHESDA

48 top This
Byzantine stela shows
that after Hadrian
had turned the Pool
of Bethesda into a
public bath, it again
became a Christian
site.

Although it is part of the Muslim quarter, the area immediately north of the Haram es-Sharif is formally owned by the French government: it was given to France by the Turkish sultan Abdul Legid in 1856 for Napoleon III's decisive intervention in favour of the Ottoman Empire during the Crimean War. This tiny Christian 'island,' known as 'Bethesda quarter'–just past St. Stephen's Gate (or Gate of the Virgin Mary)–has ruins and monuments that are extremely interesting from an function. During the Hasmonean age the pool was at its deepest, and under the Romans it was dressed with stone, which still exists. The *Gospel according to St. John* mentions the Pool of Bethesda, "by the sheep market," as the place where Jesus healed a paralytic man, thus increasing its reputation as a miraculous pool, which soon became a pilgrimage site. During Hadrian's time the twin pools were used as public baths, next to which a temple dedicated to the god of medicine, Asclepius, was built. The

48 center The
austere style of
St. Anne's, a 12th-
century church, is the
best preserved—and
most widespread—
example of Crusader
architecture in the
Holy Land.

archaeological and religious standpoint, from the Pool of Bethesda area to the adjacent Church of St. Anne, and leads to the Via Dolorosa.

The Pool of Bethesda was named after the nearby Sheep Gate (it is, in fact, also known as the Probatic Pond, alluding to the purification baths of sheep before they were sacrificed). In the prosperous period immediately prior to the Babylonian Captivity, northwest of the Temple Mount walls a pool was cut out of the rock to collect rainwater for the sacred precinct; in the Hellenistic age this cistern was flanked by another one, which was then combined with the first to form the large pool we see today. During Herod the Great's time, the pool was replaced as a source of water by a new one dug near the Temple, but retained its ritual

remains of the baths were then incorporated into a Byzantine church dedicated to the Virgin Mary, which was destroyed in 614 by the Persians, rebuilt and destroyed again by the caliph el-Hakim in 1009. During the Crusader period Benedictine nuns built a convent around the basilica area. In 1104 Baldwin I, brother of Godrey of Bouillon and his successor to the throne of Jerusalem, sent his repudiated wife there to live: thanks to the generous donations of the Crusader conqueror of Acre, the nuns were able to build a chapel in the middle of the Byzantine church. The convent church was replaced by St. Anne's in 1140. This latter was dedicated to the Virgin Mary's mother, following the traditional belief (which is probably well-grounded) that the home of Mary's

48 bottom The area
around St. Anne's
contains many ruins
dating back to a
period of at least two
thousand years.

48-49 Dedicated to
the Virgin Mary's
mother, the Church of
St. Anne lies next to

the place where Mary
supposedly spent her
childhood.

49 bottom left and
right Over the
centuries additions
were built and
superimposed around
the ancient Pool of
Bethesda.

parents, Anne and Joachim, and the site of her childhood, were near the church.

However, the new building soon proved to be too small and was immediately enlarged: the façade was therefore moved 23 feet forward. In 1192 Saladin transformed the church into a Muslim theological school (*madrasa*), as an epigraph above the entrance proves, and it served this purpose until the Ottoman period. It was later abandoned and had practically fallen into ruins by the time it was donated to the French government and the African missionaries (who still administer it). Thus this beautiful edifice in pure Romanesque style, considered the best preserved Crusader church in the Holy Land, was restored immediately, so that its austere façade is perfectly intact.

ANTONIA FORTRESS

To the west of St. Anne's is the site of the Antonia Fortress, which has virtually disappeared except for some remains under the convents and chapels flanking the Via Dolorosa. This complex, also called 'Antonia Tower,' was built by Herod the Great around 35 BC, that is, shortly after he conquered Jerusalem, over the ruins of a more ancient structure. As was his custom, the new ruler of the city built it for defensive purposes as well as for purely political motives, since in this case his aim was to control the faithful who flocked to the

sacred precinct of the Temple. The fortress, which was dedicated to Marc Anthony, the ambitious protector of the new king of Jerusalem, later became the headquarters of Pontius Pilate's *praetorium*, and was in the end beseiged and destroyed by the Romans themselves in 70 AD.

The vast area that once housed the complex is presently occupied by the Monastery of the Flagellation, el-Ummariyya madrasa, the Ecce Homo arch and the adjacent Sisters of Zion convent. The Monastery of the

50 left Traditionally connected to the Passion of Christ, the Ecce Homo arch dates from Hadrian's time.

50-51 The white dome of the Chapel of the Condemnation, next to the top of the Ecce Homo basilica, dominates the First Station of the Via Dolorosa.

50 right Two of the arches that suppport the dome of the Ecce Homo basilica lie on an arch that dates back to the time of Jesus and Herod Agrippa I.

51 top left The south wall of the Ecce Homo basilica incorporates one end of the Ecce Homo arch.

51 top right The late Crusader-period Chapel of the Flagellation lies in *the vast 19th-century Franciscan monastery of the same name.*

51 bottom right The most interesting parts of the Chapel of the Flagellation are the *stained-glass windows, vividly illustrating episdodes from Christ's Passion.*

some stones from the *Lithostrothon*, the pavement where Jesus was supposedly tried and flogged, which can be reached via the nearby Ecce Homo basilica. The Chapel of the Condemnation is generally considered the starting point of the Way of the Cross, that is to say, it is the first Station of the Cross, while some scholars still maintain that this is where the Madrasa el-Unmariya now stands.

Near the chapels is the Convent of the Sisters of Zion, built by the Franciscans around the mid 19th century over important Roman age ruins. In fact, the Ecce Homo basilica, part of the complex, lies over a part of the pavement of the eastern forum of the Roman Aelia Capitolina and includes the remains of a three-bay arch that was built sometime in the period from the reign of Herod Agrippa, king of the Hebrews from 41 to 44 AD, to the Hadrianic age. The most remarkable vestiges of the above-mentioned arch lie in the road that goes around the building: the remaining segment of the Ecce Homo Arch, which is traditionally identified as the place where Pilate brought Jesus before the crowd and uttered the famous exclamation: "Ecce Homo!" (Behold the man).

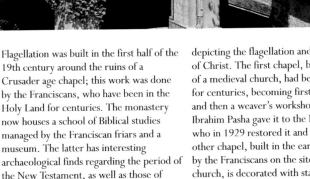

Flagellation was built in the first half of the 19th century around the ruins of a Crusader age chapel; this work was done by the Franciscans, who have been in the Holy Land for centuries. The monastery now houses a school of Biblical studies managed by the Franciscan friars and a museum. The latter has interesting archaeological finds regarding the period of the New Testament, as well as those of Herod the Great and the Crusaders, and a fine collection of coins. The large building lies next to the Chapels of the Flagellation, which have two stained glass windows

depicting the flagellation and condemnation of Christ. The first chapel, built on the site of a medieval church, had been abandoned for centuries, becoming first a sort of stable and then a weaver's workshop. In 1836 Ibrahim Pasha gave it to the Franciscans, who in 1929 restored it and still run it. The other chapel, built in the early 19th century by the Franciscans on the site of a Byzantine church, is decorated with stained-glass windows that represent angels with the instruments of the Passion, Pontius Pilate washing his hands of Jesus' destiny, and Jesus bearing the Cross. On the floor are

THE CHRISTIAN QUARTER

Once past Bed ha Bad Street, which follows the route of the *cardo*, the Via Dolorosa finally enters the Christian quarter, which covers an area of about 70 square miles in the northwestern sector of the Old City, and approaches its end, Golgotha (Calvary), with the vast complex of buildings grouped around the Holy Sepulchre. While to the north of this extremely important historical and religious site, the only building of any importance in the Christian quarter is the 15th-century el-Khanqah mosque, there are some very interesting buildings south of the heart of Christian Jerusalem.

Just southeast of the main entrance to the Holy Sepulchre is the el-Ummariya Mosque, built at the end of the 12th century by Saladin's successor in memory of Omar I, who conquered Jerusalem in 638. When he entered the Holy City, this level-headed sultan decided not to enter the Holy Sepulchre to pray so that the building would not become sacred to the Muslims. The 15th-century minaret of el-Ummariya is identical to the one beside the already mentioned el-Khanqah Salahiyya mosque, which was originally a monastery for Sufi mystics that Saladin built in 1187-89 in the area of the palace

of the Crusader patriarch of Jerusalem. The present aspect of the minarets dates from after the 1458 earthquake. Curiously enough, their tips, made of light stone, end at the same height despite the differences in ground level of their respective sites.

South of the Holy Sepulchre is the *Muristan*, which in Persian means 'hospital' or 'hospice.' This was built at the beginning of the 9th century at the behest of the king of the Franks, Charlemagne, as a token of his friendship with the caliph Harun ar-Rashid, who was made famous in the *Thousand and One Nights*. The complex originally consisted of a church dedicated to the Virgin Mary,

52 top The recently restored Church of St. John was built in the 11th century over the foundation of the most ancient Christian church in Jerusalem.

52 bottom During the Crusader period, St. Mary of the Latins with its double lancet windows, was reserved for male pilgrims.

53 top left A semicircular arch gives access to the Aftimos market, which was inserted in the Muristan area by the Greek Orthodox authorities in 1903.

53 top right The singular X-shaped intersection of the streets in the Aftimos souk has an interesting Neo-Baroque fountain.

53 bottom left The bell-tower of St. John's Church was built in keeping with the characteristic Greek Orthodox tradition.

53 bottom right The 15th-century minaret of el-Ummariyya mosque dominates the building dedicated to Mohammed's first successor, Omar I.

in the area already occupied by the Byzantine basilica. The dome in the middle of the courtyard illuminates the underlying Crypt of St. Helena, while the door in the southwest corner of the courtyard leads to the entrances of the Holy Sepulchre, via the Ethiopian and Coptic chapels.

next to which there were a Benedictine monastery and a pilgrims' hospice, but it was all destroyed in 1009 by the intolerant, 'mad caliph', el-Hakim. About fifty years later the complex was rebuilt by merchants from the Republic of Amalfi, who also had three churches built in the area, each with its own hospital and hospice: St. Mary of the Latins, built in 1070 and used to house male pilgrims; St. Mary Minor (1080), for women pilgrims; and St. John's, built in 1070, used to give aid to the poor.

In 1099 some of the Crusader knights who had been wounded during the conquest of Jerusalem and put up in St. John's hospital, decided to remain there to care for the ill. They also founded the 'Order of the Hospitallers,' also known as the 'Knights of St. John of the Hospital.' In a short time their number and power increased to such a degree that the hospital was enlarged so that it could take in 2,000 patients. St. John's church–built over the oldest Christian church in the city and enlarged by the Amalfi merchants in 1070–was left intact. After conquering Jerusalem in 1187, Saladin allowed ten knights to remain for some time to take care of the remaining ill, then in 1192 the complex was donated to the Dome of the Rock to house Muslim pilgrims. In the 15th century the hospital complex could still take in 400 persons, but it soon began to decline so much that at the end of the following century some of its stones were used to restore the city walls. In 1869, the Turkish government donated the area of the old Muristan partly to Prussia and partly to the Greek Orthodox patriarchate. In 1898 Kaiser Wilhelm II had the Lutheran Church of the Redeemer built over St. Mary of the Latins, maintaining the plan and the porch decoration, to which were added the signs of the Zodiac and

symbols of the months. In 1901 the Greek Orthodox demolished St. Mary Minor to make room for a market, and they placed a fountain in the hospice area.

Just north of the Church of the Redeemer is the Russian Mission in Exile, or 'Alexander Hospice,' annexed to a Russian Orthodox church. The building was bought by the Russians in 1859 and still has Roman ruins dating from the time of Hadrian and Constantinian: the forum of Hadrian's city Aelia Capitolina, and Constantine's Basilica of the Martyrion. A rather hard-to-find arched entranceway affords access to the area of the Ethiopian Monastery, whose rather poor aspect may strike visitors: the monks, who were evicted by the Copts from the area they once lived in, live in miserable mud huts built among the remains of a Crusader cloister erected

THE HOLY SEPULCHRE

The history of the Holy Sepulchre is no less complicated than its present-day configuration. This is due to the changes that began to be made a short time after the events described in the Gospels and continued throughout the entire history of Christianity to the present. The edifice we see today includes the places which for obvious reasons can be considered the

natural heart of the Christian religion: the circular Anastasis or Rotunda area symbolizing the Resurrection, that is, the tomb of Jesus, and Calvary, where he was crucified, a few yards southeast of the former. During Jesus' life both these sites lay outside the city walls—as the New Testament tells us—on the top of a rock whose shape, barrenness and functions earned it the name of Golgotha, or 'skull,' and they became part of the walled city during the time of Herod Agrippa, about twenty years after the Resurrection of Christ.

The first account of the architectural history of the site was handed down by the very founder of ecclesiastic historiography, Eusebius of Caesarea, who tells

us that it all began after the Council of Nicaea, in 326 AD, when the new credo of the Roman Empire was formulated. It was emperor Constantine's mother, Helena, who identified the Stations of the Cross in the Via Dolorosa as far as the sepulchre, which was brought to light together with the rock of Golgotha by cutting away the terreplein of the Temple of Venus that Hadrian had built precisely over the Stations, probably because he was apprehensive about the potentially explosive political meanings attached to the site. The tomb of Jesus was isolated from the surrounding cliff and enclosed in an *aedicule* that in turn was surmounted by a dome, connected in an east-west direction to a five-aisle basilica, covered with a roof with two pitches: the Martyrion, which was consecrated in 335. The year 614 witnessed the first destruction, when the Persians tore down most of Constantine's edifice. The reconstruction work, however, abandoned the basilica plan in favour of the asymmetrical one it still has. The façade of the new church was built south of the Anastasis, so that the complex included the

Calvary. What remained of the basilica was definitively demolished in 1009 by el-Hakim, the Fatimid caliph who was responsible for the most serious damage to the non-Muslim buildings in Jerusalem. Thirty years later, partial reconstruction began, but it took another sixty years before the Crusaders were able to build the large Romanesque church that for the most part has survived to this day. They also built the bell-tower next to the west entrance. After restoring the dome (what we see today is the result of 18th-century rebuilding), the exterior was basically left untouched until 1808, when the Rotunda was destroyed by fire. The Greek Orthodox who were charged with the reconstruction effected changes to the austere Romanesque interior that virtually erased all traces of the Crusader construction, including the tombs of the Christian kings, which were originally placed under the rock of Calvary. They also changed the middle of the original nave into the Katholikon, or Greek Orthodox chapel; the only virtue of this very questionable intervention is that it brought

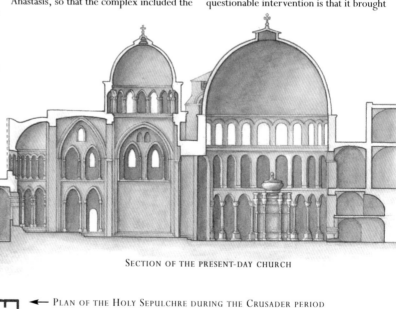

SECTION OF THE PRESENT-DAY CHURCH

← PLAN OF THE HOLY SEPULCHRE DURING THE CRUSADER PERIOD

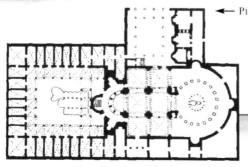

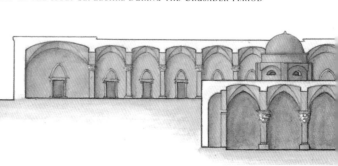

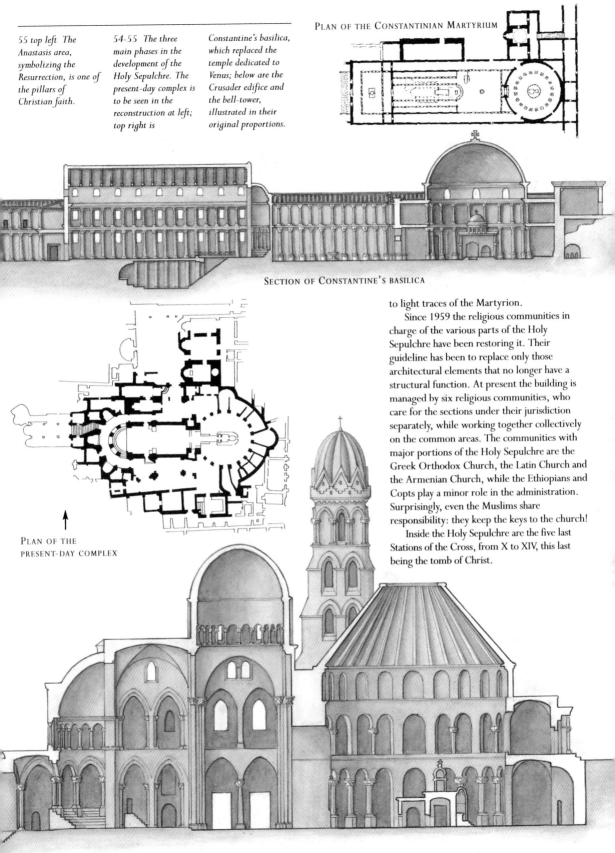

55 top left The Anastasis area, symbolizing the Resurrection, is one of the pillars of Christian faith.

54-55 The three main phases in the development of the Holy Sepulchre. The present-day complex is to be seen in the reconstruction at left; top right is

Constantine's basilica, which replaced the temple dedicated to Venus; below are the Crusader edifice and the bell-tower, illustrated in their original proportions.

SECTION OF CONSTANTINE'S BASILICA

PLAN OF THE
PRESENT-DAY COMPLEX

to light traces of the Martyrion.

Since 1959 the religious communities in charge of the various parts of the Holy Sepulchre have been restoring it. Their guideline has been to replace only those architectural elements that no longer have a structural function. At present the building is managed by six religious communities, who care for the sections under their jurisdiction separately, while working together collectively on the common areas. The communities with major portions of the Holy Sepulchre are the Greek Orthodox Church, the Latin Church and the Armenian Church, while the Ethiopians and Copts play a minor role in the administration. Surprisingly, even the Muslims share responsibility: they keep the keys to the church!

Inside the Holy Sepulchre are the five last Stations of the Cross, from X to XIV, this last being the tomb of Christ.

SECTION OF THE CRUSADER PERIOD BUILDING

The parvis in front of the entrance is flanked to the left by the bell-tower, and to the right by the chapel of St. Mary the Egyptian and the Chapel of the Franks. The bells of the tower were removed by Saladin in 1187, and an earthquake caused part of the tower to collapse in 1545. Access to the Chapel of the Franks is by means of a stairway that originally led directly to the Calvary chapel.

Once past the only remaining door in the Crusader double portal, which was partly bricked up by Saladin, one enters the vestibule, which boasts the white marble slab known as the Stone of Unction, the XIII Station of the Cross, where Jesus was supposedly laid and annointed before being buried. To the right, stairs lead to Golgotha, which is

divided into the two chapels of the Crucifixion and of Calvary, respectively the X and XI Stations of the Cross (the division of Jesus' raiment and Jesus being nailed to the Cross), and the XII Station, dedicated to Jesus' death on the Cross. The first chapel belongs to the Latin Church and is decorated with modern mosaics (only the medallion of the Ascension on the ceiling dates back to the 12th century). The second one, under the jurisdiction of the Greek Orthodox, contains a silver-plated bronze altar executed by Domenico Portigiani in 1588 in Florence for Cardinal Ferdinando de' Medici, on the base of which is a silver disk with a hole indicating the place where the Cross of Jesus was set. A crevice allows pilgrims to touch the rock of Golgotha, which is now perfectly smooth. Under the Greek Orthodox chapel is the crypt of Adam: according to tradition,

Jesus died over Adam's tomb.

Going left from the vestibule you will reach the Rotunda, which houses the *aedicule* of the Holy Sepulchre, the XIV and last Station of the Cross. The original Crusader Rotunda was apparently larger than the present-day one, because it ended in an ambulatory with a circular colonnade, while almost all the space between the columns is now walled in. Surmounted by the dome, the shrine of the Holy Sepulchre is a small, rectangular structure 26 x 19 feet, and 19 feet high, which was built by the Greek Orthodox two years after the

56 bottom left and right The slab on which the body of Jesus was annointed for burial, the hallowed Stone of Unction, is situated just past the entrance of the Holy Sepulchre.

57 top The partly bricked-up double entrance to the Holy Sepulchre was built by the Crusaders, as was the bell-tower, which was larger before it was struck by a quake.

57 center During Jesus' time the sepulchre, now part of the lavish 19th-century aedicule was situated in the rock-hewn necropolis that extended outside the city walls.

56-57 Christian and Muslim satellites seem to be keeping watch, at a respectful distance, over the Holy Sepulchre dome:

at left, the minarets of the el-Ummariyya and el-Khanka mosques soar over the bell-tower of the Church of the Redeemer.

57 bottom The dome towering over the Rotunda and the aedicule in the Holy Sepulchre, supported by austere arches, replaced the truncate cone one built in 1048 by the Byzantine emperor Monomachus, which in turn replaced the gilded dome of Constantine's basilica.

1808 fire that destroyed the 11th-century *aedicule*, which in turn had replaced the Constantinian Anastasis, which had been demolished by caliph el-Hakim. Just inside the *aedicule* is a vestibule, known as the Chapel of the Angel, from which a small door a little more than four feet high gives access to the stone tomb of Christ, which is dressed in marble. On the west apse, behind the *aedicule*, are three chapels. The central space is flanked by the Coptic chapel and the Armenian chapel and is known as the Syrian chapel. This chamber incorporates remains of the outer wall of

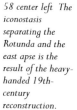

58 top The figure of the Pantocrator, the image of Christ as almighty ruler, illuminates the dome of the Katholikon, flanked by the main dome.

58 center right On the lower level of the complex, the Chapel

of St. Helena indicates the spot where the empress reputedly found the wood of the True Cross. The walls of the sacellum and the stairs leading to it are covered with crosses carved by the faithful over the centuries.

58 center left The iconostasis separating the Rotunda and the east apse is the result of the heavy-handed 19th-century reconstruction.

58 bottom left The place where Jesus

was crucified, the Calvary, is worshipped as the XI Station of the Cross.

59 A Greek Orthodox officiant facing the sumptuous iconostasis of the Katholikon. The Greek Orthodox administer most of the Holy Sepulchre.

the 4th century Rotunda, as well as 11th-century piers and columns, and is connected to the so-called tomb of Joseph of Arimathea (under the jurisdiction of the Muslims), which is the only tomb besides the Holy Sepulchre itself that belonged to the ancient necropolis.

Left of the *aedicule*, the central portion of the nave is occupied by the Greek Orthodox chapel, the Katholikon, which is covered with the smaller of the two domes

in the church. The structural elements of the Katholikon date from the Crusader age, and were built over the site of the peristyle that in the Byzantine basilica separated the Martyrion from the Anastasis. Drastically changed by the Greek Orthodox at the beginning of the 19th century, the Katholikon is divided by the iconostasis, which separates the Choir of the Greeks from the east apse of the church and its surrounding ambulatory. To the right of the

Katholikon as you face the *aedicule* of the Holy Sepulchre, just past the section of the north nave known as the Arches of the Virgin—which is supported by Hadrianic-age Corinthian columns—in the northeastern corner of the basilica, is the Greek Orthodox chapel known as the 'Prison of Christ.'

Lastly, in the east apse of the church is the Chapel of the Division of the Raiment, flanked to the northeast by the Chapel of St. Longinus and the Chapel of the Mocking of Christ (which houses the Column of the Flagellation). Next to the first chapel, which belongs to the Armenian community, a stairway leads to the austere Byzantine Chapel of St. Helena, supported by four piers surmounted by the dome that emerges in the cloister of the Coptic monks, which was once occupied by the Martyrion. Another flight of steps, decorated with numerous crosses carved by the pilgrims over the centuries, leads down to the crypt of the Finding of the True Cross. This belongs to the Latin monks and was built on the spot where emperor Constantine's mother, St. Helena, inspired by a miraculous dream, supposedly found the Cross on which Christ was crucified inside an ancient cistern.

TOURS OUTSIDE THE CITY WALLS
NORTH OF THE OLD CITY

The peripheral area north of the Old City was the second one, after the western district, that expanded outside town in the second half of the 19th century. It was divided by the 'green line,' or no man's land, during the difficult period when Jerusalem had been partitioned into Israeli and Jordanian spheres of influence, from 1948 to 1967. What could be called 'North Jerusalem,' as opposed to 'East Jerusalem' and 'West Jerusalem,' retains the signs of conflict in the 'Tourjeman outpost,' the former Israeli border station that houses a

that the quarries provided the material needed to build Solomon's Temple, even though this date seems uncertain. What is certain is that during the Roman period the quarries were exploited to their fullest when the stone was cut for Herod the Great's grandiose architectural works.

A little further north of the quarries, on the other side of Sultan Suleiman Road, is Jeremiah's Cave, the ancient cistern that was part of a group of natural caverns, where the Biblical prophet was

museum dedicated to those years of out-and-out war. Besides this relic of the recent past, the area north of Jerusalem, inhabited by a mixed Christian and Muslim population with a clear-cut predominance of Muslim culture, has many noteworthy sites, including numerous tombs that bear witness to its use as a cemetery in ancient times.

At the bottom of the escarpment outside Suleiman's walls, between Damascus Gate and Herod's Gate, is the entrance to Solomon's Quarries, a vast complex of deep tunnels that run under the small streets leading to Mount Moriah. Also known as Zedekiah's Grotto, after the king of Judah deposed by the Babylonians of Nebuchadnezzar in the 6th century BC, it is popularly believed

supposed to have thrown himself after having predicted the conquest and destruction of Jerusalem at the hands of the Babylonians. This site is sometimes indicated as the place where Jeremiah went to write the Book of Lamentations. Not far from the cave is the Tomb of Simon the Just, the high priest who lived in the 3rd century BC. About 100 yards further west, along Nablus Road, is the Garden Tomb, consisting of two adjacent chambers hewn out of a hill in an evocative skull shape, which is the reason why the Protestants claimed this site was the true Golgotha with the tomb of Christ. The layout of the innermost chamber, which has three burial niches along the walls, suggests this mausoleum probably dates back to the period of the First Temple.

Three hundred yards west of this site, at the Tourjeman outpost, is the Armenian church of St. Polyeuctus, decorated with a magnificent 6th-century mosaic. To the north is the area that belongs to the French Dominicans with the Basilica of St. Stephen, built in 638 on the site where the saint was stoned to death; this church replaced the original one built by empress Eudocia in the 5th century and destroyed by Khosru II in 614. Afterwards, the Crusaders restored the Byzantine edifice, but then destroyed it in October 1187 rather than leave it to the new conqueror, Saladin. The complex houses the important Ecole Biblique, the school of Biblical studies founded in the late 19th century by Father Lagrange, the first such institution

60 top For centuries the area north of the Old City had been a quarry and necropolis. Some scholars say that the Garden Tomb, illustrated here, was hewn out of the rock of Golgotha.

60 bottom The deacon Stephen was stoned to death in 36 AD on the site of the basilica dedicated to him, which is part of a complex built by the Franciscans in the late 19th century.

60-61 The Romanesque purity and simplicity of the nave in St. Stephen's basilica seem to show Middle Eastern and classical influences.

61 top The Garden Tomb housed persons who lived during the prosperous times of the First Temple, in the 10th-7th century BC.

61 center Massive stone blocks looking like millstones were customarily used to seal tombs.

61 bottom left and right In the 1st century BC two Ionic columns of the façade preceded the chambers and loculi of the Tombs of the Kings.

in the Holy Land. It is now an archaeological school.

Just inside the northwestern arm of Kidron Valley is the largest and most interesting cemetery in Jerusalem, known as the Tombs of the Kings, mentioned by travellers since the 16th century and studied in 1863 by French archaeologists, who are still in charge of the precinct. In reality, the eight burial chambers surrounding the vestibule were not the tombs of the kings of Israel and Judah, but were cut out of the rock to house Queen Helena of Adiabene (a region in northern Mesopotamia), who converted to Judaism in the second half of the 1st century BC and was taken to Jerusalem to be buried together with two members of her family. Cut out of the rock 26 feet under the ground, the large courtyard in front of the sepulchre can be reached by means of a flight of steps. The famous historian Flavius Josephus claimed that there were three pyramids above the façade, which was originally supported by two attached Ionic columns under the architrave, which still has its Doric frieze. In the northwest corner of the precinct is Mount Scopus ('Har-Ha-Zofim' in Hebrew, or 'mountain of the warriors'), a fine vantage point to admire the city and its surroundings toward the mountains of Judaea. After the First World War it was the site of the cemetery for the British soldiers, and around 1925 the first buildings of the Hebrew University and the Hadassah hospital complex rose up here.

EAST AND SOUTH OF THE OLD CITY: THE MOUNT OF OLIVES

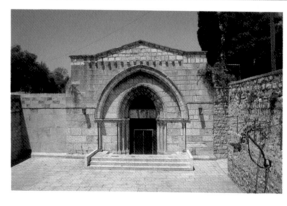

Because of its traditional association with the end of terrestrial life and with Jesus Ascension to heaven, the Mount of Olives, separated from the Temple Mount by the deep Kidron Valley, has naturally been the object of Christians' heartfelt veneration. The sacred history of the site, however, began much earlier than the advent of Christianity, and the mystical connotations that characterize it are vast indeed. Used by the Jesubites as a cemetery in the 2nd millennium BC, the hill is mentioned in the Bible as the place where David took refuge after having survived the revolt against him instigated by Absalom. Furthermore, the tombs dating from the 1st century BC to the 1st century AD, on the western slope of Kidron Valley, and the presence of huge Jewish cemeteries on the southern slopes of the hill–the theatre of disgraceful

rock above the Jewish cemetery from the 1st to the 5th century. In the 4th century the first edifices were constructed in those places that were gradually being recognized as the holy sites of Christ's life. The Byzantine age witnessed the building of the Church of Eleona ('of the Olive Grove'), a basilica partly hewn out of the rock, whose remains now lie between the Basilica of the Sacred Heart and the adjacent Pater Noster cloister. This church was followed by the original Church of the Assumption, which was probably round, founded in 378 at the top of the hill; the Basilica of Gethsemane, built in the late 4th century at the behest of Theodosius I; the Tomb of the Virgin church, also built in the 4th century; and numerous other minor churches and chapels also on the eastern slope of the Mount of Olives, such as the two

63 top The Tombs of the Prophets follow the pattern of most Jewish tombs of the time: rock-cut burial chambers around a vestibule.

62-63 Muslim veneration of Mary is the reason why the Tomb of the Virgin, a holy site since the 4th century, is still intact.

62 bottom left and right The Romanesque entrance to the Pater Noster Church precedes the cloister, where the most ancient Christian prayer is written in 36 languages.

63 bottom Facing the Temple Mount and awaiting Judgement Day, which will occur in the Kidron Valley, at the foot of the Mount of Olives, the hundreds of tombs in the Jewish Cemetery lie on the southwest side of the hill, the favourite burial site for Jews in Jerusalem.

profanation from 1948 to 1967, still being used as a cemetery–remind us that Jewish, Muslim and Christian traditions all claim that this is the place where the resurrection of the dead and the Last Judgement will take place.

It seems probable that Christian worship of the holy sites on the Mount of Olives began in the period immediately following the events related in the Gospels, as is attested by the most ancient of the sepulchres known as the Tombs of the Prophets, which were cut out of the

superposed churches at Bethany, dating from the 5th and 6th century.

Besides the Byzantine churches, the 6th century witnessed the construction of some tombs and an Armenian monastery on the site of the present-day Russian Orthodox Church of Mary Magdalene. Then, during the Persian invasion, most of the Christian buildings were either damaged or destroyed. After the Crusader conquest of Jerusalem the zone next to the *aedicule* of the Ascension was levelled off to make room for a fortress, and the *aedicule* itself

64-65 In contrast with the expanse of stone tombs in the Jewish Cemetery, are the green cypress trees and kitchen gardens around the 20th-century Church of All Nations (bottom left), dominated by the late 19th-century Russian St. Mary Magdalene Church and the Ascension aedicule (top right).

64 bottom During the 19th century the Russian Orthodox Church was supported by the czars, who founded and improved several sacred buildings. The Mount of Olives boasts two important churches built during this period: St. Mary Magdalene, seen here, and the Ascension, near the top of the hill.

65 top According to tradition, Jesus was arrested on the site of the Church of All Nations, dedicated to the universal values of faith and cooperation. Although it was inspired by hieratic Byzantine mosaic art, the modern mosaic on the tympanum is filled with pathos.

was rebuilt in its present-day form, but under Saladin the latter became a mosque and the fortress was demolished.

As is the rule in Jerusalem, the complexity of events that occurred on the Mount of Olives is underscored by the stratification of holy buildings scattered here and there, as well as by the deep-rooted persistence of evangelical traditions. The Franciscan chapel at

well, is considered a sign of the place where Christ ascended to heaven, forty days after his Resurrection.

A short way to the south is the Church of the Pater Noster, built on the site where the Lord's Prayer was first heard. The decoration in the cloister next to the church emphasizes the international character of the fundamental prayer of Christianity: 36 majolica tiles bear the

Bethphage–built over Crusader ruins on the eastern slopes of the hill facing the Edom plateau and the Judaean desert–is the starting point of the Palm Sunday procession to the Holy City to honor the tradition according to which Jesus started off from the stone kept in the chapel to make his triumphal entry into Jerusalem. From this locality a road goes to the top of the hill, dominated by the characteristic bell-tower of the Russian Orthodox Church of the Ascension, near the octagonal *aedicule* of the same name. Here, much like the footprint left by Mohammed in the Dome of the Rock, the footprint of Jesus, which is venerated by Muslims as

words of the Lord's Prayer in the same number of different languages. It seems that this had already been done in the church built by St. Helena, where the prayer was written in Hebrew, Latin and Greek.

Toward the bottom of the Kidron Valley is the place where Jesus is believed to have wept for the fate of Jerusalem, now marked by the Dominus Flevit chapel, which lies on what was a 2nd millennium BC Jesubite necropolis. This recently built church incorporates the remains of a late 7th-century chapel that was in Byzantine style, even though it dates from the beginning of the Omayyad dominion. Construction work on this tear-shaped chapel designed by the Franciscan Antonio Barluzzi in 1953, led to the discovery of remains of pavement mosaics belonging to the Byzantine chapel, as well as an inscription mentioning the priests of the Anastasis in the Holy Sepulchre.

Not far away are the six typical gilded domes of the Russian Orthodox Church of St. Mary Magadalene, built at the end of the 19th century by czar Alexander III on

65 bottom left The elevated rock-hewn chambers near the top of the Mount of Olives lie on the spot associated with Jesus' ascent to heaven.

65 bottom right In the Acts of the Apostles (I, 12) the site of the Ascension is described as being quite close to Jerusalem, "a sabbath day's journey."

the site once occupied by an Armenian monastery, a mosaic of which has been preserved. These 'onion domes' clearly point out to visitors from afar the western slope of the Mount of Olives. At the foot of the long crest of the hill, among the centuries-old olive trees that are believed to have witnessed Christ's agony, the Basilica of Gethsemane was built by Theodosius I in 385. It was destroyed centuries later by an earthquake and replaced by a Crusader church built precisely on the Rock of the Agony. From 1919 to 1924, at the site of Christ's agony and arrest, the above-mentioned architect Barluzzi built the Church of All Nations, the façade of which has a lovely Byzantine-type mosaic and is surmounted by twelve domes representing the nations that took part in the construction of the church.

At the dawn of the Christian era a crypt partly cut out of the rock of the north side of Gethsemane was identified as the tomb where the Virgin Mary lay during the Dormition, that is to say, the mystical suspension of life before her Assumption into heaven. In the 4th century the crypt was incorporated into a

Byzantine chapel, some traces of which can still be seen in the present-day Tomb of the Virgin. Much doubt has been expressed concerning the traditional belief that some niches in the present chapel were the burial places of the relatives of Jesus' mother and of Joseph, but it seems certain that the burial chamber itself housed the remains of relatives of the Christian kings of Jerusalem. It is interesting to note that, because of the Muslim veneration for the Virgin Mary, the sepulchre remained intact even during the period when the chapel was used as a mosque.

KIDRON VALLEY

This rugged depression is also known as the Valley of Jehoshphat, which the traditions of the Jewish, Muslim and Christian religions consider the future site of the Last Judgement. This link with resurrection is partly due to the fact that the valley had been used for centuries as a burial site. Besides the Muslim cemetery on the Temple Mount side of the valley outside the Lions' Gate, and the Jewish cemeteries lying on the southern end of the ridge of the Mount of Olives, the rocky valley also houses many rock-cut tombs dating as far back as the 16th century BC, and to the south of Gethsemane there are four important funerary monuments. Perhaps the most interesting of the four is the Tomb—or

Pillar–of Absalom, the best preserved funerary monument in Israel, an elegant architectural work consisting of a parallelepiped base almost entirely cut out of the rock on which lies a low tambour in masonry that ends in a curious cover in the shape of an overturned flower-cup. This singular concave dome is the funerary monument (*nefesh*) of the burial chamber contained in the base and perhaps also of the eight chambers in the so-called Tomb of Jehoshphat, the 1st-century AD rock-cut sepulchre behind the dome.

Just south of the broad façade of this tomb, decorated with a lovely relief of vine leaves and branches, is the Tomb of the Beni Hazir, the only one of the four with the correct name, since it was the burial site of some members of the powerful Beni Hazir family of Temple priests. The façade of this mausoleum evinces all the purity of the Doric style.

Cut out of the rock above another podium, it has a pair of smooth columns that support the frieze bearing the carved names of those in the burial chamber, a central rock-cut vestibule flanked by loculi that penetrate the rock for almost 50 feet. Though it is traditionally considered the place where St. James took refuge after the crucifixion of Christ as well as the tomb of the saint himself, archaeologists have dated the tomb from the Hasmonean period, around the middle of the 2nd century BC. Hewn out of the rock face just right of the Tomb of the Beni Hazir, is the monolithic Tomb of Zacharias, an isolated rock cube decorated on its four exposed sides with Ionic columns and surmounted by a sharply pointed pyramid. Some scholars say that this robust funerary monument is the *nefesh* of the adjacent Beni Hazir tombs, but it lies above its own underground burial chamber, which was

cut out of the rock under the three steps of the base in some unidentified period. It is also uncertain which of the two traditional attributions of the monument is more correct: is it the tomb of the prophet Zacharias, who lived in the 6th century BC, or of John the Baptist's father? What is certain, however, is that archaeologists have dated the construction of the work from the 2nd century BC.

MOUNT ZION

68 top These partly rock-cut rooms are traditionally considered part of the house of the high priest Caiaphas, where Jesus spent the night before being condemned.

68-69 The Church of the Dormition crowns Mount Zion, theater of the Last Supper and the symbol of the redemption of the Jews, as well as the site where Jewish tradition says the Messiah will come.

68 bottom left The Star of David woven several times on the black pall that covers the cenotaph clearly identifies the sepulchre on Mount Zion that Jews have worshipped since the Middle Ages.

At the southwest corner of the Old City, just outside the Ottoman walls, is the peak of Mount Zion. This is a holy site for Jews because it is connected to the future coming of the Messiah and the site of the so-called Tomb of David, as well as for Christians, who identify it with the place where Jesus had the Last Supper. The most ancient settlement in this area dates from the 2nd millennium BC, as is attested by traces of Jesubite fortifications found in the foundations of the first city wall, built in the 6th century BC, at the beginning of the period of the Second Temple. But in Jesus' time the hilltop now occupied by the Church of the Dormition was enclosed within the Herodian city walls. The place traditionally considered the site of the Eucharist, the Last Supper, was made part of a large 4th-century Byzantine basilica whose nave was divided by four colonnades. This edifice is shown south of the *cardo* in the famous Madaba Map. It was badly damaged by the Persians in 614, and what was left was restored by the monk Modestus and used until the beginning of Arab dominion in Palestine.

scholars claim it was a Roman-period pagan building that was later incorporated into the Byzantine basilica of Holy Zion. The adjacent Chamber of Martyrs contains a memorial dedicated to the Jewish communities exterminated in Europe by the Nazis.

As is the case with the Mount of Olives, most of the sacred precincts on Mount Zion are modern: just outside Zion Gate, the Church of the Dormition of Mary, a fine neo-Romanesque building erected over the remains of a Crusader structure to indicate the site of Jesus' mother's transition, was in fact built in the early 20th century by German Benedictine monks, as was the monastery of the same name on the southwest corner of the Catholic church.

On the southeastern slopes of Mount

It was replaced by a Crusader basilica, which in turn was rebuilt by the Franciscans in the mid 14th century. During the Mamluk period this church was converted into a mosque, but the new rulers venerated the cenotaph known as the 'Tomb of David,' which is part of the lower floor of the present-day Room of the Last Supper building, or Cenacle. The structure housing the tomb still has traces of Roman age masonry. It began to be used as a Jewish holy site in the 11th century, but the original function of the building is still debatable. Some scholars have identified what they think are the remains of a synagogue oriented toward the Temple Mount; others view it as a synagogue-church built by a Jewish-Christian sect, as was recorded by the Pilgrim of Bordeaux, who visited Jerusalem in the 3rd century; yet other

Zion, the Church of St. Peter in Gallincantu (the Crowing of the Cock) was also built in modern times, in the late 19th century, by Assumptionist monks who, during construction, brought to light the remains of a Byzantine monastery annexed to a church. Evangelical tradition links this complex to Peter's three denials of Jesus before the crowing of the cock and to the rock-cut crypt where Jesus spent the night after being interrogated by the high priest Caiaphas; this chamber was later incorporated into the Byzantine basilica. The crypt lay in a network of grottoes which in Jesus' time was perhaps used–at least partly–as a dwelling. Just north of the present-day church, archaeologists have unearthed the traces of a stepped road that connected the area of Herodian buildings and the bottom of the Kidron Valley, in the direction of the Pool of Siloam.

68 bottom right As a courtyard in the Convent of the Dormition demonstrates, the modern 'shell' of the holy edifices on Mount Zion covers much older areas and architectural elements.

69 A Byzantine basilica, Crusader church, mosque and again a Christian edifice, the Cenacle, site of the Eucharist, still bears traces of the political and religious changes in the Holy Land from the 4th to the 19th century.

70 *The water supply network is one of the most interesting and most ancient works in Jerusalem: here we see the Pool of Siloam, which is also mentioned in the New Testament.*

70-71 *This overall view gives an idea of the size of the City of David, lying between the two streets forming an oval south of the Temple Mount.*

MOUNT OPHEL AND THE CITY OF DAVID

Mount Ophel is the broad ridge that runs southward from the Temple Mount on the side of the Kidron Valley opposite the Mount of Olives. It was the original site of the Jerusalemite settlements. The hill, colonized around the middle of the 3rd millenniun BC by the Canaanites, was first mentioned in 20th-century BC Egyptian execratory texts as *Rushalimum*, the Uru-Shalim of the Jebusites. It was the last locality in Palestine to fall in the hands of the invading Israelites in the early 10th century BC, becoming the capital of the conquering king, who decided to name it the 'City of David.'

At present the most interesting ruins on the Ophel ridge are without a doubt the traces of the complex water supply network that from very ancient times guaranteed the survival of the settlement. From the distant period of the first colonization to the 2nd century BC, when aqueducts were built to carry water from the hills of Hebron to the city, Jerusalem's water supply always came only from the Gihon spring, situated on the east slope of Ophel, outside the most ancient city walls. According to the Bible, already in the period when the Jesubites were defeated the city had an ingenious and well-articulated water supply network, if it is true that David conquered it by attacking it via the *zinnor*, or water shaft. However, the Biblical account is dubious, since archaeological finds seem to prove that Warren's Shaft, the ancient vertical fissure discovered in 1868 at the foot of the Jesubite acropolis on the top of the Ophel ridge, and connected to a transverse tunnel that drew water from the Gihon spring, does not date back further than the 10th century B.C., that is, at the beginning of Israelite domination. In any case, given the intermittent nature of the spring, at a certain point in the Iron Age (1200-586 BC), in order to totally exploit the water resources, a sinuous tunnel about 420 yards long was partly cut out of the rock by following the course of the karstic cracks in the Ophel ridge; the rest of the tunnel along the base of the hill is exposed. This conduit fed the lateral canals used to irrigate the fields in the bottom of Kidron Valley and the cisterns located in the lower area south of the city. However, this supply system was too exposed to the risks of a siege–such as the impending Assyrian invasion–so at the end of the 8th century king Hezekiah built a canal named after him that is entirely

71 top right In the
First Temple period,
the Pool of Siloam,
still full of clear
water, was fed by the
Gihon spring, at the
foot of an escarpment
separating the City of
David and the floor
of Kidron Valley.

71 bottom right
Around the 8th
century BC, the need
to make the water
supply network safer
in case of siege led to
the construction of
the impressive

Hezekiah's Tunnel,
an entirely
underground canal
hewn out of Mount
Ophel.

71 bottom, left and
right At the foot of
the ancient acropolis
of the City of David
is Warren's Shaft, a
huge pre-Isrealite
fissure that connected
the Gihon
spring—the only
water source—to the
area inside the city
walls.

THE CITY OF DAVID

1 SITE OF THE CITY OF DAVID
2 POOL OF SILOAM
3 KIDRON VALLEY
4 TYROPAEION VALLEY
5 TEMPLE MOUNT

underground and ran for over 500 yards
from the Gihon spring to the Pool of
Siloam, which was part of the new
fortified area at the end of the
Tyropaeion Valley. Destroyed by the
Romans during the Jewish wars, the
pool was rebuilt during Hadrian's time,
when a peristyle was added to it. Since
the pool is considered the place where
Jesus miraculously cured a blind man, in
450 the empress Eudocia had a church
built next to it. This was demolished by
the Persians one and a half centuries
later and lay in abandon, eventually

being filled with debris, over which a
mosque was built in 1890. Today the
Pool of Siloam is like a basin of crystal-
clear water situated at the end of the
underground canal in the bottom of a
ditch bordered by stone retaining walls
accessible via a stairway.

At the top of the Ophel ridge, at
the foot of the Haram es-Sharif and
included in the Ophel Archaeological
Garden, lie the fascinating ruins of the
monumental staircase that went up the
Herodian Temple Mount esplanade, as
well as the remains of the already-

mentioned Robinson's Arch, which
supported another stairway that lead
directly to the sacred precinct of the
Second Temple.

The acropolis of the City of David
was occupied in ancient times by King
Solomon's administrative offices and
palace. The ruins in the area, however,
are mostly of dwellings dating from the
Byzantine age and later. Nonetheless,
on the whole, the modest Ophel area
has provided archaeologists with at least
twenty-one strata of ancient ruins dating
from the Chalcolithic Age—the second
half of the 4th millennium BC—to the
Middle Ages, a span of history that few
cities in the world canequal.

WEST OF THE OLD CITY

Viewing Jerusalem from a high vantage point, one will note how, by tracing an imaginary line from south to north that crosses the city more or less as the *cardo* does, there is a clear-cut difference between the growth of the modern city in the eastern sector, traversed by the Kidron Valley and rich in history, and the western one, which began to expand only in the second half of the 19th century. While the main interest in East Jerusalem lies in the abundance of archaeological and religious testimony that makes the Holy City unique, West Jerusalem is the area of recent history, characterized by the presence of modern

several stone sarcophagi were found. About half a mile to the west, Jason's Tomb was found in 1953. This dates back to the 1st century BC and is quite special in that it is the only example in Israel of a tomb with a single pier supporting the architrave instead of the usual two columns. The walls of the porch have some charcoal drawings of ships probably related to Jason's being a naval commander, as well as an inscription in Greek and others in Aramaic, including the lamentation over the deceased's death. The burial chamber with loculi, and the ossuary beyond the porch, both used until the beginning of the 1st century AD,

and contemporary monuments, buildings and parks with significant historical and political meaning.

However, even West Jerusalem has signs of the city's ancient past. Among the quarters of Yemin Moshe, at the foot of the western slope of Mount Zion, and Rehavia, at the western tip of the built-up area, there are two ancient tombs. Flavius Josephus mentions 'Herod's family tomb' as the mausoleum built by Herod the Great to be the final resting place of his father Herod Antipater and his brother, who died in 5 BC. Discovered in 1892 and now dated at the 1st century AD, this tomb is closed by a round stone larger than the ones usually used for this purpose and has a rather unusual plan compared to the other contemporaneous tombs: a vestibule flanked by four burial chambers where

72 left Jason's Tomb has a special feature: the architrave is supported by only one pier instead of the usual two.

72 top right The Shrine of the Book, part of the Israel Museum, houses the famous Dead Sea Scrolls discovered at Qumran in 1947.

72 bottom right The dome of the Shrine of the Book, designed by A. Bartos and F. Kiesler, is reminescent of the lid of jars in which the scrolls were kept.

72-73 In this splendid aerial view we can recognize: top left, the Israeli Parliament; bottom left, the Israel Museum; center, the Monastery of the Cross.

73 bottom left According to tradition, the wood used for Jesus' Cross came from a tree in the forest where the Monastery of the Cross was built.

73 bottom right During the 1948 war the Montefiore Windmill was used as an observation point by Israeli soldiers.

74 left The Israel Museum, inaugurated in 1965, boasts a rich collection of archaeological finds arranged in chronological order, from prehistoric times to the Ottoman period. This terracotta female figure, dating from the 9th or 8th century BC, comes from Shiqmona, on the coast near Mount Carmel.

74 right One of the most famous objects in the Israel Museum is this late Bronze Age basalt stela from Bet Shean.

cover an area 72 feet long and 16 feet wide in which archaeologists found Hasmonean and Herodian earthenware and coins.

Southeast of Herod's family tomb is Yemin Moshe, the first Jewish quarter to grow up outside the city walls, in the second half of the 19th century. This district was virtually created by Moses Montefiore, the English Jewish philanthropist whose name is commemorated in the last surviving construction in the original quarter, the Montefiore Windmill, which now houses a museum dedicated to him. After developing again in 1892, the area rose from the rubble of the 1948 war to become an elegant residential district in modern Jerusalem, the city's artists' quarter known for its many art galleries.

North of the Montefiore Windmill are the Mamilla and Nahalat Shiv'a quarters, between which is the Gan Haatzmaut, or Independence Park, lying over a vast pre-Crusader cemetery that was also used by the successive conquerors of Jerusalem up to the Ottoman period. Inside the ancient burial area is the Mamilla cistern, a large cavity of uncertain dating (perhaps the Herodian period) that was probably the end of a western deviation of the so-called high aqueduct, the water supply network built by the Romans that collected water from Solomon's Pools, situated about 6 miles south-southwest of the Old City. It seems that the many Christian inhabitants massacred by the Persian invaders under Khosru II were thrown into this pool, and their bodies were later placed in the nearby Mamilla church.

Heading back to the west, past Rehavia is Ben Gurion Park, named after the first prime minister of the Israeli government after the British Mandate came to an end. This park includes the Knesset, the building that houses the

75 top This simple but elegant pendant in the shape of the star of Ishtar was brought to light at Tel el-Ajjul, south of Gaza. Many 16th-15th century BC gold objects were found in the cemeteries at this site.

75 bottom Two other splendid objects in the Israel Museum are this bronze scepter head, part of a large group of Chalcolithic-Age artifacts found in the 'Cave of the Treasury' at Nahal Mishmar, and the necklace above it.

76 top left The high quality of Roman glyptic art is seen in this splendid cameo, which reproduces the haughty features of a patrician wearing a crown.

76 bottom left These two famous fragments of a mosaic pavement from the church of Kissufim, in the northern Negev, date from the 6th century AD. The Greek inscription perhaps refers to the Adventures of Alexander, a very popular book in Byzantine times that relates the heroic deeds of the Macedonian ruler.

76 right This lovely Hellenistic terracotta head reveals Phoenician influences while following the aesthetic canons imported from Greece. The three objects reproduced on this page are in the archaeological section of the Israel Museum.

Israeli Parliament, and other ministry buildings.

Just south is the Monastery of the Cross, which gave its name to the valley at the foot of the Rehavia quarter. This complex was founded in the mid 11th century by Georgian Christians and has all the features of a fortified monastery. It includes an 11th-century Byzantine-style basilica with medieval mosaics and the remains of a 5th-century mosaic pavement. The name of the monastery is related to the traditional belief that the wood used for Jesus' cross came from a tree planted here in very ancient times–some link it with Adam–on the site now occupied by the church's apse. In the same area, a few hundred yards west of the monastery, is the Israel Museum complex, with its many precious collections ranging from the country's most ancient origins to works of contemporary art. But the museum is famous above all for the separate building, known as the 'Shrine of the Book,' with its absolutely unique collection of finds: the Dead Sea Scrolls, the most ancient transcriptions of Biblical texts known to man. The parchments, which were found quite by chance in the Kirbeth Qumran caves at the Dead Sea, contain 'handbooks' of civil and military rules of the Essenes, a Jewish sect repudiated by Jews and Romans alike that grew up around the 2nd century BC and ceased to exist by the end of the 1st century AD. The scrolls also have complete manuscript transcriptions of the Bible of inestimable cultural value written in Aramaic, the language spoken by Jesus.

Once past the rise with the Giva'at Ram, the most recent seat of Hebrew University, the western outskirts of

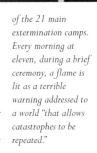

77 *The temple of a people's memory, the Yad Vashem sanctuary, standing so austerely and silently on the Hill of Remembrance, is dedicated to the six million Jews slaughtered by the Nazis. It houses a documentary center and a moving and trenchant exhibition concerning the history of anti-Semitism from the early 1900s to 1945. The Ohel Yizkor is the mausoleum: under a low cement roof is a floor bearing the names of the 21 main extermination camps. Every morning at eleven, during a brief ceremony, a flame is lit as a terrible warning addressed to a world "that allows catastrophes to be repeated."*

Jerusalem from north to south include large areas of greenery. The forests of Ramot and Jerusalem lie on the heights dominated by Mount Herzl which, 2,730 feet high, is the tallest in the Jerusalem area. It is no accident that this hill bears the name of the founder of the Zionist movement, Theodore Herzl, a Hungarian Jew who in the early 20th century literally laid the foundations of the Israeli nation by creating the conditions favorable for the purchase of land in Palestine. On the northern slope of the hill, in the military cemetery, is the grave of Yizhak Rabin, the Israeli prime minister who in 1995 was the victim of the intolerance and ideological complexity and contradictions of his own people.

One might say that the geographic tour west of the Old City and the

emotional journey into the most recent history of Judaism and of Jerusalem culminate west of Mount Herzl, on the Hill of Remembrance (Har Karon), surrounded by the Jerusalem forest and occupied by Yad Vashem, the memorial built so that the horrors of the Holocaust should never be forgotten. From the terrible and disarming simplicity of the names of the 21 extermination camps

carved on the floor of the Ohel Yizkor–the mausoleum-memorial in which a flame is lit every day during a brief ceremony–to the millions of documents concerning the history of Anti-Semitism from the beginning of the 20th century to the Holocaust, this sanctuary of memory rises up like a universal warning directed at a world that "allows catastrophes to be repeated." For that matter, if one could legitimately ascribe a meaning to the existence of a city, Jerusalem–the Holy City for three religions that are often in bloody conflict–could without a doubt be considered a symbolic site, an example at once tragic and moving, of the complexity of human nature and of the need for peace.

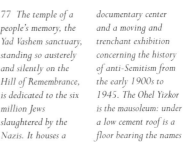

JERICHO, THE CITY OF JOSHUA

Jericho boasts two remarkable records: it is the lowest (846 feet below sea level) and the most ancient city in the world. It rose up between to 10th-9th millennia BC, when nomadic populations settled on the long ridge of Tell es-Sultan, the plateau that dominates the so-called 'Fountain of Elisha,' one of the many underground springs that still provide water for the entire area, guaranteeing fertility and a certain degree of prosperity.

The history of the city and the construction of its famous walls around the end of the 8th millennium were, of course, conditioned by its geographic position and configuration. Jericho lies near one of the ancient trade routes that went from the interior to the Mediterranean, and the fertile surroundings attracted many invaders. Archaeological digs have shown that in the late Neolithic era the modest primitive city walls were replaced by a fortified wall almost 20 feet high with a massive cylindrical tower on its western side, where the city gate probably stood.

The art of the most ancient populations here was markedly anthropomorphic, as can be seen in such artifacts as the human skulls covered with clay to simulate the facial features of the deceased, and the anthropomorphic vases, dating from the Chalcolithic to the Middle Bronze Age (4th-2nd millennia BC), which were found in the shaft graves in the necropolises on the surrounding rises. At the beginning of the 4th millennium BC, Jericho was abandoned because of some unidentified catastrophe and was then temporarily occupied by people of a more primitive culture. Two thousand years later the city suffered another calamity and was destroyed, after which time the most massive walls in its pre-Israelite history were built, probably by the Canaanites, five or six centuries before Joshua captured Jericho. The Old Testament tells us that around 1200 BC this patriarch destroyed the city utterly, so that he had to settle in the nearby locality of Galgala. Although we have no direct proof of the destruction of the walls, the fact that Jericho was obviously abandoned at the end of the Bronze Age should suffice to confirm the Biblical description. Be that as it may, it

78 bottom The abundant decoration among the ruins of Hisham's palace is often dominated by intertwining plants, especially acanthus leaves, the symbol of Paradise.

78-79 Among the vast ruins of Hisham's palace one can make out the perimeter of the main courtyard, at left, opposite the remains of the thermae and the diwan (reception hall), which have some splendid mosaics.

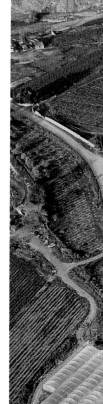

was two centuries before Jericho, during the time of Ahab, was finally occupied by the Israelites, who continued to enlarge the town up to the Babylonian captivity, in the early 6th century BC.

During the entire period of the Second Temple the city had an important Jewish community that remained there for centuries, as is demonstrated by the ruins of the synagogue found about one-half mile from Tell es-Sultan. These include a splendid mosaic pavement with a representation of the Ark of the Covenant and a *menorah*. There are also ruins of a 6th-century A.D. synagogue at Na'aran, a town about 3 miles to the northwest that was an implacable rival of Christian Jericho.

After the exile in Babylonia, ancient Jericho was no longer rebuilt, as the city took on new life in the oases and on the rises south of the *tell* where the original city once stood. In the early 5th century Jericho was made part of the Persian satrapy of Judaea and then passed under Seleucid and Hellenistic dominion, until the Hasmoneans reconquered the region.

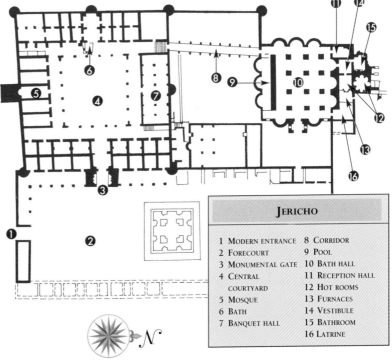

JERICHO

1 MODERN ENTRANCE	8 CORRIDOR
2 FORECOURT	9 POOL
3 MONUMENTAL GATE	10 BATH HALL
4 CENTRAL	11 RECEPTION HALL
COURTYARD	12 HOT ROOMS
5 MOSQUE	13 FURNACES
6 BATH	14 VESTIBULE
7 BANQUET HALL	15 BATHROOM
	16 LATRINE

N

During the Hasmonean period and then the reign of Herod the Great, the hills around the ancient settlement were fortified, and luxurious complexes used as the winter palace of the kings of Judah were built on the two rises known as Tulul el-Alaiq, a little over a mile southwest of Tell es-Sultan.

Having already been stormed by Pompey, during the First Jewish War Jericho was destroyed by Vespasian and was later rebuilt by Hadrian. In the 8th century A.D. the city was conquered by the Muslim Omayyads, who held it until the arrival of the Crusaders, who liberated it in 1099 without much bloodshed, since the Muslim defenders surrendered almost immediately. The Crusaders, defeated by Saladin in 1187, abandoned the city, leaving it at the mercy of desert raiders, and over the centuries it declined, becoming nothing more than a humble village.

The most interesting ruins in medieval Jericho lie about two miles northeast of Tell Jericho: the remains of Qasr Hisham, the Palace of Hisham, the Ommayad caliph who lived in the first half of the 8th century, which was razed to the ground by an earthquake in 746. This magnificent, square palace was rather complex and fortified with round towers along the ramparts. Inside is a central courtyard, surrounded by a colonnade, in the middle of which is a beautifully sculpted lintel. On the ground floor were the guest rooms, the servants' dwellings and the service and storage rooms. Access to the floor above this was gained by two stairways at the corners of the courtyard. This floor contained the most important chambers, including the royal apartment. On the east side of the courtyard was the mosque, some lovely composite columns of which have survived: they consist of

four joined shafts that originally supported the double row of three arcades on which the upper floor lay. To the south are the ruins of a smaller mosque. Going toward the north end of the palace, you will see the remains of the rooms that yielded the most precious finds, now kept in the Rockefeller Museum in Jerusalem: six mosaic pieces that decorated the pools, baths and the *diwan*, the palace reception room. Among the marvellous mosaic floors, which are particularly well preserved, is the *diwan* mosaic, which has a lively scene around a tree laden with ripe fruit, depicting a lion killing a gazelle on one side and two gazelles on the other. Besides the mosaics, the entire palace was decorated with elegant stuccowork–used for the first time in Palestine–and plaster statues that betray Western as well as Byzantine and Persian-Sassanid influences.

81 top left An elaborate fretwork stone window with stuccowork decoration in Hisham's Palace.

81 right Together with many others, this stuccoed plaster female figure decorated the dome of the diwan in Hisham's Palace. Human figures and animals are not infrequent motifs in Omayyad art.

80 The extraordinarily refined floor mosaic of the diwan is in a perfect state of preservation. It is an imitation of a carpet, with a tasseled border.

81 bottom left Archaeologists set this elegant round stone window in the central courtyard. The first Omayyad caliph, Uthman, was the third successor of Mohammed.

ST. GEORGE'S, THE MONASTERY CLINGING TO THE MOUNTAIN

82-83 The light blue domes of the Monastery of St. George stand out amid the barren natural scenery of the Wadi el-Qelt.

82 bottom left The monastery was fortified in order to defend itself from the many raids made over the centuries.

82 bottom After the destruction in 614 the monastery was rebuilt several times until 1878.

83 The nearby Monastery of the Temptation, an integral part of the laura, *is quite typical of this type of hermitage monastery.*

About three miles southwest of Jericho, perched on the barren Wadi el-Qelt escarpment, is the Greek-Orthodox Monastery of St. George, founded in the first half of the 5th century against a cliff face dotted with caves and natural recesses that have attracted hermits and ascetics for many centuries. The complex was built onto an earlier oratory erected by five hermits and was then enlarged in the 6th century, thanks to the efforts of George of Koziba, a Cypriot monk who was later made a saint, after whom the monastery was named. The complex was destroyed by Khosru II in 614 and revived to some extent only in the 12th century, when the Byzantine emperor Manuel I Comnenus restored it. The present-day aspect of the monastery dates from the reconstruction carried out from 1878 to 1901. During the period of the Byzantine restoration, many religious legends arose concerning this barren locality where the *laura* stood: prophet Elijah reputedly lived in one of the caves for three years and six months in total seclusion, and St. Joachim is said to have stopped here for 40 days, weeping over his wife's sterility on the so-called 'Quarantain' slope of the mountain, where the Monastery of the Temptation was later built. The monastery is known for its hospitality, and, unlike the Mar Saba monastery, it has always been open to women as well as men. Articulated on three levels, it houses the churches of St. John and St. George, which have 6th-century mosaic floors and a reliquary with the skulls of fourteen monks killed by the Persians. Then there is the main church, the Blessed Virgin, which boasts mosaics made during the 12th-century restoration work. The iconostasis, paintings and icons date from the 19th century, but the doors in the middle of the iconostasis were made during the reign of Alexios II Comnenus (1180-83).

BET SHEAN, EIGHTEEN SUPERIMPOSED CITIES

Bet Shean lies along one of the very ancient trade routes going from the Near Eastern countries to the Mediterranean, the Maris track, at the point in which the Jordan Valley converges with the southermost tip of the Jezreel Valley. Thanks to its strategic importance and abundance of water, this locality was already occupied in the late Neolithic era: in fact, among the eighteen archaeological layers studied, the most ancient finds on this site date back to the 5th millennium BC. They were brought to light on the Tell el-Jisn, the hillock dominating the impressive remains of the Roman and Byzantine city. Some scholars claim that the most ancient documents

that mention Bet Shean are the Egyptian Middle Kingdom 'execration texts,' 2134-1991 BC) where it is called 'As'annu,' but the certain reference to the city dates back to the New Kingdom, when it was called 'Beit Shean' in the list of Canaanite cities that were conquered and fortified by Tuthmosis III (1504-1450 BC).

The five archaeological strata studied on the *tell*, which date from the 15th to the 12th century BC, contain the remains of the Egyptian temple precinct, which was built and demolished time and time again, as well as some anthropoid sarcophagi of the pharaohs' administrators. The *Book of Joshua* and the

Book of Judges speak of the locality, excluding it temporarily from the list of cities that fell into the hands of the Israelites: "Neither did the Manaseh drive out the inhabitants… but the Canaanites would dwell in that land." Then the Bible (I Samuel) narrates an episode of the Philistine occupation, which took place at the beginning of the Iron Age, describing how the decapitated bodies of Saul and his sons were put on display on the city walls. In a later period Bet Shean finally fell under Israelite dominion, and the first *Book of Kings* includes it among the administrative centers of King Solomon's reign. A short time after the partitioning

of the Israelite kingdom into the kingdoms of Israel and Judah, during the reign of the Libyan pharaoh Shoshenq (945-924 BC), the city was again conquered by the Egyptians.

For six centuries no historic mention was made of Bet Shean, but after it was conquered by the Macedonians the city was transferred from the top of the *tell* to the flat area below, becoming Scythopolis. The Romans took this new city in 63 BC, the year when Pompey the Great made it part of the Decapolis, a confederation consisting of ten cities, all on the other side of the Jordan River except for Scythopolis. At that time the abandoned summit housed the acropolis, where there was a temple probably dedicated to Zeus, the god of Olympus

terrain, so that the *cardo* and *decumanus*, the principal streets that usually intersect at right angles, converged in the middle of Nysa at irregular angles. The asymmetrical junction of the streets at the foot of the *tell* was occupied by a semicircular temple, with a tetrastyle façade, set on a podium slightly above the level of the limestone-paved street that covers the square in front of the edifice.

and as such naturally connected to high mountains.

In 636 AD, on the so-called 'Day of Beisan,' the Arabs conquered Scythopolis, which was again given a Semitic name. But in 749 the city was almost completely destroyed by a tremendous earthquake. There was a brief revival during the Crusader age that ended in 1187, when Saladin reconquered the city. In this period a Jewish community settled in Bet Shean, replacing the former one that had disappeared at the time of the first Omayyad invasion.

During the Roman Byzantine periods Scythopolis, also known as 'Nysa,' prospered and was beautified with impressive architectural works: the city at the foot of the *tell* was laid out according to the classic Roman grid street town plan, but the architects and engineers had to adapt it to the configuration of the

84-85 The long arcaded streets of Scythopolis intersected at irregular angles at the foot of a truncate cone tell.

84 center The lower city is dominated by the tell, where the earliest settlements grew up.

84 bottom and 85 top In 749 AD a violent earthquake marked the decline of the Byzantine city.

85 center The streets of Scythopolis were lined with baths, public buildings and workshops, while the central junction was given over to the celebratory and religious life of the city.

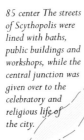

N

BET SHEAN	
1 BATHS	8 BASILICA
2 THEATRE	9 ARCADED STREET
3 ODEON	WITH WORKSHOPS
4 COLONNADED	10 PRECINCT WITH
STREET	THE OLDEST
5 TEMPLE	TEMPLES
6 NYMPHAEUM	11 GATE
7 MONUMENT WITH	
COLUMNS	

Opposite the temple, which was probably dedicated to Dionysus, were some hexagonal altars and a statue (no longer there) which the Greek inscription on the tall pedestal identifies as Marcus Aurelius.

Just east of the temple are the remains of the *nymphaeum*, an elegant structure that faces the square with a semicircular concave colonnade; it was probably built in the 2nd century AD and then completely rebuilt in the 4th century. In the 1st century AD a basilica stood behind the *nymphaeum*. It was over 213 feet long and 92 feet wide and was supported by four colonnades. Among the impressive ruins of this edifice is a hexagonal altar dedicated in 142 AD to the protective god of Nysa, Dionysus; it is magnificently decorated with the face of the god Pan. In the 2nd century the apse at the northeast end of the basilica was rebuilt to make

room for a platform 13 feet high that supported a colonnaded monument surrounded on three sides by rectangular and round niches and connected to the street by a broad stairway. No one knows what this monument looked like, but we do know that it was built with four different types of marble: at the base of the podium archaeologists found fragments of columns made of splendid cipolin

and other precious marble.

The main streets in Scythopolis were lined for their entire length with arcades that housed elegant shops and gave access to major public buildings. About halfway down the so-called 'Palladius Street,' which runs southwest from the main square, are the ruins of an odeon, a small theater used for concerts. Behind this are the remains of the public baths, the largest found to date in Israel. Although the

original complex was probably built during the Roman age, the eight rooms we see today belong to the Byzantine period and were destroyed by an earthquake in 749.

At the end of the street is the large theater built in the period from 183 to 285 AD. This is the most interesting ruin on this site and still has amazing acoustics. The theater had two particularly impressive elements: the *pulpitum* or stage, richly decorated with marble and granite imported from Asia Minor, Greece and Egypt; and the back wall of the stage, the *scaenae frons*, divided into two or three colonnaded storys. Unusual features of this edifice were the round towers flanking

86-87 The only surviving tier of seats of the three original ones boasts fine acoustics.

86 bottom left The vomitoria afforded access to the 6,000 seats in the cavea.

86 bottom right Hot air circulated in the suspensurae under the pavement of the thermae.

87 top The amphitheater, used for gladitorial combat, lies south of the city, where the Byzantine quarter rose up.

87 center The el-Husn tell offers a fine view of the center of Scythopolis: left of Palladius Street, which runs from the theater to the observatory, is the podium of the Temple of Dionysus, flanked by the semicircular nymphaeum.

87 bottom The theater must have looked like this in its heyday.

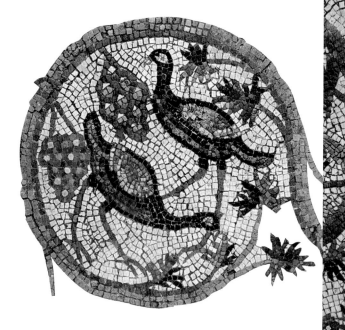

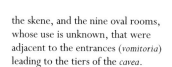

88 top and 88-89 A mosaic from the Roman-Byzantine cemetery of Tell Hammam, near the Dionysian city of Scythopolis, illustrates the yield of a rich grape harvest.

88 bottom This menorah *found in Bet Shean is flanked by palm leaves, a* shofar *(ram's horn), citron and, at right, an incense shovel.*

the skene, and the nine oval rooms, whose use is unknown, that were adjacent to the entrances (*vomitoria*) leading to the tiers of the *cavea*.

In the southern suburb of the city, which rose up in the Byzantine age and was traversed by a commercial street about one hundred yards long, are the traces of a 2nd-century amphitheater, built when the Roman Sixth Legion was based in this region. Rather than being semicircular, the amphitheater

has a singular rectangular plan; it is 335 feet long and 219 feet wide, with a seating capacity of 5,000-7,000.

Archaeologists think that the remains of the city walls found here and there around the city date back to the Byzantine period, because the Roman city was probably not fortified. Next to the inside of the northern stretch of the walls, on the Tell Istaba, are the ruins of a Christian monastery built in 576 and dedicated to the Virgin Mary. It was

spared during the Persian invasion of 614 but not by the 749 earthquake. Fortunately, the brightly-colored mosaics in the chapel and the three adjoining rooms (which were probably monks' cells)–depicting birds, the signs of the Zodiac and grape harvesting scenes–were not damaged.

Not far from the monastery, outside the city walls, are the ruins of two 6th-century synagogues. The larger one, called the 'House of Leontius,' which has a singular plan consisting of various rooms surrounding a central courtyard, has quite varied mosaics. In fact, there are not only the traditional representations of the *menorah* (seven-arm candelabrum) on the chapel pavement, with the word *shalom* (peace) in Aramaic script, but also scenes from the Odyssey and some Egyptian-style motifs in other rooms of the synagogue. This wide gamut of motifs has led archaeologists to assert that this was a hospice for pilgrims with a synagogue. The ruins of the second synagogue, with a basilica plan and oriented northeastward–that is, not toward Jerusalem–have yielded floor mosaics with geometric and floral motifs and an aedicule flanked by a *menorah*, a *shofar* and a Greek inscription written in Samaritan letters.

In the present-day city, a mosque now houses the Bet Shean Archaeological Museum, with finds from the digs and fragments of Roman and Byzantine mosaics.

BET ALPHA AND THE ZODIAC MOSAIC

The synagogue of Bet Alpha lies at the foot of Mount Gilboa, east of the Jezreel Valley and about 41 miles south of Nazareth. This site, now a national park, is best known for the mosaics that decorated the pavement of a synagogue, which are the best preserved in Israel. They were discovered quite by chance in 1929 when workers were digging an irrigation canal in the Hefzi-Bah kibbutz area. The synagogue, which is 92 x 46 feet, belongs to the latest type of the ancient synagogues discovered in Palestine, consisting of a vestibule–or narthex–followed by a main basilical hall divided into three aisles by two rows of columns, and an apse oriented toward Jerusalem in which sacred texts were

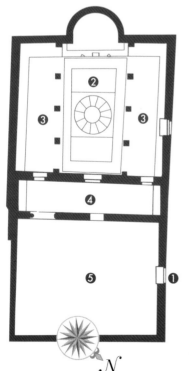

kept. All the pavements in this synagogue were covered with mosaics. The west aisle is decorated with simple geometric motifs, while the east aisle is for the most part undecorated. The naïve mosaic decoration in the central aisle is divided into three panels–framed by vine branches and geometric motifs–which symbolically represent the tripartition of Solomon's Temple: the area for the faithful, the

area reserved for rabbis, and the Holy of Holies where the Ark of the Covenant was kept before disappearing after the Babylonian invasion.

The east panel, next to the apse, depicts the Ark of the Convenant flanked by two *menorahs*, two lions and some cult objects. This is followed by the most interesting panel (the middle one), which is decorated with a Zodiacal wheel around the chariot of the sun god, Helios, and is in turn framed by the representations of the four seasons set in the corners. The last panel has a scene of the sacrifice of Isaac that is as lively as it is naïve. It includes the ram that was to replace Abraham's son on the flames of the altar, as well as the hand of God that stops Abraham from sacrificing his son. A distinguishing feature of this mosaic are the inscriptions. They not only

---

BET ALPHA

1 MAIN ENTRANCE
2 ZODIAC MOSAIC
3 VESTIBULE
4 COURTYARD

90 The Zodiac motif, which appears in the central section of the mosaic pavement in the Bet Alpha synagogue, is quite common in most Jewish art of the Byzantine age.

91 top The top panel of the mosaic features the tabernacle of the Torah, flanked by pairs of facing birds, menorahs and roaring lions.

identify the two craftsmen who executed the mosaics (a certain Marianos and his son Haninan, the same who did the mosaic pavement in the Bet Shean synagogue), but also tell us when the mosaic was laid out: during the reign of Justinian I (527-565).

TAANACH, FORTIFIED CITY

The Biblical city of Taanach lies at modern-day Tell Ta'annek, five miles southeast of Megiddo, next to the spurs of Mount Carmel. Although it was not in a strategic position, as were other fortified cities in the Jezreel Valley, Taanach still has a complex history fraught with sieges, destruction and revival. It was a fortified city as far back as the 3rd millennium BC and was also listed as one of the cities conquered and fortified by the Egyptian pharaoh Tuthmosis III in the 15th century BC. It is also mentioned in the chronicles of the undecisive victories of the ally of Jeroboam I, the pharaoh of Egypt Shoshenq, in the late 10th century. But in the Bible the city is best known for the great and, as often occurs in the Old Testament, miraculous victory of the Israelites over the Canaanites. However, on the basis of the finds, archaeologists attach less importance to the victory of the Israelites under Deborah and Barak against the Canaanite ruler Sisera: it seems that the city was not occupied by the descendants of Joshua until the 10th century, that is, Solomon's age, when it became an administrative center of the kingdom of Israel.

Taanach was also mentioned by bishop Eusebius, who desribed it in the 3rd century AD as a very large city. Archaeological digs, which began here in 1902–thus at the beginning of the archaeological exploration of Palestine–have brought to light Bronze Age fortifications and precious finds such as twelve tablets in cuneiform script, an incense altar decorated with lions' heads, gold jewellery, and an Egyptian statue–all now kept in various Israeli museums.

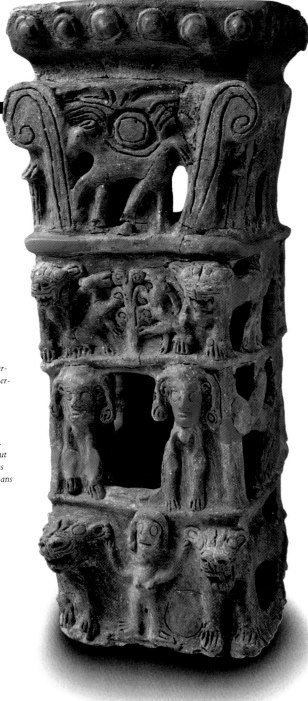

91 bottom This 10th-century, four-level incense burner-altar found in Taanach was probably used for libations during sacred ceremonies. The lions stand out among the various animals and humans represented on it.

MEGIDDO AND THE BATTLE BETWEEN GOOD AND EVIL

The rise with the ruins of Megiddo lies at the southeastern end of the long ridge of Mount Carmel, about 18 miles from Haifa, dominating from the south the broad Jezreel Valley at the crossroads of the ancient trade route that linked Egypt and Mesopotamia in a northwest-southeast direction via the Phoenician cities, Jerusalem and the Jordan river valley. If

92 top The tell of Armageddon seen from the east. The excavation in the foreground shows the progression of the archaeological dig in the many layers of ancient settlements that have created this rise.

the place name *Armageddon*—which in *Revelations* is indicated as the place where the final battle between the forces of good and evil will take place—can be correctly identified as the Mountain of Megiddo, this interpretation would be a most dramatic confirmation of the notorious history of wars and devastation of this *tell*, which boasts twenty strata of settlements dating from the Chalcolithic age (fourth millennium BC) to the early Hellenistic period (late 4th century BC).

Megiddo also makes its appearance in official history through Egyptian documents, which narrate in detail the adventurous conquest of this locality on the part of Tuthmosis III, who in 1479 BC

took the *tell* from the Canaanites after a seven month siege. Although the first recorded historic events at Megiddo are related to military actions, it seems that the city grew up as a religious center. Despite repeated invasions, the Canaanites always returned here to settle in the place where they had built their altar. Yet for some inexplicable reason no traces have been found of the defensive wall dating from the time of Tuthmosis' attack, and the lack of such a wall would befit a religious center rather than a commercial city.

In the lowest archaeological stratum there are the remains of rectangular dwellings that demonstrate—as is the case

with Jericho—the development of a true urban community. On the eastern slope of the rise, archaeologists unearthed the remains of a sacred precinct used from the time of the most ancient settlements to the 12th century BC, when the site was conquered by the Israelites. The heart of

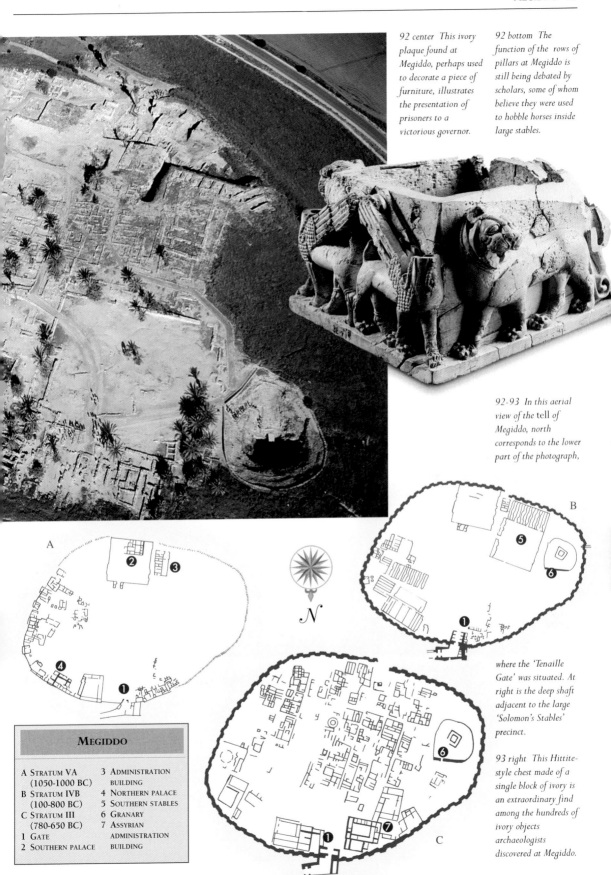

92 center This ivory plaque found at Megiddo, perhaps used to decorate a piece of furniture, illustrates the presentation of prisoners to a victorious governor.

92 bottom The function of the rows of pillars at Megiddo is still being debated by scholars, some of whom believe they were used to hobble horses inside large stables.

92-93 In this aerial view of the tell of Megiddo, north corresponds to the lower part of the photograph,

where the 'Tenaille Gate' was situated. At right is the deep shaft adjacent to the large 'Solomon's Stables' precinct.

93 right This Hittite-style chest made of a single block of ivory is an extraordinary find among the hundreds of ivory objects archaeologists discovered at Megiddo.

MEGIDDO

A STRATUM VA (1050-1000 BC)
B STRATUM IVB (100-800 BC)
C STRATUM III (780-650 BC)
1 GATE
2 SOUTHERN PALACE
3 ADMINISTRATION BUILDING
4 NORTHERN PALACE
5 SOUTHERN STABLES
6 GRANARY
7 ASSYRIAN ADMINISTRATION BUILDING

the Canaanite sacred precinct was the *bamah*, a round altar about 30 feet in diameter placed about 5 feet above the ground; it was made of rubble masonry and was delimited to the south and west by three rectangular temples. Besides its religious importance, Megiddo was also a trade center, as is attested by the rich

booty the Egyptian pharaoh Tuthmosis brought back with him, which is described in the inscriptions on the walls of the Temple of Karnak, as well as by the finds dating from the long period in which the city was a prosperous Egyptian stronghold (15th-12th century BC). The 382 Canannite ivory objects found in a

palace of that time have been interpreted as the treasure of a royal prince.

After the Israelite conquest, important public buildings and impressive structures with megalithic walls, such as the palace in the southern sector of the *tell*, were constructed in Megiddo. Solomon replaced the most ancient city wall, made of sun-

94-95 In the western sector of the *tell* is the large Canaanite shaft that afforded access to a spring outside the walls.

94 bottom At the bottom of the excavation the rocky heart of the *tell* is traversed by the canal that also supplied the city with water in case of a siege.

95 top left Using the Bible as a source, some scholars affirm that the stone basins found in 'Solomon's Stables' were troughs.

95 top right The cyclopean ruins of Megiddo date back to the period after the Israelite conquest, when the Canaanite brick wall was torn down.

dried bricks, with a massive fortification that combined the back walls of the largest edifices with stretches of the fortress itself. It is probable that in Solomon's time the only entrance to the city was a 'Tenaille Gate,' in the northern sector of the wall. It seems that this consisted of six chambers, three per side, that were protected by wooden portcullises in case of war. In the turbulent period of the division of the Israelite kingdom immediately after Solomon's death, the city became even more fortified with the construction of a massive wall over 10 feet thick and with the creation of an 'L'-shaped gate. However, these new defensive measures did not prevent the temporary occupation of Megiddo on the part of the Libyan pharaoh of Egypt, Shoshenq, as is testified by a stela dating from the late 10th century BC.

Some of the most important architectural works in Megiddo were built in the 9th-8th century BC. The water supply network of the fortress was constructed just like the one in Jerusalem: a stepped shaft and passageway led down from the southwest area of the *tell* to a canal cut out of the rock that was connected to a spring outside the city walls. It is probable that the same period witnessed the construction of the so-called Solomon's Stables, two complexes of long, narrow buildings west and northwest of the southern palace built in Solomon's time. Biblical tradition, plus the discovery of round and rectangular basins similar to troughs, have led some scholars to believe that these structures were stables for horses, while others claim they were either barracks, warehouses, or marketplaces. Lastly, in front of the Solomonic southern palace is Megiddo's public grain silo, a round cavity

with two flights of steps that go down to the bottom; this structure was originally covered with wooden roofing to protect the grain.

One of the last times Megiddo is mentioned in historical chronicles was on the occasion of the death of the king of Judah, Josiah, in 609 BC, when he attempted to check the advance of the Egyptian pharaoh Necho II toward Assyria, while the last archaeological finds date from 450 BC. The much disputed fortress city was nothing more than a small village by the Hellenistic age.

95 center Rather than stables for the king's horses, some scholars believe that Solomon's Stables may have been barracks or storehouses.

95 bottom The bamah, the altar worshipped by the Canaanites at Megiddo, consisted merely of a mound of crude stones.

CAESAREA,
THE GREAT HERODIAN HARBOUR

The magnificent ruins of Caesarea lie along the coastal plain of Sharon, extending between the modern cities of Haifa to the north and Tel Aviv to the south. Herod the Great (37-4 BC) is to be credited with the foundation of the large port basin, called *Sebastos* (the Greek equivalent of the Latin *augustus*, or 'great') and the major city next to it. In

needed to free the harbour of debris. The outer section had an elbow turn to the north and was flanked by a massive lighthouse modeled after the great one in Alexandria, which was one of the Seven Wonders of the Ancient World.

It seems that the name commonly used to indicate the impressive Herodian

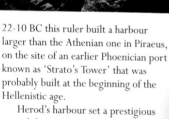

CAESAREA
1 THEATRE
2 PALACE
3 TEMPLE OF AUGUSTUS
4 PORT
5 LIGHTHOUSE
6 AQUEDUCT
7 AMPHITHEATRE

22-10 BC this ruler built a harbour larger than the Athenian one in Piraeus, on the site of an earlier Phoenician port known as 'Strato's Tower' that was probably built at the beginning of the Hellenistic age.

Herod's harbour set a prestigious record, because it is quite probable that it was the first port built entirely in the open sea without the support of bays or peninsulas that would protect the dry dock. These were replaced by two enormous parallel breakwaters that pointed westward from the coast and were built with cemented blocks and huge masses of rubble used as filling. The articulated *Sebastos* harbour consisted of a large basin divided into three sections. The innermost one was built partly over the previous Hellenistic installation and had quays to load and unload cargo, as well as warehouses. The middle section opened out southward with a sluice gate that regulated the flow of the water

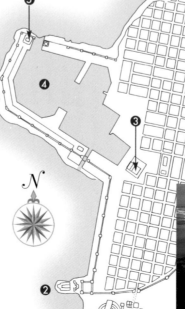

96 top The massive breakwater of the Sebastos harbor, which jutted in a sharp bend to protect the bay, ended in an equally impressive lighthouse.

96-97 Caesarea is a typical Herodian city, rich in Roman architecture adapted to the megalomaniacal taste of the king.

96 bottom One of the two aqueducts in Caesarea extended for the ten miles along the coast separating Mount Carmel from the port town.

ruins, *Caesarea Maritima*, was unknown in ancient times: in fact, to distinguish this locality from those of the same name that had risen up in the Near East, the Latin sources used the name *Caesarea Palestinae* for the most part.

Herod's city contained all the features of a typical Roman city, from the grid street pattern to the efficient sewer system, buildings and major public areas and works. Notable examples are the clearly classically inspired theatre; the amphitheatre, used for gladitorial combat; an aqueduct that collected water from the spring waters on Mount Carmel about 10 miles away; and the forum, situated by the harbour and dominated by a temple

97 top This inscription on the main aqueduct states that the structure was restored by the Tenth Legion (Fretensis).

97 bottom left A detail of the aqueduct shows how Herod the Great applied the principles of Roman town-planning

combining functionality and monumentality.

97 bottom right Caesarea Maritima

lacks none of the characteristic features of a Roman city. This photograph shows the suspensurae of the great city baths.

98 top left and bottom right The main port in Herod's kingdom was ideal for cultural and political propaganda; for example, it abounded in statues dedicated to the august rulers of Palestine.

98-99 The perfection of each architectural element in Caesarea reflects the power of Rome in the period bridging the end of the Republic and the Imperial Age.

99 top Although Caesarea continued to prosper in the Byzantine and Crusader periods, the local statues are mostly pagan.

dedicated to the deified Rome and Augustus Caesar. In keeping with the best tradition of Herod's cities, Caesarea also had a grandiose palace the ruler used as a pleasure garden that jutted into the sea between the south bay and the theatre.

At first, the administration of Caesarea was modeled after the Greek city state, the *polis* of the classical age, perhaps in order to vie with the political power of Jerusalem, but after Herod's death it became the residence of the Roman procurators of Judaea, among whom was the notorious Pontius Pilate. In the first decades of the Christian era the city was linked to the tragic events that preceded and followed the First Jewish War (66-70 AD), when indiscriminate massacres on the part of the Romans took the lives of an estimated 5,000-13,000 of the city's inhabitants, almost all of whom were Jews. Albeit less ferocious, other mass executions occurred during the Second Jewish War, which ended in 135.

Caesarea was also linked to personages

99 right This red porphyry statue may have been a portrait of Hadrian.

99 bottom left The mosaics at Caesarea also have secular themes and motifs.

in the New Testament. Peter converted centurion Cornelius here, and the apostles Phillip and above all Paul were here, the latter being imprisoned for two years before being sent to Rome to be executed. But the main connections with the new Christian religion regard the Church Father who was active in the city around the mid 3rd century, Origen, and Eusebius of Caesarea, the founder of ecclesiastic history and the city's bishop in the first half of the 4th century.

The great economic development that had characterized the decades following the end of the bloody Jewish Wars favoured cultural growth as well, which concerned both the Jewish communities that had returned to the city, founding rabbinical schools and synagogues, and the Christian population, which was increasing rapidly. After the Council of Nicaea, Caesarea became one of the leading intellectual and cultural centers in the Near East. By the 5th and 7th century the city was prevalently Christian, and

there was conflict with the Jewish and Samaritan minorities until the Byzantines under emperor Heraclius briefly occupied the city from 627 to 639-641, when they were driven out by the Muslims. Caesarea then fell into obscurity, like so many other cities in Palestine at this time, and revived temporarily during the First Crusade, when the harbour was cleared of the sand that over the centuries had blocked it and the Byzantine walls were replaced by new ramparts which, however, enclosed a much smaller area than the Herodian and Byzantine city.

The historical events that followed were linked to the vicissitudes of the Crusades. First Saladin occupied the city; this was followed by Richard the Lion-Hearted's conquest, caliph el-Malik's plunder and the brief dominion of Louis IX of France. The Muslims, led by the sultan Baybars, reconquered the city in 1265 from the Christian troops, razed it to the ground and it was abandoned for centuries. In 1837 the ruins of Caesarea were further damaged by an earthquake. However, from 1884 to 1948 the city was the home of a community of Muslim Bosnian refugees, which was dispersed during the 1948 war, as well as of a fishermen's kibbutz

100 top left and right The cross-vaulting of the inner passageways in the Crusader gates at Caesarea is still intact. The accessways to the fortified city were laid out in such a way that direct entry would be impossible.

100 center The massive Crusader walls, a great deal of which have been preserved, protected a much smaller area than that of Herod's city.

100 bottom The Crusader structures on the side facing the sea have almost completely disappeared, except for the outer jetties.

founded in 1940 south of the ancient site. The members of this latter community, taking advantage of the Roman and Crusader breakwaters, built a pier, thus initiating the rediscovery of the ancient city and its massive harbour installations, which, as Herod the Great certainly had intended, had resisted the assaults of time to bear witness to the splendor of his reign.

101 The fortifications in Christian Caesarea were built by Louis IX of France, who promoted the eighth (and last) Crusade. Outside the east gate of the city, the arches that supported the bridge over the moat are still intact.

DOR, THE PHOENICIAN HARBOUR

The ancient port town of Dor lies on a squat promontory–a rarity on the uniform Israeli coast–that juts into the Mediterranean north of Caesarea, in a stretch of coastline with three bays protected by natural reefs and islets. The name of the locality was first recorded in an inscription of the Egyptian pharaoh Ramses II (1304-1237 BC), and much later it became part of the Greek world, its foundation being ascribed to Doros, the son of Poseidon, the god of the sea. Archaeological surveys have shown that Dor began to be used by the Phoenicians or the Canaanites around the 13th century BC, and that at the beginning of the following century it was conquered by the Sikuli, one of the Mediterranean populations–generically called 'Sea Peoples' by the ancient Egyptians–who in this period invaded Asia Minor and Syria and even posed a threat to Egypt. Evidence of an attack on the port town in the mid 11th century seems to confirm that Dor was reconquered by the Phoenicians, who were supplanted by King David a few years later.

landing at Dor and Jaffa, which were constantly battered by southwest winds and often ran aground. However, history tells us that after 10 BC Dor went through a dramatic decline and by the end of the 4th century was totally abandoned. Despite such decadence, it seems that it still remained a harbour to some degree: the Crusaders occupied it and built a castle they named 'de Merle,' after the fief holders who had granted the town to the Templars. These latter still owned it when the castle was destroyed by Saladin in 1187.

Archaeological digs have revealed that since very ancient times the underwater rocky land formations were enlarged with stone structures to protect the slips, which lay in three adjacent bays. Just south of the north bay, which is shallow and suitable for small boats, researchers brought to light traces of a Roman theater and the remains of a purple dye factory (the Phoenicians were world-famous for this activity), which was of fundamental importance to the economy of Dor. In the small central

102 center left and bottom A port already in the Bronze Age, under the Phoenicians the three contiguous bays at Dor were furnished with complex harbor facilities as well as industrial plants to produce purple dye and wash dyed cloth.

Despite all these changes, Dor continued to be a prevalently Phoenician seaport until the 3rd century, when Ptolemy II Philadelphus conquered the city and rebuilt it in keeping with Greek town planning canons. It was then taken by Alexander Jannaeus (103-76 BC) and in 63 BC was annexed to the Roman province of Syria. According to Flavius Josephus, one of the reasons behind the construction of *Sebastos*, the port of Caesarea, was the difficulty ships had in

102-103 The prosperity of the Phoenician port town attracted many enemies, but the constant scourge of Dor has been the sea, which has eliminated at least 15% of the coastline.

103 This bust of Aphrodite found at Dor was also made by local Hellenistic artisans.

DOR

1 RESIDENCES	5 TEMPLES
2 GATE	6 RESIDENCES
3 RESIDENCES	7 ARSENAL
4 HARBOUR WAREHOUSES	8 THEATRE

bay archaeologists found a quay consisting of three parallel rows of cut stones that was probably used for laying up large ships. Lastly, the broad south bay of Tell Dor was used as the main harbor.

Given the long history of the harbor, the sea has also yielded many finds from different ages: heavy anchors dating back to the 20th-6th century BC; Persian amphoras lying on the sea bottom that came from at least two shipwrecks that occurred in the 6th-5th century BC; Roman, Byzantine, Crusader, Arab and even modern finds, such as the foodstuffs transported onto a Greek vessel that sank at Dor in 1664, and the arms that Napoleon threw into the sea during his retreat from Acre in 1799.

At the Nashoim kibbutz, next to the archaeological site, the Center for Nautical and Regional Archaeology boasts many finds from the digs and research carried out in this area. Moreover, inside the kibbutz itself are the remains of a 4th-century AD Byzantine church built over the ruins of a Hellenistic temple.

BELVOIR,
THE STAR OF JORDAN

*104 center left
Lacking springs inside
its walls, Belvoir used
rainwater collected in
its cisterns.*

*104-105 Belvoir was
accessible from the west
via a drawbridge, and
from the south through
a gate defended by the
barbican.*

The Crusader castle of Belvoir–also known as the 'Star of Jordan' (Kokhav ha-Yarden in Hebrew)–was built on the top of a scarp 1,640 feet high that dominates the Jordan Valley. From this strategic position its massive glacises controlled the hills of Samaria to the southwest, Mount Tabor to the northwest, Lake Tiberias and the Golan up to Mount Hermon to the north, and the Yarmuk Valley, which marks the Syrian-Jordanian border, to the northeast.

The history of this fortress is complex. In 1140 the Velos family from Tiberias founded a strongly fortified

farmstead on the hill and then sold the property in 1168 to the Knights Hospitallers, who transformed it into a grandiose castle. During the campaign of conquest in the Beisan Valley, as a diversionary maneuver Saladin attacked the fortress, without succeeding in taking it, in 1182-83. Then, after his victory at the Horns of Hattin, the Ayyubid sultan again laid siege to the castle, finally managing to take it after two years by mining the tower that defended the entrance ramp, the barbican that had been considered unassailable. The defending Crusader knights negotiated a surrender whereby they were allowed to take refuge in Tyre. The Muslims demolished the castle only in 1217-18, when they systematically dismantled all the

fortresses in the Holy Land so that the Crusaders could not use them again. However, the latter were able to take possession of what remained of Belvoir in 1241, after negotiating a treaty with the Muslim governors of Palestine, but they did not stay long enough to rebuild it and it was abandoned definitively.

The heart of the complex was the keep, with four corner towers that

enclosed a square parade ground surrounded by rooms that served as the kitchens, refectories, storehouses and the chapel. The courtyard surrounding the keep was like a moat in masonry that separated it from the outer fortification, which was more or less pentagonal and ran for a maximum length of 472 feet from the west wall to the end of the barbican; the width

104 bottom left The outer walls housed large communicating chambers used as workshops, storehouses and shelters.

104 bottom right The heart of the fortress was the keep, the massive castle that housed the Crusader garrisons.

105 center The Crusader loopholes, of Oriental inspiration, were set inside deep niches.

105 bottom Just like the arches illustrated here, the entire structure of Belvoir consisted of alternating layers of limestone and basalt.

BELVOIR
1 MAIN GATE
2 OUTER TOWER (BARBICAN)
3 OUTER TOWERS
4 CISTERN
5 OUTER COURTYARD
6 INNER TOWERS
7 KITCHENS
8 INNER COURTYARD
9 REFECTORY
10 KEEP
11 WEST GATE
12 DRAWBRIDGE
13 MOAT

between the corner towers was 328-367 feet. There were towers at every corner and in the middle of the outer walls, with the barbican at the east end of the castle. The curtain wall was surrounded on three sides by a deep dry moat. The narrow passageways under four of the outer towers allowed the defenders to make sorties, which were quite useful in case of a siege.

Since the slope underneath was so rugged and seemingly impassable, the eastern side of the castle was considered safe, but this proved to be a costly mistake that led to the conquest of Belvoir. Shrewd strategist that he was, Saladin chose precisely the side that was supposedly the strongest, to make a breach in the Crusaders' defense.

The castle was built with different material, but most of it consisted of blocks of black basalt dug during the creation of the dry moat, as well as stones taken from the nearby Jewish village of Kokhava. Among the latter was a lintel from the local synagogue; it was decorated with a *menorah* flanked by an inscription in Aramaic.

Today a tour of the ruins begins by crossing the drawbridge that led to the secondary entrance facing west, which in turn gave access to the first of the two concentric circles around the keep. The vaulted spaces between the outer and inner walls were used for barracks, storage and workrooms, while those in the keep itself made it a totally self-sufficient fortress, with storehouses for food, a cistern that collected rainwater and, naturally, a chapel.

NAZARETH, THE HOME OF JESUS

"Can there any good thing come out of Nazareth?" The question in the *Gospel according to St. John* found a clear and overwhelming answer in the great number of Christians who for two thousand years have come to pray in this village–or better, in this urban area of almost 100,000 souls. This is the place where Jesus spent his childhood and began his preaching, and in the surroundings the Christian pilgrims can visit dozens of localities connected to the life and miracles of Christ. However, it would not be improper to use the word 'obscure' when speaking of this ancient village: according to the Gospels, Nazareth was precisely that in Jesus' time, and the name of the town does not appear at all in the other authoritative chronicles of the time, from Flavius Josephus to the Jewish commentaries.

The modern-day town lies about 20 miles from the west shore of Lake Tiberias, in a fertile valley among the foothills of Galilee, within sight of Biblical Mount Tabor to the east and Mount Hermon to the north, and dominating the broad Jezreel Valley to the south. Today Nazareth is inhabited by Arabs, who live in the interesting old town, by Jews who live in the modern suburb of Illit, and by

Christian communities that administer the many sacred edifices. But until the 4th century AD the population of this village was exclusively Jewish. Therefore, it was a Judeo-Christian sect that initiated the worship of the holy sites mentioned in the Gospels, identifying a group of caves used as dwellings in the 1st and 2nd centuries as the Holy Cave of the Annunciation and the home of Mary. Most likely this site was included in a synagogue-church that was replaced by a Byzantine basilica,

which in turn was incorporated into the large Crusader cathedral built by Tancred after 1099. It is not surprising that, during the Crusader period, Nazareth, like so many other towns, changed hands so often and so quickly, from Saladin's reconquest of Palestine to the destruction of all the Christian edifices effected by the sultan Baybars I in 1263.

106 top right The modern Basilica of the Annunciation was finished just before the outbreak of the Six-Day War.

106 center right On the ground floor of the Basilica, the cave dwelling considered the home of Mary is a holy site.

106 center left and bottom right Only five column capitals and a French effigy of the Trinity were salvaged from Saladin's destruction of the Crusader church in Nazareth.

106 bottom left The Greek Orthodox Church of the Assumption houses the Fountain of

the Virgin, where Mary was said to have heard angel Gabriel's voice.

106-107 More massive than attractive, the Basilica of the Annunciation consists

of two superimposed churches designed by the Italian architect Giovanni Muzio.

107 bottom Nazareth offers a good view of Mount Tabor, the mountain of the

Transfiguration, now crowned by a modern basilica built over Byzantine foundations.

The Christians were able to rebuild their sacred buildings only in the second half of the 17th century, when the Franciscans built a monastery and church over the remains of the Annunciation cathedral, around which modern-day Nazareth grew up. This complex was enlarged in the 17th and 18th century, and was then demolished–after four years of meticulous archaeological research at the site–in order to make room for the largest Christian church in the Middle East, the Basilica of the Annunciation, designed by the Italian architect Giovanni Muzio and consecrated in 1968. Mention must be made of the laudable ecumenical spirit shown by the Israeli government, which sponsored the public financing of this large complex. The heart of the basilica is the Holy Cave, the ancient cave dwelling that the Crusaders turned into a chapel. Other holy sites in the town are the church dedicated to St. Joseph, which was built on the site that late Christian tradition identified as the place where the house of Jesus' putative father stood, and the Fountain of the Virgin, which lies inside the Greek Orthodox Church of St. Gabriel. In the surroundings of Nazareth there are two localities traditionally considered the sites of the miracle of the water turned into wine: Khirbet Qana, five-and-one-half miles northwest of Nazareth, a rather important town during the Roman period; and Kafr Kana, about four miles from the town, where a 19th-century Franciscan church lies over the place which around the 5th century was occupied by a synagogue converted into a church in the following century and into a mosque under the Ottoman rulers.

BET SHE'ARIM AND ITS ANCIENT NECROPOLIS

On the western side of the Jezreel Valley, about twelve miles southeast of Haifa, the catacombs of Bet She'arim are a direct and moving testimony of the trials and tribulations of the Jews under Roman rule. Many of the Jews who had survived the two bloody Jewish Wars, which ended in 70 and 135 AD, took refuge in Galilee. In particular, the locality among the low hills of southern Galilee that Flavius Josephus called 'Basara,' which had already been the administrative center of the land belonging to Queen Berenice, became famous in the 2nd century as the seat of the Sanhedrin (the supreme

rabbinical council) and an ancient rabbinical school. Since the Romans prohibited Jews from entering Jerusalem, the latter decided to build a vast necropolis in Galilee, and Bet She'arim was chosen as the alternative, most probably because illustrious rabbis had already been interred in the local cemetery during Herod the Great's time. As they wanted to have their final resting place in the land of their ancestors, many Jews who had gone to live in various parts of Palestine and in foreign countries during the Diaspora in the 2nd-4th century, had their remains taken to be buried next to the tomb of the patriarch Judah I (Judah ha-Nasi), whose death coincided with the growth of the necropolis.

Archaeologists have been able to identify many of the places of exile of the pious Jews buried in Bet She'arim, thanks to the epigraphs. They range from Ezion Geber, a locality at the mouth of the Jordan River in the Gulf of Aqaba, to the south, to Antioch in Syria, to the north, and Nahardea, on

the Tigris River, to the east. The corridors of the catacombs, which were cut deeply in the limestone slopes of the hill at Bet She'arim and the nearby rises, are lined with hundreds of sarcophagi that are for the most part intact despite the destruction wrought by the Byzantine tetrarch Constans

108 left The eternal resting place in the Promised Land: for the pious Jews of the Diaspora, being buried at Bet She'arim was like returning to native land.

108-109 Bet She'arim was the burial site of many illustrious people in the Herodian period, but its fame grew in the 2nd century AD, after the death of the patriarch Judah I.

Gallus, who in 351 AD ruthlessly put down a new revolt in Palestine. After that time, the necropolis was used less and less and, naturally, there was a decline in the town's leading industry, funeral and burial services. Both the cemetery and its related activities fell into oblivion in the Byzantine epoch.

Access to the catacombs was gained through an entrance with decorated sides, the lintels of which sometimes bore carved epigraphs, as well as three stone doors cut so as to imitate the design of common wooden doors. Once past the entrance, there is a decorated courtyard leading to the corridors and adjacent burial chambers. In the

108 bottom left In many cases the entrance to the catacombs had stone doors carved to resemble wooden ones.

108 bottom right The refuge of the Jews that survived in 70 and 135 AD, Bet She'arim did not manage to avoid being destroyed by Constans Gallus.

109 top The varied size and workmanship of the catacombs reflect the social status of their owners.

109 bottom Characteristic features of the architecture of the 3rd-century synagogues are the three arched doors giving access to the main catacombs.

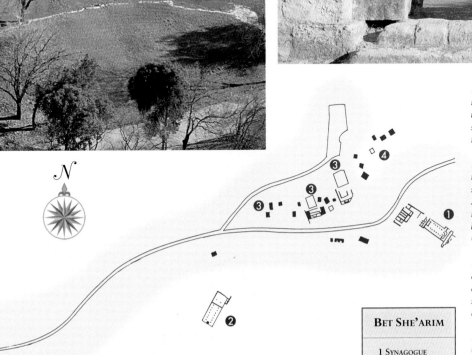

N

BET SHE'ARIM

1 SYNAGOGUE
2 BASILICA
3 CATACOMBS
4 CISTERN

underground catacombs, which are now numbered, the burial sites vary from the open loculi hewn out of the walls, to the tombs set into the pavement. But certainly the most interesting aspect of the catacombs are the sarcophagi in the corridors or the burial chambers, some of these latter being more than 13 feet high.

Although the first catacomb was public, the social status of most of the deceased interred in the other parts of the necropolis (persons who could afford the transport of the corpses from such distant places and the burial itself, which were quite expensive) is underscored by the elegance of some sarcophagi and by the decorations on the walls of the catacombs. Large *menorahs* carved into the limestone, representations of the Ark of the Covenant and of cult objects such as the *shofar*, the ram's horn that commemorates the interrupted sacrifice of Isaac, as well as decorative motifs drawn from nature and architectural elements–all alternate, on the walls and on the tombs, with mythological scenes, and zoomorphic and even anthropomorphic figures. The presence of the last-mentioned motifs shows that in the early Christian era, the Jewish

110 top and center At Bet She'arim the figures sculpted on the sarcophagi and walls depart from the Jewish precepts prohibiting the representation of living beings.

precepts against idolatry were less strict than in the past. The Greek-Judaic, Hebrew and Aramaic epigraphs found everywhere were also executed with refinement and are extremely interesting manifestations of the social, economic and religious conditions of the Jewish people in the period after the Diaspora.

On the slopes of the Bet She'arim hill, archaeologists discovered the remains of a complex that included an unidentified public building called a

110-111 The catacombs contain hundreds of sarcophagi that line the corridors or lie in the funerary chambers.

110 bottom Pairs of facing lions are a common motif in the Bet She'arim sarcophagi.

'basilica,' as well as a synagogue, and other edifices that lined the streets of the ancient town. The large basilica is 131 feet long and 49 feet wide and dates from the end of the 2nd century AD, that is, the 'golden age' of Bet She'arim. It was rebuilt several times up to the mid 4th century, when it may have been destroyed by Constans Gallus. The slightly smaller synagogue, which has a basilica plan, met with the same fate. It was built in the 3rd century northeast of the basilica. The ruins have yielded some marble tablets, originally on the colored stucco walls, which bear the names of the patrons of the construction.

111 top and center The seven arms of the menorah, which is a sort of universal symbol of Judaism, were also sculpted to sanctify the final resting place of the persons buried at Bet She'arim.

111 bottom Although they were often influenced by Hellenistic art, the sarcophagi have many purely religious symbols, such as the flanking columns depicting the Ark of the Covenant.

SEPPHORIS
AND THE MONA LISA OF GALILEE

The historic village of Sepphoris, now the town of Moshav Zippor, situated just northwest of Nazareth, was deeply influenced by the presence of the Jewish communities that lived there almost uninterruptedly from the late Iron Age to the 5th-6th century AD. Sepphoris was an important city before Tiberias was founded: it was the capital of a district under the Hasmonean kings and again during the Roman dominion of Palestine up to the end of the Roman Republic. Sepphoris prospered under Herod Antipas and somehow stayed clear of the disastrous Jewish wars by siding with emperor Vespasian. After the destruction of the Temple, the city became the residence of

Tiberias, only to be defeated the following day by Saladin at the Horns of Hattin. Thanks to a special treaty, the Knights Templars were allowed to return to the city in 1240; they remained there until the Mamluk sultan Baybars conquered it in 1263. *Sephorie* castle, which became the Muslim Safuriyye, was rebuilt for the last time by the son of Dahar el-Omar, the Bedouin sheikh who tried to make Galilee his personal fief.

In the upper part of the city, east of the castle that dominates it, lie the ruins of a Roman theater with a seating capacity of 4,000-5,000. It was built in the 1st century AD under Herod Antipas, when part of the tiers and seats were hewn out

112 top Sepphoris had two aqueducts that conveyed water into underground cisterns; the hydraulic cement that lined the inside walls is still intact.

112 center The residential area of Sepphoris (in the foreground) is flanked by the tell on which one can recognize the Roman theater and the square Safuriyye castle.

112 bottom Parts of the cisterns were hewn out of the natural cavities and recesses.

the powerful priestly Jedaiah family. Its fame as a cultural and religious center grew when Rabbi Judah ha-Nasi (135-217) moved there around 200 AD from Bet She'arim. For seventeen years this great religious leader had managed the affairs of the Sanhedrin and completed the codification of the *Mishna*, the first Hebrew oral law.

The city was greatly damaged by an earthquake in 363 and was only partly rebuilt. But it still maintained its eminently Judaic character until the 6th century, when a Christian community settled there and the city became a diocese.

The Crusaders built the *Sephorie* castle from which their army set off on July 3, 1187 to aid to the besieged town of

of the hill, and was then enlarged in the 3rd-4th century. However, the gem of ancient Sepphoris is the large patrician mansion that lies immediately south of the theater, because the pavement mosaics in the dining room—which is flanked by rooms on three sides and has a peristyle

courtyard with an ornamental pool on the fourth—are among the most beautiful and best preserved in Israel. The fame of these mosaics rests mostly on the representation of the face of a woman that is so incredibly expressive and sensual it has been called the 'Mona Lisa of Galilee.' But the entire composition is remarkable, with its vivacious hunting, mythological and Dionysian cult scenes.

Another interesting mosaic pavement, found among the ruins of a huge Byzantine building at the foot of the hill, has scenes set on the Nile River and even the representation of a nilometer, the pillar inscribed with a scale used to determine the height of the river during its seasonal flood. Digs carried out on the

112-113 A nilometer stands out in the middle of this magnificent mosaic panel: the

vivacious mosaics with their Nilotic setting are among the most precious treasures in Sepphoris.

113 bottom left The tiers of the Roman theater were cut out of the rock of the tell.

113 bottom right This mosaic, found in a 3rd-century Roman villa, has exquisite portraits.

This female face in particular is so fascinating it was called the 'Mona Lisa of Galilee.'

top of the hill west of the castle have unearthed the remains of a residential quarter that was partly Hellenistic and mostly Roman. The many stepped and stuccoed ritual baths (*mikveh*) show that this area was the ancient Jewish quarter of Sepphoris.

TIBERIAS, A CENTER OF JUDAIC LEARNING

In 18-20 AD, Herod Antipas, the son of Herod the Great, founded his capital, which he dedicated to his august patron Tiberius. According to the authoritative Flavius Josephus, the city was situated amid a landscape of "…incommensurable natural beauty." The fertile land, now with subtropical vegetation, had been famous for some time: 695 feet below sea level, the western bank of Lake Tiberias was inhabited already during the Natufian epoch, around the 8th millennium BC. Again, further south of ancient Tiberias are hot springs that were known and appreciated at least from the Iron Age on.

Tiberias, the newly built Hellenistic-type capital that replaced Sepphoris, had to face a serious problem from the outset: since it lay over ancient burial grounds, the Jews were reluctant to live there because they considered it impure, so Herod Agrippa (about 100 AD) had to resort to compulsory measures. In the meantime, the city was not affected by the terrible Jewish Wars, and after the death of Herod Agrippa even benefitted from its peaceful acceptance of Roman administration. The city was purified in the mid 2nd century, so that during the

following century even the Jewish supreme council, the Sanhedrin, the Jewish Patriarchate and the Talmudic school left Sepphoris and set up their headquarters in Tiberias.

The city continued to prosper both commercially and culturally. Almost all of the Jerusalem Talmud was compiled here, and Tiberias became a leading religious center, the city of the preachers, poets and cantors of the sacred Hebrew texts.

In the first century AD the *thermae* locality of Hammat Tiberias also acquired considerable religious importance when two major synagogues were built in the coastal area south of the Herodian city. One of these edifices has a magnificent 4th-century mosaic divided into three panels that is virtually intact. The traditional representation of the Ark of the Torah is flanked by cultic objects (*menorah, shofar, lulav and ethrog*). This is followed by a Zodiacal circle which, surprisingly enough, revolves around the figure of the pagan sun god Helios on his celestial chariot. In the four corners of the square area in which the Zodiac is placed, are the faces of personifications of the seasons, which miraculously remained intact even after the construction of a dividing wall in the middle that broke the unity of the work, concealing Cancer, Capricorn and the sun chariot. The last panel has a long Greek inscription with the names of the founders of the synagogue, flanked by a pair of facing lions.

But in 1033 it was badly damaged by an earthquake and a few decades later the Crusaders rebuilt the city further north, where the present-day town lies.

Much smaller than ancient Tiberias, the city built during the Crusader period suffered the successive waves of conquerors so common in Palestine, which began in 1187 with Saladin and ended in almost definitive fashion with the dreadful sultan Baybars in 1247. The buildings of the Crusader-founded city have all disappeared, except for traces in the foundations of some Muslim edifices, such as the 19th-century el-Bahri mosque, and in the area now occupied by the Church of St. Peter. Even the name Crusader Castle, given to the fortress built by Dahar el-Omar, is deceptive: its site, in fact, is the same one where Tancred's castle stood, but the complex was built in 1745, as was the partly preserved city wall. The brief 'illuminated' period under el-Omar–who was so tolerant in religious matters that the el-Omri mosque, built a few dozen yards west of the Church of St. Peter, was donated to him by the Jewish community–was followed by the Egyptian invasion in the early 19th century and, a few years later, by a terrific earthquake that destroyed most of the city.

Today Tiberias is entirely Jewish and looks quite modern, so that it seems to have fewer monuments and ancient ruins than other localities in the Holy Land. However, in the heart of the modern city are the tombs of 'cultural heroes' who are still venerated. Two of these are rabbi Akiva, the martyr of the anti-Roman Bar Kokhba revolt (135 AD), and the great physician and philosopher rabbi Mosè Ben Maimon, a scholar who lived in the Crusader epoch and was highly respected by Christians and Muslims as well.

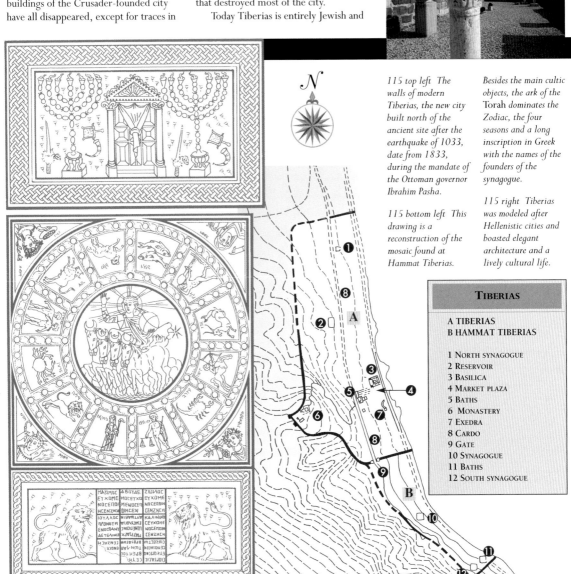

115 top left The walls of modern Tiberias, the new city built north of the ancient site after the earthquake of 1033, date from 1833, during the mandate of the Ottoman governor Ibrahim Pasha.

115 bottom left This drawing is a reconstruction of the mosaic found at Hammat Tiberias.

Besides the main cultic objects, the ark of the Torah dominates the Zodiac, the four seasons and a long inscription in Greek with the names of the founders of the synagogue.

115 right Tiberias was modeled after Hellenistic cities and boasted elegant architecture and a lively cultural life.

TIBERIAS

A TIBERIAS
B HAMMAT TIBERIAS

1 NORTH SYNAGOGUE
2 RESERVOIR
3 BASILICA
4 MARKET PLAZA
5 BATHS
6 MONASTERY
7 EXEDRA
8 CARDO
9 GATE
10 SYNAGOGUE
11 BATHS
12 SOUTH SYNAGOGUE

TABGHA AND JESUS' MIRACLES

Just south of Capernaum, on the northwestern bank of the Sea of Galilee, is a locality that is extremely important in Christian tradition: first of all, the name Tabgha evokes images of the miraculous multiplication of the loaves and fish, together with one of Jesus' most powerful and meaningful sermons, which he gave to a multitude of people stunned by the novelty of his message not far from Tiberias. Today, this site, which is traditionally considered the place where Christ worked one of his most sensational miracles, is occupied by a modern church modeled after the Byzantine basilica that was built there in 5th century over the ruins of a 4th-century church. The archaeological excavations that began in 1932 have demonstrated that the original church was a simple structure with an aisleless nave. What is more important, they brought to light some splendid mosaics depicting the flora and fauna of the Sea of Galilee and a symbolic representation of Jesus' miracle: two fish flanking a basket of bread loaves. The stone that pilgrim Egeria

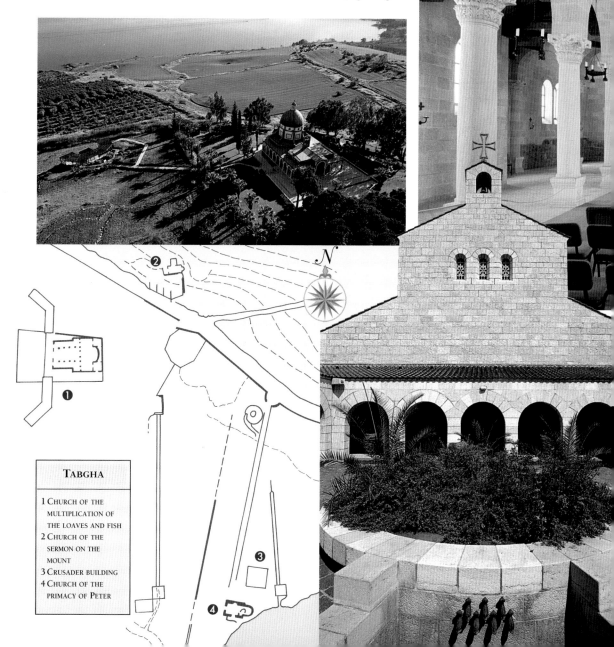

TABGHA

1 CHURCH OF THE
  MULTIPLICATION OF
  THE LOAVES AND FISH
2 CHURCH OF THE
  SERMON ON THE
  MOUNT
3 CRUSADER BUILDING
4 CHURCH OF THE
  PRIMACY OF PETER

116 top right In the 4th century, a Byzantine church with mosaics with naturalist and cultic motifs, stood on the site of the present-day Church of the Multiplication of the Loaves and Fish.

described in the late 4th century, considered the table on which Jesus placed the loaves, is now kept under the altar of the present-day Benedictine church.

Another major episode in the Gospels, Jesus conferring spiritual leadership of the church to Simon Peter, who is considered the first vicar of Christ on Earth and hence the first Christian pope, is

116 center The Church of the Sermon on the Mount lies where Jesus supposedly gave his famous sermon, but this interpretation clashes with the account made by pilgrim Egeria.

116 bottom and 116-117 The Church of the Multiplication of the Loaves and Fishes was built in 1982 over the holy edifice that contained the famous mosaics, but it was modeled after the Byzantine basilicas.

commemorated by the Church of the Primacy of Peter. Here too the building is modern and also houses a sacred rock that is worshipped as the stone table around which Jesus reputedly gathered together his disciples to teach them and comfort them after his resurrection.

"Blessed be the meek, for they shall inherit the earth," Jesus said from the top of the Mount of Beatitudes during his famous Sermon on the Mount, which according to modern tradition was delivered in the place where the Church of the Sermon on the Mount was built in 1938. The church has an octagonal plan that refers to the eight Beatitudes, yet it is far away from the cave that the authoritative pilgrim Egeria–whose accounts have been confirmed by archaeological discoveries–describes as the site of the Sermon on the Mount. Indeed, according to the most ancient Christian tradition, the place where the sermon was given lies on the road linking Tabgha and Capernaum, well below the Franciscan Church of the Sermon on the Mount; this claim is also attested to by the ruins of a 4th-century chapel that was used up to the 10th century after being restored and rebuilt several times.

117 top and center The Church of the Primacy of Peter, near the shores of the Sea of Galilee, lies in the place where Jesus entrusted Peter with the spiritual leadership of his church. It houses the rock-table where Jesus gathered his disciples.

117 bottom The symbolic prefiguration of the Eucharist, the loaves and fish that Jesus multiplied, are the central motif of the mosaic kept in the Church of the Multiplication.

HAMMAT GADER, THE CITY OF BATHS

In the 4th century, the Roman baths at Hammat Gader, a locality southeast of Tiberias, were considered among the most beautiful in the Roman Empire. The site was inhabited already in the Bronze Age because of its numerous sulphur hot springs, but became famous in ancient Greek and Roman times: it was mentioned by Strabo, Pliny the Elder, Origen and Eusebius. The baths continued to be used even after the city was conquered by the Muslims after the battle of Yarmuk, in 636. They began to decline about a century later, and were abandoned in the 10th century. The

known as 'the roasting spring'); the cooler ones, with an average temperature of 68° F, lie to the north and west. The baths were conceived as a combination of grandiosity and luxury, and the *caldarium* and *tepidarium* (the hot and warm rooms) were surrounded by halls and pools of varying sizes and shapes.

In 1932 a 5th-century synagogue built over an older edifice was discovered on the top of the tell that dominates the archaeological park. It has a basilica layout, with the nave divided by two rows of four columns each, and a third row parallel to the back wall. The holy ark, facing east, stood on a two-step platform over the pavement. With the exception of a panel with two lions, the pavement is covered with mosaics with geometric patterns and motifs and also with four inscriptions bearing the names of the donors. In the vicinity are the ruins of a Roman theater, which has fifteen rows of basalt seats and a seating capacity of 2,000.

A few miles from Hammat Gader, above the valley where the hot springs lie, and in Jordanian territory, are the ruins of ancient Gadara, now called Umm Qays. This city was founded in

118 top This fountain, which filled the basin of the large Oval Pool in the Roman baths, resembles a small altar.

118 center Here we see the Corinthian columns of the basilica of Gadara and, in the background, those in the Quadriporticus.

HAMMAT GADER	
1	ENTRANCE
2	FOUNTAIN
3	RECEPTION ROOM
4	HALL OF INSCRIPTIONS
5	ANTECHAMBER
6-7-8	POOLS
9	SPRING RESERVOIR
10	HOT SPRING
11	CANALIZATION
12	POOL

neighboring city of Gadara, one of the cities in the *Decapolis* after which Hammat was named, also declined in the same period. The archaeological precinct of Hammat Gader, now a national park, has Roman ruins at the bottom and top of the hill known as Tell Bani: the baths, a synagogue and a theater. Inside the park there is a modern spa and a crocodile farm.

The ancient baths were built in the 2nd century AD between two groups of hot springs and were then expanded and modified several times up to the 8th century. The hottest springs, to the south, have a temperature ranging from 77 to 125.6° F (in fact, the site was

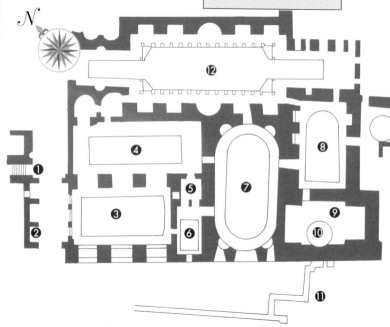

the 4th century BC by veterans of Alexander the Great's Macedonian army and was quite prosperous in Roman times. In antiquity it was famous as the birthplace of the philosophers Menippus and Philodemos and the poet Meleager. The many archaeological finds testify to the glorious past of this rich commercial and trading center. For the most part, they date from the first half of the 2nd century AD, that is, the golden age of the city's economic and building activity. Gadara was a bishopric in the 4th century and was destroyed by a violent quake in 746. Among the most interesting monuments are the tombs in the East Necropolis (including those of the Germanus family, the patriarch Modestus, and Kaireas), the north and west theaters, the colonnaded street, the baths, the *quadriporticus*, the basilica, the *nymphaeum*, the west gate with its adjoining *hypogeum* (a spectacular underground Roman mausoleum), the monumental gate, and the hippodrome.

118 bottom The western theater at Gadara, built in black basalt, is rather well preserved.

118-119 The Oval Pool at Hammat Gader was covered with a vault flanked by two half-domes.

119 left This is what remains of one of the pools in the Roman baths.

119 right Clouds of steam surround the hottest springs at Hammat Gader.

CAPERNAUM, THE CITY OF ST. PETER

120 top A rare example of cooperation in the Holy Land: at Capernaum the synagogue was built with the help of Gentiles.

120 bottom The eagle carved on the lintel of the entrance anticipates the iconographic variety of the decoration in the interior.

Present-day Kfar Nahum, on the northern banks of the Sea of Galilee, is known as the birthplace of the apostles Peter and Andrew, where Jesus often preached. Since it was situated right on the Galilee border, along the trade route linking this region and Damascus, Capernaum had a military garrison and a customs house. After the second Jewish War (135 AD) many Jews took refuge in Galilee, and Capernaum, where the new Christian religion had found many converts, went

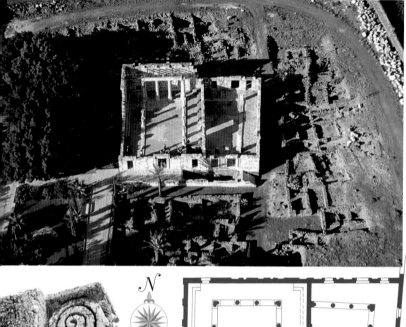

CAPERNAUM	
1	PORTICO
2	MAIN ENTRANCE
3	PRAYER HALL
4	COURTYARD

120-121 The synagogue lies over Roman period foundations, perhaps of the synagogue frequented by Jesus, next to the octagonal church built over the supposed house of Peter.

through a period of prosperity.

Coexistence between Jews and Romans was based on tolerance and mutual respect, so much so that between the 4th and 5th century the Gentiles helped build the large synagogue which the local Jews could not have afforded by themselves. In the meantime the Christians had chosen the house of Peter as their place of worship and had built a church on the site. Both buildings were destroyed in the period of the Arab conquest of Palestine in the 7th century, which brought about the decline of Capernaum. The Crusaders were of course interested in the city, but did not develop it because of its dangerously exposed position. Only in 1894 did the Franciscan Custody of the Holy Land purchase the site where the house of Peter had stood, and about ten years later began archaeological digs in the area of the synagogue and the Byzantine church. Father Orfali continued the excavations in 1921 and they were resumed in 1969 by fathers Corbo and Loffreda, whose exploration of the area under the floors of the synagogue revealed ancient Roman ruins. The two scholars had set out to find the synagogue mentioned in the *Gospel according to St. Luke*, which had been built by the Roman centurion and frequented by

121 top During the liturgy the worshippers sat on two superposed steps that formed a bench at the base of the walls of the synagogue.

121 center The door illustrated here connected the synagogue with a school, to the east,

arranged on three sides of a paved courtyard.

121 bottom A few yards west of the synagogue and the church, this millstone was part of the daily life in the large quarter that surrounded these places of worship.

Jesus. After this discovery they came to the conclusion that the synagogue lay under the one rebuilt in the 4th-5th century.

The present-day archaeological precinct is dominated by the remarkable ruins of this synagogue and by those of the adjacent Byzantine basilica. These two monuments are surrounded by the remains of a large village that has been only partly explored and brought to light. The synagogue was in an elevated position. It was built of blocks of white limestone, which stood out among the surrounding black basalt houses. There was a large, rectangular basilican interior (79 x 59 feet) built in Graeco-Roman style. The façade had three doors and the exterior had a lot of finely carved decoration. The nave was divided by two rows of seven columns with Corinthian capitals, and

there was a third two-column row along the back wall. Several well preserved friezes decorated the walls. These include the decoration with faces of the Medusa, the eagle on the entrance lintel, statues of lions, Hebrew symbols, vine branches and grapes, roses and geometric motifs. However, the most exceptional decorative element, because of its rarity, is a representation of the Ark of the Covenant on a four-wheel cart. In a later period a small building used as a school was built on the east side of the synagogue; it had a paved courtyard surrounded by a peristyle with Doric columns.

The 5th-century Byzantine church was built over what is traditionally regarded as the house of Simon Peter. The interior consisted of two concentric octagons surrounded on five sides by a colonnade and had several entrances. A small baptistery was built along the east wall in a later period. The floor and colonnade of the church were covered with mosaics whose style is reminiscent of that in the Church of the Multiplication of the Loaves and Fish in Tabgha. The central mosaic has a peacock set against a background of geometric patterns and bordered by lotus flowers. The ruins of the church are now protected by an original octagonal structure that architect Ildo Avetta completed in 1990 with the two-fold aim of preserving the various superimposed archaeological strata and offering a place of worship that can contain about 400 persons.

QASRIN, A VILLAGE REBORN

In Central Golan, about ten miles north of Lake Tiberias, is the archaeological site of Qasrin, which was excavated and studied systematically only after the Six-Day War, in the early 1970s, when the most important monument in this ancient Jewish village was brought to light–a well-preserved synagogue. This edifice was founded in the early 3rd century AD and rebuilt two centuries later. It was badly damaged by an earthquake in 746, left in ruins, and then transformed into a mosque in the 13th century. The present-day structure dates from the 5th-century reconstruction, with a more or less rectangular plan. The synagogue, made of blocks of black basalt, has a three-aisle interior with two rows of four columns with curious Ionic capitals that is surrounded on three sides by the traditional stonework benches. The entrance still has its original jambs and monolithic lintel, in the center of which are carved a round garland between two amphoras and two pomegranates. The

122 center This kitchen shows how the accurate restoration work effected by archaeologists in Qasrin allows us to understand the lifestyle of the local ancient communities.

122 bottom The exterior of House B in the reconstructed ancient village of Qasrin. This building dates back to the 7th century AD, that is, the early phase of Arab penetration in Palestine.

122 top Some dwellings in the village discovered next to the synagogue of Qasrin were reconstructed, and replicas of ancient furniture and implements were placed in them.

CHORAZAIN, THE BASALT CITY

The archaeological site of Korazim, about two miles north of Lake Tiberias and a short distance from Capernaum, owes most of its fame to the ruins of a large 3rd century AD synagogue. The history of this locality, which was perhaps founded in the Hellenistic period, is rather uncertain; we know that in the Roman period the city, mentioned in the New Testament, was mostly Jewish and it was almost totally destroyed during the Bar Kokhba revolt. Chorazain was rebuilt, and then razed to the ground in the mid 4th century during the conflict between Jews and Christians. It rose again during the Byzantine age but was abandoned in the 8th-13th century. The general structure of the ruined synagogue, made of blocks of basalt, is similar to the one in Capernaum: it is oriented on a North-South axis and the façade faces Jerusalem, while the nave is divided into three aisles by two rows of five columns. Near the synagogue archaeologists found a necropolis dating back to the 6th-4th millennium BC, as well as the ruins of a Roman-Byzantine city, with streets, buildings, cisterns and hypogea.

interior also has remains of the mosaic pavement, and fragments of capitals and decorative stone elements lie on the floor. In 1983-1990 many houses, dating from the Byzantine and Mamluk periods, were discovered in Qasrin. Three of these (Houses A, B and C), which were built in the 4th-8th century, were subjected to intense anastylosis (the restoration of ruins with the fallen elements) and fitted with replicas of ancient furnishings and implements.

Qasrin is famous in Israel not so much for its synagogue, as for the interesting Golan Archaeological Museum, which illustrates the history of human settlements in this region from prehistoric times to the Byzantine age. It also features a reconstruction of a Chalcolithic dwelling with all its various furnishings.

123 top and bottom left *The monastery of Kursi—the basilica of which can be seen in these two illustrations—was built in the late 5th century and destroyed two centuries later.*

123 center left Korazim boasts fine ruins of the Roman-Byzantine city.

123 center right As can be seen in this photo, the synagogue at Korazim was carefully reconstructed by archaeologists.

123 bottom right Some of the columns inside the synogogue at Korazim were raised by archaeologists.

KURSI, THE BLACK MONASTERY

Lying on the east shore of Lake Tiberias, the small village of Kursi is known for the ruins of a monastery built in Byzantime times and brought to light only in 1970. The monastic complex was defended by a rectangular wall (393 x 459 feet) made of black basalt blocks.

Curiously enough, the small inner courtyard was plastered and frescoed with plant motifs. The entrance was in the middle of the western side, and was protected by a watchtower. The area inside the enclosure consisted of the monks' cells and, in the middle, a large three-aisled basilica preceded by a large colonnaded atrium. The church boasts the remains of splendid pavement mosaics and a crypt, which is also decorated with mosaics.

GAMLA,
THE MASADA
OF THE NORTH

124 top The oil presses found at Gamla are always associated with ritual baths, because for the Orthodox Jews, oil was part and parcel of this practice.

124-125 Gamla was perched on the Khirbet es-Salam ridge, which was apparently invulnerable but was the theater of a mass suicide by the locals when besieged by the Romans.

124 bottom The heavy basalt of the millstones and oil presses was ideal for pressing and crushing, which was carried out by revolving the cone-shaped millstone at right inside the massive oil press, which had an opening out of which the oil flowed.

125 top The ruins of the synagogue dominate the valley floor towards the Sea of Galilee, about six miles as the crow flies. The elevated position offers a view of the magnificent valleys and forests.

125 bottom The number of oil pressing facilities found at Gamla reveals the religious and economic importance of this age-old industry, which must have made the desolate site a pleasant place in Jesus' time.

The site now known as Khirbet es-Salam—a sharp, rugged ridge dominating the northern end of Lake Tiberias (the Sea of Galilee)—is so much like a camel's hump that it was called 'Gamla,' or 'camel,' in ancient times. According to Flavius Josephus, Vespasian laid siege to Gamla with three legions in 67 BC but had a hard time subduing the population, part of which (perhaps as many as 5,000 persons) even decided to commit suicide rather than surrender to the Romans. This tragic episode is similar to what occurred at the more well-known Masada, and in fact Gamla is often called 'the Masada of the North.'

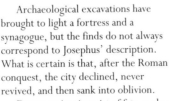

GAMLA

1 CITY WALL
2 GATE
3 SYNAGOGUE
4 MIKVEH
5 OIL PRESSES
6 RESIDENTIAL QUARTER
7 PRODUCTIVE AREA

N

Archaeological excavations have brought to light a fortress and a synagogue, but the finds do not always correspond to Josephus' description. What is certain is that, after the Roman conquest, the city declined, never revived, and then sank into oblivion.

Due to an ironic twist of fate, a place so tragically affected by war and violence, literally erased from history, was brought to light again thanks to another war. During the Israeli-Syrian conflict at the Golan heights, Israeli soldiers chanced upon the traces of a city, which were thoroughly studied in 1970, three years after the war.

Because of its elevated and almost inaccessible position, Gamla had only one wall, built perhaps in the Herodian period, on its eastern side. In front of the wall was a rectangular building that was colonnaded and had stepped benches on its sides. This must have been a synagogue, since the three entrances led to a courtyard with a ritual bath (mikveh) fed by rainwater collected on the roof. The synagogue, built in the 1st century BC, may be one of the oldest in the Holy Land, along with those in Masada and Herodium. It was converted into a house by the Jewish rebels who survived the first Jewish War. The roof was made of stone slabs, just like those on the Nabatean buildings in the Negev. In the courtyard, next to the ritual bath, is an olive oil press that has been dated to the 1st century AD. In the archaeological area, houses and several other presses flanked by ritual baths have been found. Olive oil was an essential part of Jewish religious ritual, and this is why it had to be produced by persons who were ritually pure.

MEIRON AND THE *ZOHAR*

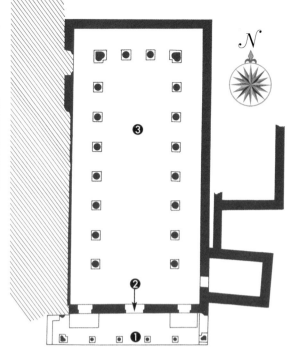

The thousands of pilgrims who on the occasion of the Lag ba Omer feast, 33 days after the Jewish Passover, go in procession with the Scrolls of the Law from Safed to nearby Meiron, are proof of the deep-rooted bond between these two mystical centers. Inhabited since 200 BC and mentioned by Flavius Josephus in 66 AD as a fortified city, Meiron flourished two centuries later because of

its quality olive oil production. But the city's fame is based on the figure of Rabbi Simeon Bar Yokhai, the compiler of the fundamental text of Kabbalistic studies, the *Zohar*, or Book of Splendor.

The large, white-domed building in which the great sage lies together with his son still attracts many pilgrims. Meiron also has the remains of a 3rd-century AD synagogue with a basilica plan. Its massive façade is the only surviving section of a monument which, judging by the ruins, must have been the largest synagogue in the Holy Land. The three entrances are made of huge blocks of basalt. The jambs of the central door are more than 10 feet high, and the lintel is cracked and seems about to collapse. But popular legend has it that should this happen, it would signal a remarkable event, the predestined coming of the Messiah.

SAFED, THE CENTER OF THE KABBALAH

A few miles northwest of Lake Tiberias, not far from the Lebanon border, situated among the highest hills in Galilee, is one of the four holy cities of the Jews—mystical and legendary Safed. Always cloaked in a palpable aura of sacredness, such mountain localities also offered refuge to persecuted Jews, and Safed, the highest city in Israel, was certainly no exception to this rule. It had already taken in some priestly families after the destruction of the Temple, and then provided refuge for many Spanish and Portuguese Jews after the ruthless persecution of the infamous inquisitor Torquemada. Little is known of the history of the city in the period preceding this major event. The name of the town appeared in the list of places Tuthmosis III had conquered, and the city took on military and strategic importance only in the mid 12th century AD, when the Crusaders built a fortress there. This structure shared the fate of all the Christian castles from Saladin's time on: it was taken and demolished. But what counts most in Safed was its spiritual and cultural dimension, not its material history.

At the end of the 15th century the city became one of the focal points of Talmudic mysticism, becoming the home of some of the leading erudites of the time: Rabbi Joseph Caro, who compiled the *Shulhan Arukh*, the basic collection of daily Jewish rituals; the Spanish Rabbi Isaac Abuhav; and the

126 left The massive basalt blocks of the Meiron synagogue, perhaps the largest one in the Holy Land, have weathered two terrible earthquakes.

126 right The synagogue of Rabbi Isaac Luria, rebuilt after the tremendous 1837 quake, houses an elaborately decorated holy ark.

126-127 The colorful furnishings in the synagogue of Abuhav reflect the outstanding centuries-old religious and cultural life of Safed.

Kabbalistic scholars, the greatest inquirers into the secret meaning of the Old Testament, who were disciples of the great Rabbi Isaac Luria. Known as Ha Ari, 'the lion,' Luria had taught his doctrine for three years at Safed, making a lasting impression on Jewish culture despite his premature death at the age of 38. Poets as well as scholars, the sages at Safed were so active that in 1563 they made the first printing press in the Holy Land, and 100 years later the city boasted 21 synagogues and 18 Talmudic schools run by no fewer than 300 erudites from the entire Jewish world. The city's cultural vitality was interupted in 1747 and 1759 respectively by an epidemic and earthquake, but at the end of the century there was a revival thanks to the arrival of a large group of *Hassidim* ('pious ones'), Polish Jews who were followers of Rabbi Israel Baal Shem Tov, and of a group of Lithuanian members of a rival sect headed by Rabbi Elijah Zalman. Almost nothing of the synagogues dedicated to each of them survived the disastrous earthquake of 1837, except for the wall facing Jerusalem that is part of the rebuilt synagogue of Abuhav that has perhaps remained intact to bear witness to the mysterious powers of the great sages who in 5 centuries made Safed the magical city of the Kabbalah.

127 center right
The entrance to the Ari Sephardi shows that the exteriors of the synagogues at Safed are also particularly colorful.

127 bottom left In the Ari Sephardi synagogue, the drapes concealing the tabernacle are embroidered with

symbolic representations of the Scriptures, flanked by menorahs and emblems of regality.

127 bottom right
One of the most important synagogues in Safed, in the heart of town, is dedicated to Rabbi Joseph Caro. In the past Safed boasted 21 synagogues.

ACRE, THE CRUSADER CITY

Lying along the northern tip of the Bay of Haifa, Acre (or Akko) is one of the most ancient cities in the world. Despite its extremely long history, the most Arab city in Israel has maintained its age-old fascination, wrapped in an aura of ancestral abandon and intriguing Levantine torpor. Crowned by the Crusader walls, and more tranquil than nearby Haifa, with which it has competed for at least 23 centuries, Acre gazes upon the vastness of the Mediterranean from the privileged vantage point of history. In fact, human settlements in the Bay of Acre area date back to remote times: as early as the Palaeolithic era the first member of the Homo sapiens species, in particular *Homo sapiens neanderthalensis*, occupied the caves on the slopes of Mount Carmel and then went into the surrounding territory. The Natufian culture, whose members were Neolithic cave dwellers, replaced the first population around the 9th millennium BC and colonized the area until the onset of the major changes that occurred in the Chalcolithic Age (4th millennium BC) and Bronze Age societies. The primitive hunters-gatherers were supplanted by farmers, herders and the first merchants,

Within the maze of streets in St. John of Acre, ancient Akko, were the large courtyards of the commercial and military quarters.

whose commerce was based on the flourishing industrial activity along the coast. Ancient Akko developed quite rapidly in this period, so much so that during the Egyptian Middle Kingdom (2040-1650 BC) the city was mentioned as one of the city-states that could be a potential threat to the pharaohs' dominion in the region, which lay at the crossroads of the spheres of influence of the great powers of the time. Tuthmosis III, Sethos I and Ramses II conquered Akko, which was also claimed by the Israelites: according to the Old Testament, the important port resisted Asher's attempted

128 bottom The slender arches of an aqueduct built by the Turks stand out against the countryside around the city.

128-129 The White Mosque watches over the intricate quarters of the old city: the vessels at right are anchored inside the ancient southern breakwater.

conquest, but it seems that during the reign of David and Solomon it was finally annexed to the United Kingdom of Israel.

Given its exceptional commercial importance, from then on Akko changed hands many times. The successive conquerors of the prosperous Phoenician port town were the Assyrians, Persians, Seleucids, and Romans (under whom the city regained its independence, albeit only nominally). Herod the Great began the conquest of his kingdom precisely from Akko, and a few decades later Vespasian made it his headquarters when he set out to subdue the first Jewish revolt after

massacring 2,000 Jewish citizens. In 636 AD the Omayyids took the port and named it 'Akka,' a name which lasted until the arrival of the Crusaders under Baldwin I, who in May 1104 conquered the city after a twenty-day siege and renamed it St. John of Acre. The city was taken by Saladin in 1187 and then by the Crusaders four years later, becoming the capital of the Latin Kingdom of Jerusalem and a lively and composite religious center. But this change by no means diminished Acre's commercial importance; indeed, in the Crusader town plan the quarters reserved for the

129 top left At the southern end of the eastern section of the Crusader rampart, to be seen at left, was the massive Land Gate, the main access to the city by land.

129 top right Beyond the Burj el-Kuraijim tower, in the foreground, is the vast and luminous Bay of Acre.

129 bottom Bordered by outcrops, the eastern section of the city walls is the only one facing the open sea.

monastic and knights' orders lay next to those occupied by the Italian mercantile guilds of the maritime republics of Genoa, Pisa and Venice. The Brothers of the Order of St. John had settled in the middle of the Crusader city, to the east were the Teutonic Knights and to the north the Knights of the Order of St. Lazarus, while the commercial colonies lay along the southern coast.

Little remains of the city of that time, which was much larger than present-day Acre. Most of the city walls were destroyed to make room for new buildings (in fact, what is left of the walls, north and east of the old city, dates back to the Ottoman period) and all the

Crusader edifices suffered the same fate, as they were loaded with filling material by the Turks to reinforce the new buildings. However, thanks to the technique employed, the subsoil has kept some of the pre-Crusader and Crusader chambers in a good state of preservation. Under the Turkish citadel, the most noteworthy building in the city, the austere rooms of the refectory of the Knights of St. John building were cleared of the masses of debris. The pre-Crusader underground passages going northward to the city wall and southward to the port, were likewise cleared of rubble. Near the refectory, six underground chambers, all parallel to one another and called 'el-Bosta,' date from the period just prior to the arrival of the Crusaders and are probably all that remains of a Fatimid period caravanserai that was later used by the Crusaders as an infirmary and was partly rebuilt in line with European

architectural canons.

After centuries of ancient splendor and one hundred years of Christian dominion, the glorious city was destined to pass through a long period of decadence after the Mamluks razed it to the ground in 1291 so it could not be recaptured by the Crusader troops. Acre came back to life only in the 18th century thanks to two singular figures: Dahir el-Omar, a rebellious Bedouin sheik who established an independent sultanate with

Acre as its capital; and the Albanian Ahmed, better known in historical chronicles as 'el-Jazzar,' or the 'Butcher,' who killed the tolerant el-Omar in 1775 and took possession of the city. Both these rulers took on the task of rebuilding the residential quarters of Acre and constructing fortifications. In 1799, the walls built by el-Omar resisted Napoleon's siege, partly thanks to the aid of the British fleet. But in 1832 the city had to surrender to the onslaught of

THE HOSPITALLERS' FORTRESS	
1 MODERN ENTRANCE	7 KITCHEN
2 STREET	8 REFECTORY
3 GREAT MOSQUE	9 CLOISTER
4 11TH-CENTURY GATE	10 DORMITORY
5 HOSPITAL	11 KNIGHTS' HALLS
6 MUNICIPAL MUSEUM	12 TOWER

130 left In the half-light of the Crusader refectory one can see the three petals of the French fleur-de-lis.

130-131 After the fall of the Ottoman Empire, the debris in the refectory of St. John's, which was almost as high as the cross vaults, was removed.

130 bottom The Crusader halls resisted time, serving as the foundation for Ottoman buildings.

131 top and bottom The dark passageways that echoed the footsteps of the Teutonic Knights, the Knights of the Order of St. John and the Hospitaller Knights, now house an interesting museum. The little that has been preserved lies within the perimeter of ancient Akko.

Ibrahim, Pasha of Egypt, and in 1840 was again conquered by the Ottoman Empire.

This period in the troubled history of Acre witnessed the foundation of the White Mosque, which el-Jazzar built in 1781, perhaps over the foundations of the Crusader Church of the Holy Cross. This beautiful and luminous edifice with a white interior and exterior is decorated in the purely geometric style of the late Ottoman period. It is the third largest mosque in Israel and is second in importance only to the al-Aqsa Mosque in Jerusalem. The Roman columns in the

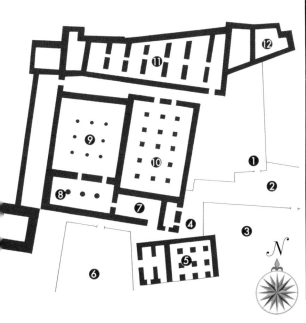

peristyle of the surrounding courtyard were taken from the ruins of Caesarea and Tyre, just as the column shafts supporting the *mihrab* come from Herod's port town. El-Jazzar also built baths in the city, the Hammam el-Pasha, which now houses a museum.

In the late 19th and early 20th century the Turks transformed the military, monastic and commercial quarters of Acre into *khans*, that is, *caravanserai*, typical Ottoman constructions that can be seen from Istanbul to Cairo. Near the port

is the Khan el-Umdan (Inn of Columns), which was probably built over the Crusader Courtyard of the Chain, so named because of the type of barrier that in the 12th century blocked the entrance to the port when necessary. This broad courtyard, which was originally part of the Genoese quarter in Acre, is dominated by a clock tower the Turks erected in 1906; it is similar in style to other edifices built in the same period throughout the Ottoman Empire.

Immediately northeast of this *khan* is the Khan el-Faranj (Inn of the Franks), in the central square of the Venetian quarter. In the second half of the 13th century—toward the end of the Crusader epoch—one of the guests in this area

132 top Linear patterns and sober colors are the distinguishing features of the late Ottoman style, as exemplified by the marble inlay in the White Mosque.

132 center At the northern edge of the old city, the White Mosque is surrounded by a trapezoidal arcade built over the foundation of the Holy Cross cathedral.

inhabited by the merchants of the Queen of the Sea was none other than Marco Polo, then unknown but destined to achieve lasting fame, who at Acre received the papal letters he was to take to the Kublai Khan at his fabulous capital. Further along in the same direction, is the largest caravanserai in Acre, the Khan es-Shawarda, which lies over the remains of a nuns' convent. To the north of this latter *khan* was the German quarter, which no longer exists. Two other areas that suffered the same fate were the Templar and Pisan quarters (the former, situated northwest of the port, had its own citadel): they were used as quarries to provide building material for the new city walls.

As had occurred at the end of the

Crusader 'golden age,' after the Turkish conquest Acre had to bear the negative consequences of centuries of wealth and strategic importance that had led to great progress: weakened by the continuous battles that blocked maritime traffic and by now obsolete, no longer able to accommodate the large modern ships, the harbor ended up being supplanted by the Haifa port. When the Ottoman Empire collapsed shortly after the end of World War One, the inhabitants of Acre numbered only one-sixth of its medieval population, which has been estimated at 50,000. The silted-up ancient harbor has regained some of its former glory only recently, as the hordes of besiegers have been replaced by the peaceful invasion of tourists.

132 bottom Although he was notorious for his ferocity, el-Jazzar promoted refined architectural works.

132-133 Nothing is excessive in the White Mosque, illuminated by the reflection of its predominant white;

the only non-geometric elements are the fasciae and the tile panels with inscriptions.

133 top right Inflexible but stimulating rules imposed on the Ottoman craftsmen produced masterworks.

133 bottom left The Crusader harbor could be blocked by a taut chain placed at the port entrance.

133 bottom right The medieval Genoese quarter was occupied by the Ottoman Khan el-Umdan.

MONFORT, THE CASTLE OF THE TEUTONIC KNIGHTS

The Crusader castle of Monfort lies in Upper Galilee, along the Naharya-Safed road in the Nahal Keziv valley. It was built on a narrow ridge in 1226 by a French family, the Courtenays. Two years later they sold it to the Teutonic Knights, who turned it into their headquarters, setting up the archive and treasury of their order, and named it Starkenberg, the German translation of the French placename. The castle had no strategic value to speak of because it was small and stood far from the main communication routes in the region, but it was important from an administrative standpoint. The German knights enlarged it in keeping with the

MONFORT	
1 DEFENSIVE WALL	5 CHAPEL
2 ENTRANCE	6 WINE PRESS
3 TOWER	7 KEEP
4 HALL	8 MOAT

latest techniques in military architecture, so that in 1266 it was able to resist the siege of the Muslim troops headed by Baybars. However, five years later the sultan launched another attack and the garrison was forced to surrender. The Teutonic Knights were allowed to go to Acre with their archive and treasures. Baybars had the walls torn down and Monfort was never again occupied.

The fortress, which ran along the rugged ridge, was defended on the valley side by the natural cliff about 590 feet high, and was protected on the side facing the mountain by a short but deep moat; in its inner concentric circle there was also a wall, in the northwestern section of which was the main entranceway with a front gate.

The few remaining ruins are quite fascinating. On the western end a semicircular wall may be part of what was the residence of the governor, who was the treasurer of the knights' order. Next to this is a tower, which is virtually intact. It has recessed balconies outside and vaulted rooms in the interior. Eastward is a building whose upper floor had a vault supported by a central octagonal pier. This was probably the Teutonic Knights' assembly hall. Adjacent to this body of the complex lay the chapel, the nave of which was divided by two rows of four octagonal columns. Further east there was a series of service rooms. The keep stood on the eastern tip of the bluff, overlooking the moat that was hewn out of the rock of the col. Under the floor of

the keep there was a cistern for the water supply. In 1926 American archaeologists found, at the base of the tower, traces of pre-Crusader structures that may have been there even before the Roman conquest. The finds discovered during the excavation are on display in the Rockefeller Museum in Jerusalem and the Metropolitan Museum of Art of New York. At the foot of the castle, on one side of the *wadi*, are the remains of a two-story 13th-century building. The ground floor was used as a mill whose grindstones worked with the water from the weir built across the *wadi*. When the Teutonic Knights purchased the castle, they built a hall with Gothic vaults on the top floor and the building was used to accommodate guests.

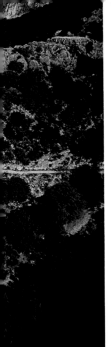

134-135 The ruins of Monfort lie along a narrow ridge among the hills of Upper Galilee.

134 center A bust found among the fortress ruins evokes the presence of the knights who defended it until 1271.

134 bottom Standing like a sentry at the eastern tip of the ridge, the keep lies over a site that may be pre-Roman.

135 top Nimrud, like Monfort, is perfectly suited to the configuration of the narrow spur.

135 bottom Facing eastward, the south wall of Nimrud runs along the col up to the massive keep.

NIMRUD, THE CLIFF FORTRESS

The strategic position of the Nimrud fortress has been exploited by military leaders of many different cultures and periods, from its mythical founder, the great hunter Nimrud, who according to the Old Testament founded an empire in Babylonia and Assyria, to the Syrians and Israelis, who used the ancient castle as a base during the Six-Day War in 1967. The largest Crusader castle in Israel dates from 1129, when the Christian knights transformed the pre-existing Qaalat Subeib, or 'Cliff Fortress,' built by the Arabs on a rocky spur on the slopes of Mount Hermon.

Although the Crusaders had intended to make it an outpost to control the northern border of the Latin Kingdom, they were unable to hold it for any length of time. It was taken again by the Arabs and dismantled by the Ayyubid sultan el-Malik al-Muazzam in 1219. Nimrud was rebuilt by the Arabs in 1228-1230 and 1239-1240, taking on the configuration that can still be seen in the ruins. After the Crusaders had abandoned St. John of Acre in 1291, Nimrud lost its strategic importance, so much so that in the following two centuries the Mamluks used it as a prison.

The plan of the fortress, which lies on the ridge of the hill, is perfectly adapted to the conformation of the terrain. The entrance is situated on the western section of the outer walls and has two towers built by the Mamluks,

who expanded and remodeled the original Ayyubid structures. In fact, two distinctly different building phases can be seen in the large vaulted cistern at the corner of the right-hand tower: its northern part is covered with barrel vaulting, while the southern one has cross vaulting. The cisterns were vital for the very survival of the garrisons stationed at Nimrud, whose water supply depended exclusively on

rainwater, which was collected from the sloping roofs and channeled into the many catch basins in the towers and in the two courtyards. Proceeding counter-clockwise from the large cistern, one comes to the area housing the kitchens, which is flanked by a space used to store provisions. In this stretch the wall is defended by a series of small towers, some of which are round. The original entrance to the fortress lay on the eastern section of the wall and was defended by an extremely well-fortified, massive keep: should assailants have succeeded in breaking through this area, they would have had to get over an inner wall and then cross a ditch, only to arrive at a second defensive line consisting of a wall with six towers. The round tower on the tip of the ridge is the most interesting one from an architectural standpoint: two massive piers support six bays with cross vaulting. The northern section of the outer wall, built on the steepest side of the rise, has only one tower because it would have been virtually impossible to attack the fortress from this side.

NIMRUD	
1 MODERN ENTRANCE	5 OLD ENTRANCE
2 SOUTHWEST TOWER	6 INNER WALL
3 CISTERN	7 KEEP
4 DEFENSIVE TOWERS	

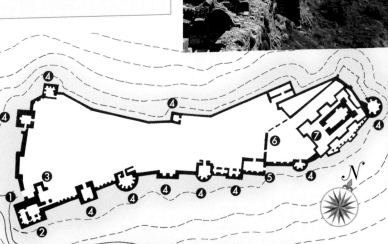

BARAM, A SYNAGOGUE IN GALILEE

This site in Upper Galilee, whose name means 'Son of the People,' is situated near the Israel-Lebanon border. Baram boasts the ruins of an impressive synagogue that was said to have been founded by the famous Rabbi Simeon Bar Yokhai. Furthermore, according to one medieval tradition, the locality has the tombs of Esther and the prophet Obahdia, but the exact sites have not

been identified. The kibbutz that lies a short distance from the ruins, houses the Bar David Institute of Jewish Art, which also includes a museum with ancient finds discovered during digs here.

The synagogue was preceded by a portico supported by eight columns with Attic bases, six along the façade and one on either side. The façade is oriented southward, that is, it faces Jerusalem. The tabernacle (now totally destroyed), which contained the scrolls of the *Torah*, was pointed in the same direction. The façade of the synagogue has a central entrance and a minor one on both sides. The lintel of the former is decorated with a round garland that was originally supported by two winged victories which were deliberately effaced by the iconoclasts. Above this is a convex frieze depicting vine shoots emerging from an amphora. On the

sides of the lintel, on which is an arch that served as a large window, are two brackets in the shape of a double volute. The two side doors are simpler and similar: the convex frieze on the left-hand one is decorated with rope-like patterns, while the one at right has laurel leaf decoration. Above each of the side entrances is a rectangular window; the one at left still has a monolithic lintel over it that is decorated with vine shoots in relief. On the sill of the window at left is an inscription in Aramaic that reads: "Built by Elazar, the son of Judah." The floor of the prayer hall is made of stone slabs; the wide nave was divided into three sections by three rows of columns, two laid out longitudinally and one crosswise. There is no trace of the upper floor of the synagogue, but it is evident that the façade ended in a tympanum and that the building had a roof with two slopes.

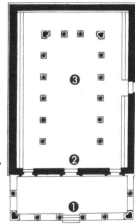

136 bottom The fourteen columns in the interior supported the upper floor of the synagogue.

137 top Grape vines decorate the panel of classic inspiration above the only intact window on the façade.

137 bottom left The rope-like decoration on the west door is counterbalanced by the classicizing leaves on the east door.

137 bottom right Of the eight columns once in the portico, one still supports part of the trabeation.

BARAM

1 PORTICO
2 MAIN ENTRANCE
3 PRAYER HALL

Some 19th-century travellers described another, smaller synagogue about 1,300 feet north of the large one. The only trace of this is an inscription in Hebrew (now kept at the Louvre): "May there reign peace in this place and in all of Israel. Yose the Levite, son of Levi, made this inscription. May his work be blessed. Shalom."

On the hill opposite the synagogue is a Maronite church that was abandoned in the 19th century. The façade is still intact. The lintel of the portal has a cosmic cross with the four cardinal points indicated by rosettes; on either side are traces of low-relief and other crosses.

136-137 The 4th-century ruins of Baram offer a fine example of the first synagogues, the most ancient of which date back to the 1st century AD.

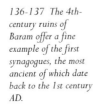

HAZOR, THE CANAANITE CITY-STATE

At the end of the 19th century Tel el-Quedah, about nine miles north of the Sea of Galilee, was recognized as the site of ancient Hazor, a large Canaanite and Israelite city that is mentioned in Egyptian documents as early as the 18th century BC but which is really much more ancient. Excavations carried out here have in fact brought to light 21 archaeological strata of successive settlements. These range from the 29th century BC to the Hellenistic period and have allowed scholars to establish that the city was divided into the upper city on a rise and the lower one at its feet, the latter being inhabited in the 18th-13th century BC. The fame and splendor of Canaanite Hazor—resulting from its location on the trade route linking Babylonia and

Egypt—reached their height in the 14th century BC, when the city was probably the largest in Canaanite territory. However, in the second half of the 13th century BC, all this wealth attracted the Israelite tribes, who according to the *Book of Joshua* devastated the lower city and left it partly abandoned: indeed, the Israelites probably did not settle permanently on the *tell* for at least three centuries, when the city finally recovered under Solomon and was included in the

138 left On Tel el-Quedah (center), the ruins of upper Hazor dominate the less ancient lower city, to be seen above left.

138 top right Cut out of the solid rock of the tell, a stepped tunnel gave access to a spring outside the walls.

138 bottom right Much like the pillars in the 'stables' at Megiddo, the two parallel rows of piers found on the tell probably belonged to a storehouse.

United Kingdom of Israel. Attacked and destroyed by the Aramaeans in 885 BC, Hazor was rebuilt by Omri. But this revival lasted barely a century: the city was damaged by an earthquake and then razed to the ground in 732 BC by the Assyrians. Hazor was abandoned and in the following centuries housed only temporary settlements, such as small garrisons stationed there to guard the major trade routes at the foot of the *tell*.

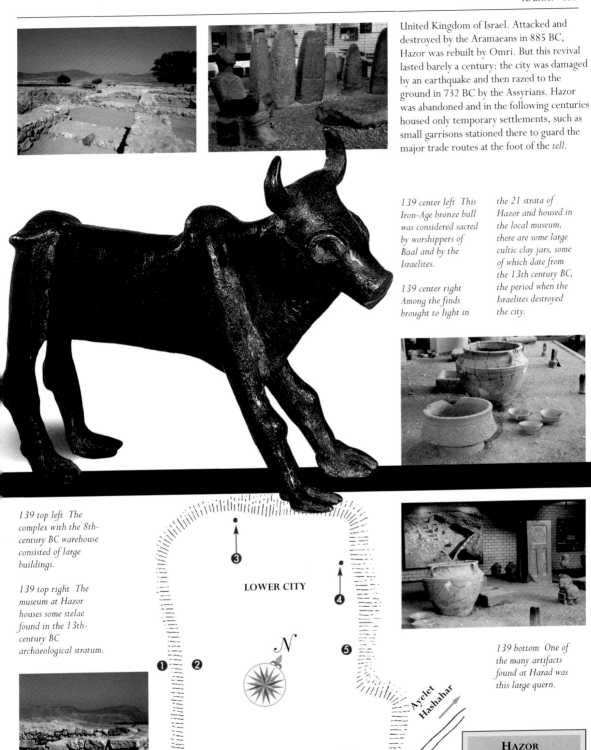

139 center left This Iron-Age bronze bull was considered sacred by worshippers of Baal and by the Israelites.

139 center right Among the finds brought to light in *the 21 strata of Hazor and housed in the local museum, there are some large cultic clay jars, some of which date from the 13th century BC, the period when the Israelites destroyed the city.*

139 top left The complex with the 8th-century BC warehouse consisted of large buildings.

139 top right The museum at Hazor houses some stelae found in the 13th-century BC archaeological stratum.

LOWER CITY

N

139 bottom One of the many artifacts found at Harad was this large quern.

Ayelet Hashahar

UPPER CITY

Rosh Pinna

HAZOR	
1	MOAT
2	EARTHEN RAMPARTS
3	TEMPLE
4	CITY GATE
5	EARTHEN RAMPARTS
6	CITY GATE
7	EARTHEN RAMPARTS

MAR SABA, THE DESERT MONASTERY

The most impressive monastery among those that dot the barren landscape of the Judaean Desert, is the *laura* of St. Sabas, a veritable fortress situated seven and one-half miles east of Bethlehem. A monastic institution typical of the vast desert region of Judaea, and more in general, of the Orthodox Church, a *laura* consists of a series of hermits' cells that lie around a common church and are linked by paths and passageways.

as palm branches and rushes for their daily work. In fact, they spent their solitary days making rope, baskets and mats that were then sold at the Jerusalem market to finance the monastery.

The complex is said to have been founded by St. Sabas, who was born in 439 in Cappadocia, Turkey and went to Palestine when he was eighteen. After spending twelve years in the monastery of Theoctistus, this holy man moved to a

140 top The main church in Mar Saba houses the mortal remains of the founder of the monastery, who came from another region known for its many important monasteries— Cappadocia.

The origins of Mar Saba monastery go back to 290 AD, when the recesses and caves along the steep cliff face of the gorge, created by the Kidron river as it flows toward the Dead Sea, attracted many hermits who were followers of St. Hilary. The monastery thus rose up as a center of communion among the anchorites who meditated in isolation in the many cell-caves, remaining inside from Monday to Saturday, when they left their solitude to gather together. The complex had a church, a meeting hall, a bread oven and a cell for storing food. The hermits spent all night Saturday praying together, and at Sunday dawn they celebrated mass and then assembled. Sunday evening they returned to their caves after gathering the necessary provisions of food, as well

cave in the Wadi Mukellik, where he stayed for five years. He then settled for good in a cave in the Kidron Valley, remaining in total solitude for five years, after which time he decided to allow other hermits who had gone there, attracted by his holiness, to settle nearby. This marked the birth of the great *laura*.

Sabas immediately set about building a tower and a small church (483). At that time about 70 monks lived in the monastery, but the number increased so much that in 490 the saint used a large cave as a church so that all the hermits could take part in the communal prayer. Thanks to a legacy from his mother, Sabas was able to build a hospice in 491, and when two architects arrived at the monastery, a bakery, a hospital, some

cisterns and a large church were added to the original complex. The church, which could take in 250-300 hermits, was dedicated to St. Nicholas in 501 and thirty-one years later the remains of St. Sabas, who was almost 100 when he died, were housed there.

With time the monastery prospered, housing up to 8,000 persons, including historians, poets and musicians. One illustrious guest was the theologian St. John Damascene (675-749), one of the last Fathers of the Church, who wrote most of his works in the cave that was later named after him.

The present monastery, which was restored after the 1834 earthquake, counts about twenty Greek Orthodox monks and is open only to male visitors. Under the brilliant light blue of the domes that lend a

because of its abundance of natural caves, ideal for meditation.

141 bottom left St. Sabas and the other illustrious guests and inhabitants at the monastery are still the object of heartfelt veneration.

141 bottom right Transferred to Venice by the Crusaders, since 1965 the embalmed body of St. Sabas has been in the monastery.

140 left In the 7th century, 8,000 monks lived at Mar Saba, which is now run by only about twenty.

140 right Built in 1929 opposite the main church, this hexagonal shrine marks the first burial site of St. Sabas.

140-141 The awe-inspiring cliff on which the complex is perched was chosen by the hermits in the 3rd century AD.

refreshing note to the surrounding cliffs, Mar Saba is enclosed within an enormous wall that immediately reveals the defensive nature of the monastery: the wall is quite thick and well planned, the windows are so narrow that they look more like slits, and the low and narrow entrances are protected by massive portals. A steep stairway leads from the main entrance to the central courtyard, with the shrine built in 1929 in honor of St. Sabas that lies near St. Nicholas church and in front of the main church of the monastery. The saint's body was originally interred in the local cemetery. It was then taken to Venice by the Crusaders, and only in 1965 was it brought back to Kidron Valley, and now lies, embalmed, in the *Theotokos*, the main chapel of the monastery.

The apse of St. Nicholas is hidden behind a lavishly decorated iconostasis that dates back to the 15th century, the same period of the five icons above the wooden fascia that decorates the wall facing it. Many of those who went to

142-143 A common feature of Greek Orthodox churches is their lavish decoration: the chapels at Mar Saba glitter with the gold of the innumerable icons placed in sumptuously decorated settings.

142 bottom right In non-Orthodox churches the iconostasis (the screen of icons, or images) has been replaced by the simpler balustrade.

143 top left Some of the finest icons were donated to the monastery by the Russian government in the 19th century.

overlooks the *wadi*. Another stairway leads to some small chapels of uncertain date.

The monastery gets its water from fourteen large Byzantine cisterns that are still used. The monks also adopt an age-old technique: two aqueducts collect the rare rainwater from the slopes of Kidron Valley, which is added to the water that runs off the roofs and other parts of the monastery itself.

The complex has three large buttresses that retain the walls of the refectory, kitchen, storehouse and oven. At the base of this fortress-monastery, in a walled-up area near the bottom of the *wadi*, is the tiny 'holy spring.'

The cave where St. Sabas lived in solitude for the first five years in the Kidron Valley is in the cliff opposite the monastery: it is a bare, natural cave now protected by a metal grille. Inside, two ladders take you up a 19-foot shaft. The cave is tiny and simple, with only a rock-cut bench along one wall and a prayer niche cut out of the east wall.

Of the 45 cavities that served as cells, St. Sabas' is the only one that is so small. Although the others were usually used by only one hermit, they were large enough for two or even three persons: for example, for an old monk and his disciples.

143 top right The sacristy of St. Sabas chapel is also an ossuary: the reliquaries seen here house the skulls of the monks martyred centuries ago.

143 center The succession of icons decorating the chambers in the monastery clashes with the austere simplicity of the natural caves along the rock faces of the wadi, which have been the home of anchorites for centuries.

142 bottom left The overdecorated 16th-century iconostasis of the St. Sabas chapel separates the presbytery from the area for the faithful.

Mar Saba to lead a monastic life stayed for good. The skulls of the monks killed by the Persians and Arabs are on display in the sacristy, near their bones, which lie behind a grille. The winding steps that lead from St. Sabas' cell to the upper cave of the church has been closed. The northern narthex has a chapel and sacristy, but originally it was probably conceived as a single chamber. From here the stairs give access to various rooms: the refectory, kitchen, bread oven, and the gallery that

QUMRAN AND THE DEAD SEA SCROLLS

In the Bible the Dead Sea is called the 'Salt Sea,' while the ancient Greeks and Romans called it the 'Asphalt Lake' and for the Arabs it was 'Lot's Sea.' The unique chemical composition of this sea aroused the curiosity of ancient scholars such as Aristotle, Strabo, Pliny the Elder, Tacitus, Pausanias and Galen (the last two, in the 2nd century AD, called it by its present name).

144 top Five excavation missions, carried out in 1951-56, were needed to bring to light all the ruins of Qumran, which cover a surface area of 328 x 262 feet.

144-145 The striking barrenness of the rise where the Qumran complex lies, a few hundred yards from the caves, was the best guarantee of safety for the inhabitants.

144 bottom Fortress, the residence of a rich Jewish family, or caravan route way station: these are the hypotheses regarding the function of the buildings at Qumran facing the west coast of the Dead Sea.

After the Byzantine and Crusader periods it was known as the 'Devil's Sea' and was the subject of legends and popular beliefs that were disproved only in 1848 by an American scientific mission. The shores of the Dead Sea boast remains of civilizations dating from prehistoric times. On the west bank, about twelve miles south of Jericho, is the most famous locality, Qumran.

145 top and bottom A cave housed two bronze vases that were perhaps abandoned by the Bar Kokhba rebels.

145 center Next to the vases seen here, archaeologists found a bronze mirror still in its case.

QUMRAN

1 DECANTATION POOL	8 PANTRY
2 RITUAL BATH	9 RITUAL BATH
3 TOWER	10 OVEN FOR CEREMONIES
4 BENCH ROOM	11 LOCATION OF POTTER'S WHEEL
5 SCRIPTORIUM	12 CISTERNS
6 KITCHENS	13 LAUNDRY
7 REFECTORY	

Besides its ancient settlement, the fame of this city is due to the discovery made from 1947 to 1958 of numerous manuscripts that were hidden in eleven caves. Although scholars almost unanimously agree that these documents are connected to the Jewish religious sect of the Essenes, Qumran continues to arouse heated controversy. Indeed, despite the fact that the numerous archaeological finds lead to the conclusion that Qumran was the home of a homogeneous community, scholars have not yet found any direct links between the Essenes and this archaeological site. What

is more, some scholars point out that indisputable connections between the Essenes themselves and the religious group mentioned in the Dead Sea Scrolls, are still lacking. According to one interpretation, Qumran was a caravan way station founded in the 8th century BC and frequented by travellers on the 'Salt Route' from Jerusalem to Arabia and the Horn of Africa. Other scholars have suggested that the locality was the summer residence of a rich family from Jerusalem, or that it was a military fortress. It is also probable that Qumran was the city of Salt, one of the six towns in the Judaean desert mentioned by

Joshua (15, 61-62).

Archaeological studies have confirmed that the site was inhabited during the Israelite period and was abandoned after the fall of the Kingdom of Judah, so that it was continuously inhabited by the Essenes from the 2nd century BC until the suppression of the First Jewish Revolt in 68 AD, with the exception of a brief period following an earthquake that struck the site in 31 BC. As for historical references, the Essenes are cited by Jewish chroniclers such as Philo Judaeus and Josephus Flavius, and are also mentioned by Pliny the Elder. According to these eminent scholars, the Essene sect had over 4,000 members scattered throughout Palestine. They fiercely opposed the Hellenization of Jewish culture and scrupulously observed the Law, living in communal dwellings. Membership was reserved for men, and it was necessary to

146-147 The Bible speaks of six Judaean cities in the desert: Qumran is the 'city of Salt,' Ir ha-Melah.

146 left The Qumran scrolls are still intact thanks to the protection afforded by the jars they were kept in.

146 bottom left An inkpot found on the site may prove that the manuscripts were written by local scribes.

147 top In 1947 a young shepherd entered this cave and discovered the first scrolls.

147 bottom The Dead Sea Scrolls contain thousands of lines concerning religious and civic matters, from dogma to prophecies and rules of social life, as

well as almost all the books of the Old Testament written in Aramaic from the 2nd century BC to 68 AD. But who wrote them is still an open question: Pliny the Elder says they belonged to the dissident Essene sect, whose members were scrupulously obedient to the Law and led a communal life in the desert.

which lies on a promontory jutting eastward toward the Dead Sea, consisted of a gate, which had a fortified tower nearby. There were two other entrances. The backs of the houses served as defensive walls which enclosed several courtyards. Among the community buildings there was a huge kitchen with five fireplaces; nearby were a large hall that has been identified as the refectory, and a smaller room that contained over a thousand earthenware objects–jars, plates, jugs, beakers, cups, bowls and vases–that were perhaps used for communal meals. The site also had a pottery workshop. Archaeologists brought to light a long assembly hall that may have been used as a *scriptorium*, since a long writing table and three inkpots were found inside. The system used to ensure a constant water supply for the settlement was rather sophisticated: water reached the buildings via an aqueduct that entered through the northwest corner of the site and flowed to a decantation pool, where it was purified and then channelled to seven cisterns by means of a series of canals.

Next to the settlement is a cemetery with over one thousand tombs arranged in regular rows, each marked by a small pile of stones. In general the sepulchres contained the remains of males, with very few women and children.

go through a trial period before being admitted as a bona fide member. New adherents donated all their possessions to the sect and had to turn over any later earnings as well.

It is commonly believed that the Dead Sea Scrolls were hidden in the caves near Qumran by the inhabitants of the village around 68-70 AD. Some scrolls, like other similar ancient documents discovered earlier, such as the Damascus Manuscripts, set down a series of rules for social life, while others expound religious dogmas that differ from those commonly practised by Judaism at the time.

The main entrance to the settlement,

EN GEDI, AN OASIS
AT THE DEAD SEA

hundred yards northeast of Tel Goren, archaeologists found the best preserved ruins in the area, a site occupied by the synagogues that replaced one another from the 2nd-3rd century to the second half of the 6th century AD. Besides the many sacred objects—bowls, *menorahs*, inscriptions in Aramaic and coins—some well preserved pavement mosaics were found; the finest of these, dating from the 5th century AD, depicts four birds placed in a medallion which in turn is set within two squares arranged so as to form an eight-point 'star.' At each of the corners of one square are two facing peacocks

The list of the cities of Judah includes En Gedi–which lies along the western coast of the Dead Sea–among the localities in the desert area, but the name of this site derives from the presence of water there. The archaeological site, which is now a national park, has some springs, one of which, known as the 'spring of the kid goat,' gave its name to the site; and the most ancient settlement found in the area, a Chalcolithic-Age sacred precinct with a circular altar in the middle, is situated a short distance from this spring.

Mentioned in historic chronicles since the 7th century BC, the original settlement flourished thanks to its production of dates and local balsamic plants, as well as the salt and bitumen extracted from the nearby shore of the Dead Sea. The five archaeological strata found on Tel Goren, the hillock occupied by the village, comprise traces of some industrial facilities, perhaps for the

production of perfume, which date back to the Iron Age (7th-6th century BC), and the ruins of a large Persian Age edifice with a surface area of 1,802 square feet that consisted of numerous rooms, inner courts and storehouses.

En Gedi was destroyed around 400 BC and revived during the Hasmonean period, when the top of the *tell* was occupied by a fortification that at the beginning of the Herodian age became a bona fide citadel made of large blocks of stone. During the Roman period the village suffered at least two catastrophes: the first at the hands of the Sicarii, the violent Zealots who sacked the town and slaughtered much of the population during the First Jewish War, and the second during the Bar Kokhba revolt, when En Gedi was destroyed.

There are ruins of Roman baths near the Dead Sea coast, a long, narrow building whose rooms were, curiously enough, arranged in a long row. A few

with grapes in their beaks. The lack of Zodiacal representation, a common motif in the contemporaneous synagogues found in other localities, from Tiberias to Bet Alpha, seems to demonstrate the strict attitude of the local Jewish community, which may have rejected the 'pagan' representation of the Zodiac out of respect for the purest Jewish tradition. Perhaps it was this very religious inflexibility that brought about the destruction of the synagogue in the mid 6th century during emperor Justinian's persecution.

148 left In place of the Zodiac, a common motif in 5th-century synagogues, the En Gedi mosaic has less 'pagan' images: peacocks holding grapes in their beaks.

148 right En Gedi thrived thanks to the springs that fed the oasis, which was famous for its dates.

148-149 A bronze menorah found in the Byzantine-period synagogue, which was perhaps destroyed during Justinian's persecution.

149 top The En Gedi oasis emerges behind the ruins; the spring that made life possible here lies about 660 feet above the Dead Sea.

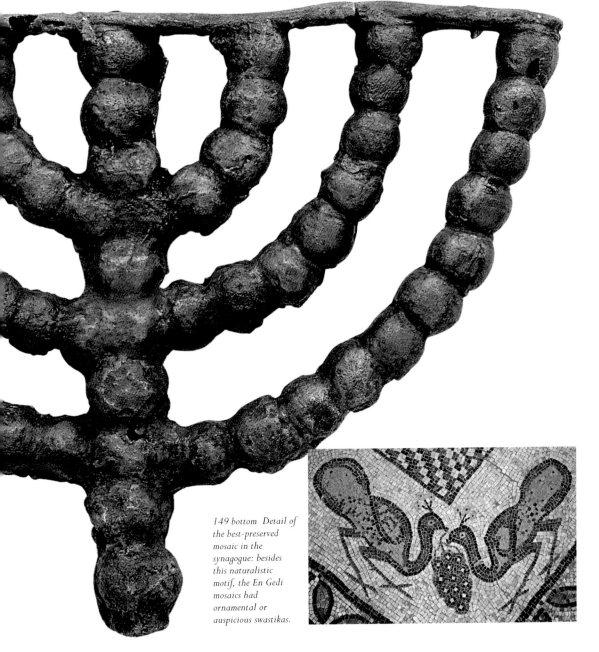

149 bottom Detail of the best-preserved mosaic in the synagogue: besides this naturalistic motif, the En Gedi mosaics had ornamental or auspicious swastikas.

HERODION, HEROD THE GREAT'S ILLUSION OF GRANDEUR

An ambitious voluptuary always seeking the favour of the Romans, King Herod became famous for the splendid and lavish architectural works he commissioned during his reign. Without a doubt, his most original creation is the grandiose palace he built about seven miles south of Jerusalem that was named *Herodion* after him. Seen from afar, in the barren landscape of the rises surrounding it, this singular architectural structure looks much like a curiously regular truncate-conical hill at the foot of which are the ruins of a palace, an immense pool, storehouses and baths. The superb complex, built around 20 BC, was

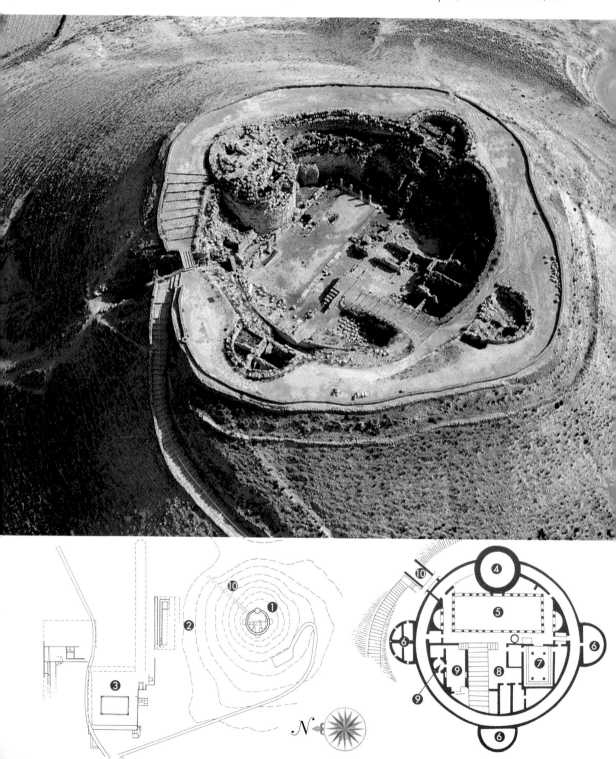

N

conceived as a fortified palace that was intended to be the monarch's mausoleum upon his death. However, despite the historian Flavius Josephus's description of Herod's funeral procession, and the innumerable exploratory studies made by archaeologists, his tomb has never been found.

The edifice stands on the top of a semi-artificial hill about 197 feet above the surrounding countryside and enclosed within two concentric circular walls with a diameter of 203 feet. The walls were dominated by a round tower, which archaeologists reckon must have been about 52 feet high, and by three smaller, semicircular towers that jutted out from the outer wall. The hill took on its

150-151 Seen from above, the uniqueness of the fortress in Herodion *is quite apparent.*

151 top The regular configuration of the tell *on which* Herodion *stood, much like a volcanic cone, reveals that the rise was half artificial.*

peculiar shape because of the debris from the excavation of the foundation and from the construction of the palace which, together with other fill material, was dumped along the slopes to make them steeper. Access was possible only by means of a vaulted underground passageway, the entrance of which lay at the bottom of the hill.

The interior of the round palace had two wings: one was occupied by a garden surrounded by columns, a veritable oasis in the desert, while the other consisted of luxurious apartments with elegant bathrooms on the ground floor. The floors were decorated with mosaics with geometric motifs and the walls were covered with painted relief stuccowork. Water for the entire complex was provided by large cisterns cut out of the hill.

The lower part of the *Herodion* was equally magnificent, dominated by a large pool in the middle used not only for swimming but for small boats as well. The pool was surrounded by a garden with many buildings and large baths. Inside the semi-artificial hill archaeologists discovered a labyrinth of secret passageways that partly incorporated the underground cisterns Herod had built: these were cut out of the rock by the Jewish rebels led by Simeon Bar Kokhba during the second Jewish revolt, which broke out in 132 AD throughout Palestine. Among the many finds were tools, weapons, and coins minted during the revolt.

Later on, during the Byzantine period, a small monastery was erected over the ruins of the palace. The religious community probably abandoned the *Herodion* sometime in the 7th century.

HERODION

1 HERODION
2 LOWER PALACE
3 POOL PAVILION
4 MAIN TOWER
5 PERISTYLE COURTYARD
6 SEMICIRCULAR TOWERS
7 SYNAGOGUE
8 CRUCIFORM HALL
9 BATHS
10 UNDERGROUND PASSAGEWAY

151 bottom Herod's fortress-mausoleum was protected by four towers that increased the robustness of the wall and was accessible from the base of the tell *via an underground passageway.*

"Hic de Virgine Maria Jesus Christus natus est (Here was born Jesus Christ of the Virgin Mary):" this inscription at the Messiah's birthplace epitomizes the mystical fascination of Bethlehem, the cradle of Christianity in both a literal and metaphorical sense. But this is not all. The modern-day city, now quite close to the southern suburbs of Jerusalem, is also one of the holiest sites for Jews and is worshipped by Muslims because of Rachel, the prototype of long-suffering Jewish mothers, and David, the great king of Israel who was born in Bethlehem 1,010 years before his direct descendant Jesus. Among the prophecies attributed to Micah (8th-7th century BC), there is one that indicates Bethlehem as the future birthplace of the Messiah, an event that according to our modern calendar should have occurred around

which she built the first basilica, which it seems had a nave with two lateral aisles enhanced by magnificent mosaics on the pavement and walls. In 590 Justinian built the Church of the Nativity we see today, whose original structure has remained intact due to a series of fortunate circumstances, which makes it one of the oldest surviving churches in the world. In 614 the Persian king Khosru II devastated practically all the sacred buildings he saw during his invasion of the Holy Land, but spared the basilica because the Magi on the façade were wearing Persian clothes. And in the 11th century the Crusaders rebuilt very little of the church, which was spared later during the waves of Muslim conquest–though several times its stones were taken away to be used as building material.

Once past the forecourt, access to the narthex of the Church of the Nativity is gained through a door only four feet high, which was perhaps an expedient to prevent defilers on horseback from entering. From the vestibule a medieval wooden door sculpted by Armenian artisans leads to the interior; this consists of a nave with

150 top left The place where Mary gave birth to Jesus is marked merely by a silver star and brief Latin inscription.

150 bottom left The present-day Nativity Cave, run by Greek Orthodox monks, belies the humble place described in the Gospel.

the year 7 BC. In an attempt to tranform the holy character of the cave where Jesus was born–already venerated in the 2nd century BC–Emperor Hadrian consecrated the site to the cult of Adonis. However, in doing so he ended up indicating the exact spot that had been worshipped by the early Christians. Consequently, in 325 Queen Helena had no trouble identifying the cave, over

152-153 The dozens of lamps and votive candles afford some light in the Nativity Cave. Opposite the altar over the silver star at left, are the Chapel of the Manger and the Chapel of the Magi.

153 top and bottom In what is perhaps a unique event in the history of religious conflict in the Holy Land, the sacredness of the Church of the Nativity dissuaded the Muslim invaders from destroying it.

BETHLEHEM	
1 LOWERED ENTRANCE	6 ENTRANCES TO NATIVITY CAVE
2 NARTHEX	7 GREEK ORTHODOX ALTAR
3 WOODEN DOOR (1227)	8 REMAINS OF CONSTANTINIAN MOSAIC PAVEMENT
4 CLOISTER	
5 4TH-CENTURY BAPTISMAL FONT	

east is the tiny apse, on the marble pavement of which is the star with the Latin inscription quoted above, surmounted by 15 lamps that represent the Christian denominations, while on the opposite side are the altar of the Manger, where the infant Jesus was laid, and the altar of the Magi. Inside the cave one can see traces of a 12th-century mosaic depicting the Nativity. Part of a network of natural caves used as dwellings as early as the 6th century BC, the main cave communicates with other crypts, one of which is dedicated to the memory of the victims of Herod's supposed Massacre of the Innocents.

Proceeding along the network of caves, one reaches the Church of St. Catherine, access to which is also afforded from the left-hand apse of the basilica. This modern building was built in the 19th century over the foundation of a monastery dedicated to St. Jerome, but the light-filled cloister opposite dates back to the Crusader period. Southwest of the complex is the 19th-century Franciscan 'Milk Church,' built over the ruins of an Early Christian chapel and corresponding to the cave of the same name where Mary presumably suckled Jesus before the Holy Family fled to Egypt. It is a popular belief that the light color of the rock was caused by milk that had dropped from the Holy Child's lips.

four side aisles marked off by four rows of yellow marble columns and piers that are lavishly decorated in a surprising mixture and variety of styles, the result of the contributions made by the members of the various Christian denominations during centuries of pilgrimage. The most ancient part of the edifice is the nave itself, which has traces of the mosaic pavement with geometric patterns dating from the Constantinian period, as well as some representations of saints painted on the columns.

On the sides of the choir, situated in the transept in the middle of the three Justinian period apses, are two stairways leading to the Cave of the Nativity, a rock-cut crypt with masonry vaulting and partly dressed in marble along the walls. The cave has three chapels: to the

151 right Christ in the guise of a Crusader king towers over a pilgrim's staff from the Church of the Nativity.

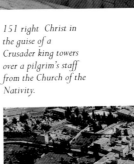

ASHQELON, HEROD THE GREAT'S BIRTHPLACE

Almost two miles southwest of the modern city of Ashqelon is the ancient site, which is like a vast semicircle bordered to the west by the Mediterranean and surrounded on the other sides by the remains of the Crusader walls. Ancient Ashqelon was built at the end of the Chalcolithic age, around 3500 BC, and in the middle of the 2nd millennium BC it was a Canaanite city in the sphere of influence of the New Kingdom pharaohs of Egypt, remaining in this condition until about 1175 BC, when the Philistines conquered the major localities in the Holy Land and established the *Pentapolis*, a federation of five city-states. Despite the Israelites' attempts at conquest, the *Pentapolis* resisted, losing its independence only in 711 BC, when it was taken by the Assyrian king Sargon II. After the Persian conquest of 558 BC, Ashqelon was ceded to the Phoenicians, whose culture became a predominant influence. During the Hellenistic period the city was under Ptolemaic and Seleucid rule. The city placed itself under the protection of Rome in the 2nd century BC, and in 73 BC Herod the Great was born there. According to the historian Flavius Josephus, this ruler later beautified the city with "thermae and magnificent fountains, as well as colonnades remarkable both for their scale and craftsmanship." During the First Jewish War the city remained loyal to Rome and thus

enjoyed a period of prosperity and power in the centuries of the *Pax Romana* that followed, when it became a center of learning and religion. In 636 AD Ashqelon was captured by the Arabs and in 1153 by the Crusaders, who fortified it. During the entire Crusader period the city was bitterly contested, until the sultan Baybars razed it to the ground in 1270, which marked the end of the city. Tell Ashqelon National Park is interesting from both an archaeological and naturalist standpoint. The ancient site has yielded traces of all the settlements from the Canaanite to the Crusader periods. In the northern section are the ruins of the massive walls built in the middle Bronze Age (around 2000 BC), while to the south are the remains of the ancient harbor, some large columns of which are lying on the ground. Next to the medieval walls are the ruins of the Crusader Church of St. Mary the Green, rich in fragments of sculpture used to rebuild it, and of the theater. The Forum, which dates from the late 2nd century AD, was marked off on all four sides by colonnades supported by monolithic columns about 26 feet high. Some of the colonnades were elevated during the archaeological excavations. The original level of the pavement has been preserved in a small section at the southern end of the square, the site of the basilica (a sort of City Council Chamber), a large edifice with a large apse. Among the finds on display in the Forum area, now a very interesting open-air museum, are the 2nd-century AD low-reliefs that decorated the basilica; they represent the Egyptian goddess Isis with the infant Horus and two Winged Victories, one of which is standing on a globe held up

154 top Ashqelon has traces of settlements dating as far back as the 4th millennium BC, but the most significant ruins belong to the Roman-Byzantine period.

by Atlas. In the 4th century the basilica collapsed due to natural causes, but one century later the original pavement became the auditorium of a theater that was destroyed in the 7th century by the Muslims, who incorporated the area into a mosque.

Modern Ashqelon and its suburbs also have yielded important finds. In the Afridar residential quarter there are two finely wrought Roman marble sarcophagi decorated with mythological scenes and scenes of battles with the Celts. Not far from the city is the Painted Tomb, dating from the 3rd century AD. This is a vaulted chamber measuring 10 x 13 feet used to house four sarcophagi, which were missing when the tomb was discovered. The chamber is named after the wall painting decoration depicting some nymphs seated next to a stream where animals have come to drink, while among the grapevines decorating the ceiling are such mythological figures as Demeter, Medusa and Pan.

154 center The interesting remains of Roman Ashqelon, with its fine architecture, also include magnificent minor sculpture pieces.

154 bottom A winged victory rests on Atlas' shoulders: this is a part of the bas-reliefs that decorated the Basilica and are now in the Forum.

154-155 Around the cavea of the Roman theater, now lacking its marble dressing, is Ashqelon National Park.

155 bottom left Ashqelon park, famous for centuries for its mild climate, combines archaeology and natural beauty.

155 bottom right Figures connected to the mystery cults, Isis and her infant son Horus (called 'Harpocrates' by the Greeks), appear on a bas-relief fragment.

RAMLA AND ST. HELENA'S CISTERN

The city of Ramla, or 'sandy place,' was designed and founded in 715-717 AD by Suleiman, one of the sons of the Omayyad caliph Abd el-Malik. Since there were no springs in the area, the architects had three cisterns hewn out of the rock to collect rainwater. One of these is the Cistern of St. Helena, which was completed in 789. In ancient times it was 82 feet long, but in the early 20th century the southern section of the bays that protected it collapsed. The roof of this large underground cistern was rebuilt by the Crusaders, who used cross-vaulting, thus contributing to the development of the Gothic pointed arch. The roof of each of the twenty-four bays has a square hole that allowed many people to draw water with buckets at the same time.

156 The inscription at the entrance of the minaret in the White Mosque dates the edifice back to 1318. Other epigraphs found in situ suggest that during Baybars's time the tower was topped by a dome.

156-157 Besides the damage caused by invasions and conquest, in the 11th century Ramla was hit by a series of quakes so disastrous that the Crusaders had to rebuild and fortify most of the city.

157 Lydda, ancient 'Lod' mentioned in Egyptian texts and the Old Testament, was renamed Georgopolis in honor of St. George, who was supposedly born here and buried in the crypt of the local Greek Orthodox church.

LYDDA, ST. GEORGE'S CITY

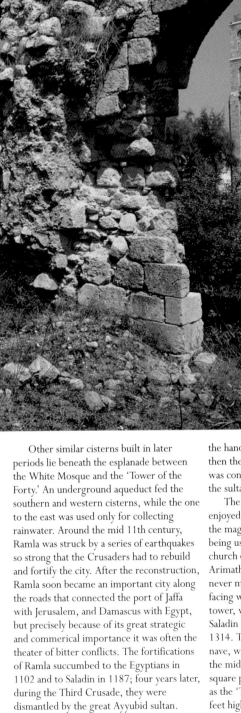

The name of ancient 'Lod' was mentioned for the first time in the 15th century BC, in the list of the cities conquered by the Egyptian pharaoh Tuthmosis III. It was occupied by the tribe of Benjamin in biblical times, destroyed by the Assyrians in the 8th century BC, rebuilt in the 5th century BC, and occupied by the Greeks, who gave it its present name. It was then conquered by the Maccabees. In the 1st century BC Lydda became a center of Talmudic studies and in 67 BC was occupied by the Romans led by Pompey. A Christian community quickly grew up in Lydda, which was one of the stops made by St. Peter while he was sermonizing, and in the 4th century it was already a bishopric. The pagan name of the city, *Diospolis*, or 'city of Jupiter,' was chosen in the 2nd century by Settimius Severus, and during the Byzantine period it was called *Georgopolis*, 'the city of St. George,' who was supposedly born in Lydda and whose tomb lies there. Gradually overshadowed by

Other similar cisterns built in later periods lie beneath the esplanade between the White Mosque and the 'Tower of the Forty.' An underground aqueduct fed the southern and western cisterns, while the one to the east was used only for collecting rainwater. Around the mid 11th century, Ramla was struck by a series of earthquakes so strong that the Crusaders had to rebuild and fortify the city. After the reconstruction, Ramla soon became an important city along the roads that connected the port of Jaffa with Jerusalem, and Damascus with Egypt, but precisely because of its great strategic and commerical importance it was often the theater of bitter conflicts. The fortifications of Ramla succumbed to the Egyptians in 1102 and to Saladin in 1187; four years later, during the Third Crusade, they were dismantled by the great Ayyubid sultan. When Richard the Lion-Hearted arrived, he found an abandoned city, which he used as a base for his attempt to conquer Jerusalem. In the space of a few years, Ramla passed into

the hands of the Muslims, then the Crusaders, until it was conquered definitively by the sultan Baybars in 1268.

The prosperity the city enjoyed during this period can be seen in the magnificent Great Mosque, which is still being used. Originally it was the Crusader church dedicated to St. Joseph of Arimathaea, whose basic structure was never modified. Next to the main entrance, facing west, there was probably a bell-tower, which may have been demolished by Saladin in 1191 and replaced by a minaret in 1314. The White Mosque, with a two-aisle nave, was built in 1318. Quite nearby, in the middle of the northern side of a vast square plaza, is the tower commonly known as the 'Tower of the Forty,' which is 88.5 feet high. Different interpretations have been given for this name: for the Muslims it is a clear reference to the Prophet's companions, while for the Christians refers to the forty martyrs of Cappadocia.

the nearby city of Ramla, in the 7th century Lydda was conquered by the Omayyads and had to wait five centuries before being retaken by the Crusaders, who built the French Romanesque church dedicated to the saint who killed the dragon. Only a few years later the city was taken by Saladin. After defeating the Ayyubid sultan at Arsur, Richard the Lion Hearted regained possession of the city in 1191 and rebuilt it, but only a few decades later, in the second half of the 13th century, the Mongols' pillage of Lydda marked the beginning of its decline. In the center of the town, in the crypt of the Greek Orthodox church dedicated to the patron saint of England, is St. George's tomb, built in 1870 over the ruins of the Crusader church destroyed by Saladin. A short distance away is the el-Khadr Mosque, built over a 4th century church.

BET GUVRIN, THE CITY OF CAVES

In the vicinity of biblical Maresha–which was devastated by the Assyrians in 701 BC, recovered after the Babylonian captivity and was then destroyed for good by the Parthians in 40 BC–lies Bet Guvrin, the 'city of free men' mentioned for the first time by Flavius Josephus, who in his *Jewish War* describes the locality as a village in the heart of Idumaea. During the Roman period it was an important town on the road linking Jerusalem and Ashqelon, and in 200 AD Septimius Severus named it *Eleutheropolis*, the future capital of *Palaestina Tertia* during Theodosius's time. This district extended from the shores of the Dead Sea to the coastal area behind Gaza and was the largest ever created in the region. Bet Guvrin soon became Christian and continued to prosper in the Byzantine age, up to the Omayyad

conquest in the 7th century, when it was given a name that was a corruption of its ancient name, Beth Gibrin, again modified by the Crusaders in Bet Giblin (or Gibelin). Now quite small (the city fortified by Fulk of Anjou was about one-fifteenth of the surface area of the Roman-Byzantine city), Bet Guvrin began to decline at the end of the Crusader period. Now the name of the ancient city has been taken over by an active kibbutz near the archaeological site.

In the northwestern area of Bet Guvrin is the intact exterior of the Roman amphitheater, an oval-shaped edifice with a barrel-vaulted double ring that gave access to the *vomitoria*. Other unique features of the archaeological precinct are the so-called bell caves, a large group of caves with a characteristic

shape and function that have been variously interpreted: in the past it was thought they were granaries, cisterns or dwellings, but today scholars tend to think they were chalk quarries excavated in the 4th-7th centuries. Indeed, the configuration of the caves is the result of the excavation technique employed at that time. In order to keep the chalk moist enough to be extracted easily, laborers cut a round hole about three yards in diameter into the hard crust of the terrain (called *nari*) which in various localities in Palestine covers the chalk deposits. Once they reached the chalk, the quarrymen removed the chalk in regularly cut blocks that were lifted up through the hole. The shape of these excavations was such as to allow the laborers to exploit the structural principles of a dome, so that a cave-in was unlikely to occur. Although smoothed out by erosion, the walls of these 800 bell caves still have the marks of the tools used. Several caves are communicating, because the quarrymen often broke through the rock walls while excavating. The extracted chalk was fired in kilns to make mortar and cement, but in the Bet Guvrin area archaeologists found very few such facilities, which indicates that the chalk was probably sold crude

158 top left The bell shape of the chalk caves was due to the excavation technique and the nature of the terrain.

158 top right The maximum and minimum radius of the Roman amphitheater arena were 82 and 65 feet respectively.

159 The round holes cut into the very hard crust of the land typical of this region, the nari.

158 bottom left Most of the hundreds of caves in Bet Guvrin are artificial.

158 bottom right The extracted chalk was fired in kilns to make mortar or sold crude.

and processed elsewhere. Exploited from the Byzantine period (7th century) to the 10th century, the caves contain numerous inscriptions which show that the local workmen were Christians who spoke Arabic.

The Bet Gurvin area also has the remains of one of the three Crusader castles built by Fulk of Anjou. It was destroyed by the Mamluks in 1244 and rebuilt by the Ottomans three centuries later. The Crusader St. Anne's Church lies in nearby Tel Maresha, where there are also the ruins of the water supply network and the remains of Hellenistic-age residential areas. In the area around

Tel Maresha digs have unearthed some extremely interesting tombs and various *columbaria*. West of the rise is the best designed *columbarium*, which is also one of the largest. It consists of a narrow corridor cut out of the limestone with the same technique used to open the bell caves; it has hundreds of tiny niches which, as the name indicates, were used to raise doves. Indeed this activity thrived in the region

up to the 3rd or 2nd century BC: it has been calculated that there are about 50,000-60,000 niches in the Maresha *columbaria*. This tunnel is accessible by means of rock-cut steps and is connected to a cistern and to a nearby olive processing installation.

The burial area east of Tel Maresha contains some truly spectacular tombs built in the Hellenistic age. The largest and most richly decorated of these consists of an entrance passageway that affords access to a vestibule flanked by three burial chambers arranged in the form of a cross. Along the walls of these three chambers are 31 long loculi with a characteristic shape and, beyond a colonnaded entrance topped by a tympanum on the back wall, three smaller burial chambers. The most interesting feature of this tomb are the paintings: the entrance to the small burial chambers is flanked by two cinerary amphoras in the lower register and, above, by two eagles on an undulating garland that decorates the entire corridor. Under the volutes of the garland is a series of hunting scenes, palm trees and various wild and exotic animals, such as an elephant and rhinoceros. Similar in structure but smaller, the nearby Tomb of the Musicians owes its name to the lively painting of a woman playing a lyre preceded by a flutist, both wearing clothes with bright, multicolored vertical stripes. Next to this painting is a drinking scene and figures of a tripod and a *kantharos*.

160 right The thousands of niches in the columbaria *were opened only in the upper section of the walls to prevent predators from catpuring the birds.*

160 left This painting in the largest tomb in Maresha shows a determined knight about to lance his prey, a leopard already wounded by an arrow.

160-161 The light of the lamps lends spectacular liveliness to what was a tomb, thanks to the variety of exotic animals depicted on the walls.

161 top A crudely but effectively rendered lion stands on one of the Greek inscriptions illustrating the motifs of the frieze.

161 bottom left There are 14 loculi along the walls of the mortuary chamber.

161 bottom right
Other animals in the
predatory scenes are
a deer, a porcupine
and a rhinoceros
enlosed between a
garland and a Greek
inscription.

MASADA, THE FORTRESS THAT DARED TO CHALLENGE ROME

162-163 In order to capture such a formidable fortress like Masada, the Romans *built the huge ramp seen at right, one of most prodigious obsidional apparatuses ever created.*

The fortress that Herod the Great built a short distance from the Dead Sea on the rock of Masada, is to this day one of the most vivid symbols of the Jews' heritage as well as the most famous archaeological site in Israel. It was here that 960 men, women and children committed suicide in 73 AD rather than succumb to the soldiers of the Tenth Roman Legion. This was the last chapter of a rebellion that had reached its peak three years earlier with the destruction of Jerusalem by Titus' troops. Already during the Hasmonean period the site, in an ideal position on the flat top of an isolated rock that was virtually invulnerable on all sides

162 bottom left The grandiose Northern Palace was built as Herod the Great's personal residence.

162 bottom right The arrows found among the ruins of Masada bear the signs of the fire that devastated the fortress.

163 top left Among the names written on these ostraka (shards) is that of Eleazar Ben Yair, the head of the revolt against Rome.

163 top right This view from the north shows the winding course of the wall, which follows the contour of the rock.

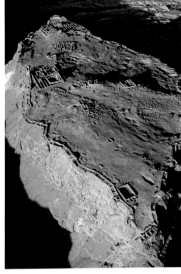

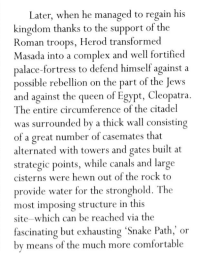

Later, when he managed to regain his kingdom thanks to the support of the Roman troops, Herod transformed Masada into a complex and well fortified palace-fortress to defend himself against a possible rebellion on the part of the Jews and against the queen of Egypt, Cleopatra. The entire circumference of the citadel was surrounded by a thick wall consisting of a great number of casemates that alternated with towers and gates built at strategic points, while canals and large cisterns were hewn out of the rock to provide water for the stronghold. The most imposing structure in this site—which can be reached via the fascinating but exhausting 'Snake Path,' or by means of the much more comfortable

163 center Herod's large fortress required weapons and considerable supplies of food, which were kept in the long, narrow rooms attached to the Northern Palace.

163 bottom One of the Corinthian capitals in Herod's palace still bears traces of the stucco used to dress the interiors, often painted so as to look like marble.

because of its sheer cliffs, had become a military stronghold. In 40 BC Masada played a fundamental role in the life of Herod who, having to flee from the Parthian army, was forced to leave his family there in safety while he went to Rome to seek military aid. His family, together with the 800 soldiers who had orders to protect them, were about to die of thirst during the Parthian siege, when a timely rainstorm filled the empty cisterns.

cable car—is certainly the splendid royal palace that rises up on the northern tip of the rock. This architectural masterpiece—built on three levels—boasts quite advanced building techniques and a spectacular distribution of space. The top floor comprised a rectangular hall, which on the side adjacent to the floor underneath opened onto a large apse bordered by a Corinthian colonnade that offered an extraordinary view of the Dead Sea depression. This is still a vantage point, as the remains of the hall has been transformed into a panoramic terrace with a breathtaking view of the Dead Sea and

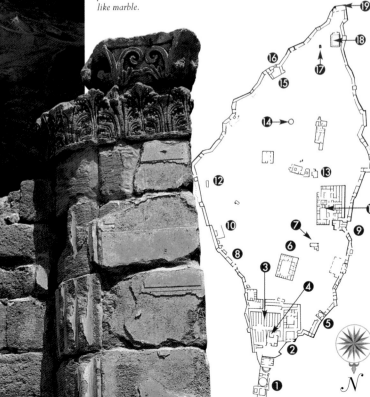

MASADA

1 NORTHERN PALACE	10 ZEALOTS' LIVING
2 WATER GATE	QUARTERS
3 STOREHOUSES	11 WESTERN PALACE
4 BATHS	12 OPEN-AIR CISTERN
5 SYNAGOGUE	13/15 MIKVEHS
6 LARGE BUILDING	14 COLUMBARIUM
(USE UNKNOWN)	16 SOUTH GATE
7 BYZANTINE CHURCH	17 COVERED CISTERN
8 SNAKE PATH GATE	18 LARGE POOL
9 WEST GATE	19 SOUTHERN BASTION

the entire region; one can also see the borders of the Roman camp and the circumvallation (*vallum*) built by the besiegers around the rock to discourage any assaults on the part of the Zealots. A covered stairway links this wing of the Northern Palace and the middle level, which is a round terrace that is also surrounded by columns and surmounted by a bell-shaped roof. It should be pointed out that the modern metal steps and the roofed passageway linking these two levels follow a different course from the original one. The lowest level of the palace was more or less square and had an inner courtyard in the middle surrounded by a peristyle with pilasters

against which elegant Corinthian half-columns were placed. Next to this was a small but luxurious bath-house. The inside walls and the columns of the palace were dressed with lively polychrome stuccowork, most of which was made to look like precious marble, while the

164 bottom From the ruins of the apsidal hall there is a view of the desert as far as the Dead Sea.

165 The Suspended Palace is one of the greatest architectural achievements of Herod, who built many grandiose works.

164 top center Situated on the middle floor of Herod's palace, the round hall was used to receive and entertain guests.

164 top right The lower building, laid out around a peristyle court, was flanked by a bath-house.

164 center This reconstruction illustrates how spectacular Herod's palace was (aptly called 'Suspended Palace').

floors were decorated with black and white mosaics with geometric motifs. Traces of the original decoration can be seen here and there.

The bath-house constructed slightly south of the upper level of the palace is also extremely interesting. It is undoubtedly one of the best preserved among the various Roman sites discovered so far in Israel. The complex, which comprises four rooms and a courtyard with a peristyle on three sides and a small pool, was mostly restored in the 1990s, and the precise anastylosis effected at that time makes it easier to understand the functions of the various chambers. The dressing room, or *apodyterium*, decorated with stuccowork on the walls and white and black tiles on the floor, is followed by the *tepidarium*, the warm room, and the *frigidarium*, the coolest room, which has a large stepped pool (with stone seats). In the *calidarium* (hot room) is the *hypocaust*, the pavement supported by small columns (*suspensurae*), beneath which the hot air from the furnace circulated.

Near the bath was a vast complex of long, narrow rooms that were used not only to store food and wine, but weapons and valuable objects as well. This section of the fortress, including the royal palace proper (Western Palace), the baths and the storehouses, was separated from the rest of the citadel by a wall and gate.

166 top The guest rooms lay around an inner court of the Western Palace.

166-167 The niches of the columbarium may have housed the ashes of the Gentile soldiers who died at Masada.

166 center The main gate of the fortress lies on the edge of the cliff on the western side of Masada rock.

This sumptuous complex was used for feasts and as a display of Herod the Great's power and wealth. But at the same time it had been conceived as the last bulwark should invaders succeed in getting past the main walls. The Western Palace, on the other hand, was intended to be more functional and contained the royal apartments and the guests' apartments, service rooms, workshops and storerooms, as well as halls used for administrative purposes, such as reception rooms for official visits. Here again the floors were enhanced by lovely mosaic work, and it has been demonstrated that some parts of the edifice were several storys high. In the vicinity were three other structures, one of which housed a *mikveh*, the typical room used for Jewish ritual baths.

The most serious problems for Masada—where it might have been necessary to house as many as a thousand persons at one time—were provisions and water supply. The citadel was not only in the desert, where rainfall was seasonal and slight, but it was also situated on a plateau on the top of a mountain. Consequently, Herod's architects devised a drainage system that conveyed rainwater from the weirs built in the surrounding *wadis* to a network of twelve cisterns at the base of the rock that could contain 1,412,588 cubic feet of water. From here the water was transported by men on foot or by muleback along a winding path to the basins inside the citadel.

166 bottom left Near the Western Palace was the large pool used for the Jewish ritual bath, the mikveh, reached via a stairway.

166 bottom right Some fragments of sacred texts were found buried under the synagogue, in the northwest section of the site.

167 top One of the towers on the west wall, near the main gate, bears traces of a silo for food storage.

167 bottom In the 5th-6th century the rock was occupied by Byzantine monks, who built a church near the Western Palace.

changes can still be seen in different areas. Furthermore, the Zealots built two ritual baths and a structure that may have been used as a *beit midrash*, a hall for theological studies. The synagogue, on the northwestern part of the rock, has been partly reconstructed. It faced Jerusalem and may have been built by the Zealots on the site of a temple dating back to Herod's time.

Masada is an exceptionally precious archaeological site not only because of its architectural ruins: among the many finds discovered here that were preserved thanks to the dry climate, there are pieces of clothing, including prayer shawls and leather sandals, as well as pottery and wicker baskets. Archaeologists also found a large

number of coins that were struck on the spot by the Jewish rebels. Of fundamental importance for the study of the various texts of the Bible are the remains of fourteen scrolls discovered in different parts of the citadel. Furthermore, during the excavation campaign researchers brought to light over 700 *ostraka* (shards with inscriptions) that provide more information on the life led by the rebels who were trapped on this rock by the besieging Romans. Most of these *ostraka* are written in Aramaic or Hebrew, but some are in Greek or Latin as well. The majority

As we have already seen, Masada was fortified by massive walls that enclosed all the edifices on the esplanade, with the exception of the Northern Palace, which was impregnable. The perimeter was 4,920 feet long and contained 70 casemates, 30 towers and four gates. When the Zealots conquered the fortress during the anti-Roman Jewish revolt, which lasted six years, they effected many changes in Herod's original complex. In order to house the greatest possible number of families, all the rooms in the walls were transformed into living quarters and many halls in the palace were partitioned to create smaller rooms for the same purpose. Many traces of these

of them were found near or in the storehouses, and they seem to show that there was a system of food rationing during the siege. The researchers also found various large *ostraka* with names accompanied by numbers, which seems to indicate they were administrative lists.

However, the most sensational discovery were the eleven fragments, each with only one name, that were found next to the doors of the storehouses. One of the names is Ben-Yair, the leader of the Zealot rebels at Masada. Some scholars maintain that these shards prove that, on the last day of the siege, when it was clear that the

Romans would conquer the citadel, ten men were chosen by lot to initiate the procedure of mass suicide. In his *Jewish War*, Flavius Josephus relates that each of these men selected by lot had to kill the members of his own family and that in the end, "they obeyed the same rule, choosing by lot from among themselves: the winner was to kill the other nine first and then commit suicide." Around the rock are ruins confirming Josephus's account of the siege headed by the Roman general Flavius Silva. The men of the Tenth Legion built eight fortified camps around the base of the mountain and then a continuous wall connecting them, which had twelve sentinel towers. In this way the rebels could neither penetrate the camps nor leave the citadel, while replacements and supplies

could be sent to the besiegers without any danger. Since the only accessway, the Snake Path, could not be used by a large number of soldiers all together because it was so steep and devious, and the war machines absolutely had to be taken to the top of the rock in order to

168 left Some fragments of wall painting give us an idea of the lively decoration in the rooms of the large bath-house.

168 top right The building in the northeastern corner of Herod's palace was the home for many families during the Roman siege, and contained everyday tools and Jewish coins (shekels).

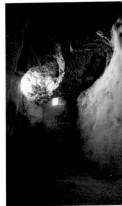

169 top left The dry desert climate has preserved the sandals belonging to a Jewish defender of Masada.

169 top center Some mosaics survived the destruction wrought by both Man and time.

169 top right The large rock-cut cistern guaranteed the vital water supply for the inhabitants of Masada.

169 bottom This small room in the bath-house of the Western complex was used by the king's guests.

168 bottom right This elegantly wrought bronze kitchenware, probably taken from Herod's palaces, was found in the rooms inhabited by the Zealots.

168-169 In the large baths at Masada, modeled after the Roman ones, the columns of the hypocaust are still intact.

make a breach in the wall, Flavius Silva had a huge ramp built on the western side of the mountain. The soldiers who carried out this task were protected by the cover of the catapults placed on a nearby promontory. Once the ramp was finished, the war machines could be positioned and in a short time the Romans made a breach in Herod's walls. The Zealots made one last attempt to defend themselves, building a wall of boards and sand in great haste. In vain; this was destroyed and Masada fell to the Romans.

BEER SHEBA AND ABRAHAM'S WELL

About halfway between the Dead Sea and the Mediterranean, modern Beer Sheba is surrounded by three important ancient settlements. At Abu Matar, southwest of the city, along the course of the *wadi* Beer Sheba, are some underground dwellings dating from the late Neolithic and Chalcolithic eras. They were partly cut out of the friable clayey earth and accessible via shallow pits which were like outer courtyards, and were connected to one another by tunnels. Even though it was variable and seasonal, the water of the *wadi* was used for the primitive agriculture of these peoples, who also raised livestock.

At Bir Safadi, south of the modern city,

archaeologists found similar contemporaneous settlements and houses built on the land.

The biblical town of Beer Sheba was discovered at Tel es-Sheba, just east of Beer Sheba. The Bible mentions Beer Sheba for the first time in connection with Abraham and a famous transaction. According to *Genesis*, Abraham settled near the *tell* and made a pact with the local lord, the Philistine Abimelech, to whom he gave seven ewes for the privilege of using the well. The etymology of the word Beer Sheba is interpreted as 'well of the seven (ewes)' or 'well of the oath.' Later on, Isaac built an altar at Beer Sheba in memory of

8th century the city was totally destroyed by the Assyrian ruler Sennacherib. In subsequent periods defensive fortifications were built there: in the 4th century BC a Persian fortress, and in the 2nd-3rd century AD a Roman one. Archaeological excavations have brought to light the original Middle Iron-Age city (10th century BC). Among these ruins is one of the city gates, with three pillars of equal width, with two guard posts on either side and an outer protective gate. Outside the gate a deep well was found; it was dated from the 12th century BC, which, if exact, would mean that it was being used in the biblical period of the Patriarchs, so that it could be identified as Abraham's well. However, it is still difficult to explain why the well lay outside the walls.

When the city was rebuilt after Sheshonq destroyed it, the outside gate was abandoned, but its two pillars were reinforced. During this period the original wall was also reinforced with casemates (two parallel walls whose chambers could be filled in case of danger). Once past the gate there was an open space from which the the streets branched off. A ring street passed between two houses and led to a group of 9th-8th century four-room houses (now reconstructed) in the western quarter. On the side opposite the gate there were three storehouses much like those found at Hazor and Megiddo. In front of these, but on a higher level, one can recognize the paved entranceway of the Roman fort (2nd-3rd century AD). Most of the local archaeological finds are kept in the Negev Museum in Beer Sheba. The homogeneous quality of most ancient earthenware and copper and ivory objects found in the area has led archaeologists to distinguish a local Beer Sheba culture.

170 top left Considering the number of houses found, archaeologists think that Tel es-Sheba had a population of 400.

170 top right The site of biblical Beer Sheba was inhabited from the Chalcolithic era to the 9th century AD.

170 bottom left The western sector of the tell had private houses built against the wall.

170 bottom right The outer ring of buildings followed the contour of the top of the tell.

God's promise and Jacob had a vision that encouraged him to take his family to Egypt. According to the Bible, the city was then made part of the territory of Simeon, and then passed under the dominion of Judah.

Given its role as a frontier settlement, Beer Sheba was exposed to continuous attacks on the part of the Philistines and Amalekites, until David secured Israelite control over the region. However, the city was destroyed by the Egyptian pharaoh Sheshonq in 925 BC, and it took three centuries for it to regain its former vitality and prosperity. Dating from the 9th and 8th centuries BC is the horned altar kept in the Israel Museum, Jerusalem, which consists of cut stones and therefore does not comply with biblical law, which states that an altar must be "of whole stones, over which no man hath lift up any iron." At the end of the

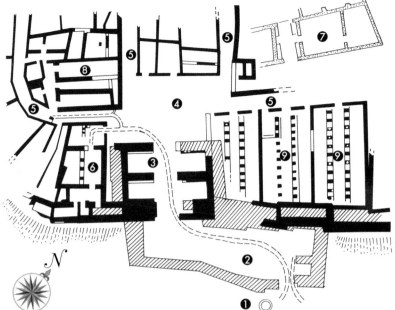

171 center right The exceptionally large Canaanite city lay at the foot of the tell, seen here in the background, on which the Israelite citadel was built in the 10th century BC.

171 bottom right The subsoil around the Dead Sea covers an extensive aquifer: a deep 10th-century BC Israelite well made this 'natural reservoir' available to Arad.

ARAD, THE ISRAELITE CITY DEFENDING THE SOUTH

In the Arad area on the southern slopes of the hills flanking the Dead Sea to the west, the very ancient and the modern face each other a short distance from one another. The Israeli city, the vanguard of town planning and efficiency both from an industrial and recreational-touristic standpoint, is less than six miles from the seventeen layers of ancient settlements that in five millennia have risen up over one another on the *tell* that dominates the farmland west of the modern city. The most ancient layer dates back to the Canaanites, pioneer shepherds, farmers and merchants who at the dawn of the Bronze Age settled in the lower part of the hill, where the impermeable nature of the rock allowed them to collect water running down the slopes. The discovery of Egyptian jars dating as far back as the First Dynasty shows the remarkable commercial expansion of Egypt, as well as the importance of Arad, which during the Canaanite period covered a surface area of 958,000 square feet that was protected by walls 3,937 feet long reinforced by semicircular towers. The three successive Canaanite settlements were followed by the Israelite conquest of the prosperous *tell* in the 10th century, which was again fortified but was smaller than the previous city.

From the 9th to the 6th century BC the Israelites used a well 69 feet deep that penetrated the aquifer; from here the water was transported to the acropolis and poured into a cistern. The city was laid out with the civic buildings in the center and the private dwellings in the periphery. The main public building found by archaeologists was a double temple, much like the one discovered at Megiddo, consisting of two rectangular halls with entrances to the east. Next to this complex was a large edifice, perhaps a palace. The dwellings had a common layout: a living room area with a bench running along the four walls, a kitchen-storeroom, and a courtyard the pavement of which was higher than the living room. The buildings had no windows and the doors opened towards the left, as can be seen by the position of the stone socket in the jamb. The roof was supported by a central wooden pole that lay on a stone base.

Most of the archaeological finds from Arad date from the Israelite period and are kept in the local museum. Over and above the abundance of finds, archaeologists also made a singular discovery in the citadel: the remains of a 10th-century BC sanctuary, used up to the 7th century, which is similar in many respects to the Temple in Jerusalem. In fact, it was the only temple contemporaneous with Solomon's Temple that had an outer courtyard followed by a hall that gave access to the Holy of Holies, where the Ark of the Covenant was kept.

The Romans used Arad as an outpost at the edge of the desert, then the city was conquered by the Nabataeans and became a caravanserai. During the Byzantine age Arad was fortified with a massive wall but was not able to withstand the Omayyad invasion, which marked the beginning of the city's decline into oblivion.

MAMSHIT, THE NABATAEAN CITY

Mamshit, the Semitic name of the
Greek placename *Mampsis* which appears on
the Map of Madaba mosaic, was founded by
the Nabataeans in the Negev desert, about
thirty miles southwest of Masada and the
Dead Sea, along a caravan route that
connected Arabia Petraea with southern
Palestine and the Mediterranean.

The discovery of coins that were minted
there during the reign of the Nabataean
ruler Aretas IV, sets the date of the city's
foundation between the end of the first
century BC and the beginning of the
Christian era. However, there may have
been a more ancient settlement there that
left no remains because it consisted of
tents, the traditional shelter of the
Nabataean nomad-merchants.

The traces of the original town consist
of the ruins of a building on the highest

point, which was probably a fortress, and of
a defensive tower. Other constructions
dating from the same period are the
Nabataean burial precinct about half a mile
north of the above ruins, which is one of the
three cemeteries on the site, and a cistern.
Toward the end of the Nabataean period, at
the end of the 1st century AD, the town
plan was changed: the new North-South
orientation of the main street separated the
residential area to the west from the zone
occupied by public buildings. The eastern
sector of the site includes three especially
important complexes. In the vicinity of the
northeastern part of the Roman walls and
partly below them, is a late Nabataean bath-
house that was also used during the Roman
and Byzantine periods; this is flanked by a
pool, which was built at the same time, or a
short time later. Proceeding southward, one
arrives at the ruins of the most important
late-Nabataean edifice in Mamshit, a vast
complex with a perimeter of 131 feet per
side, which included rooms with different

*172 top Nothing
remains of the most
ancient settlement,
which consisted of
tents that the
Nabataeans replaced
with imposing
buildings after
abandoning their
nomadic lifestyle.*

*172-173 Mamshit
has another, curious
name: 'Kurnub,' the
Arabic name for a dish
of milk and dates.*

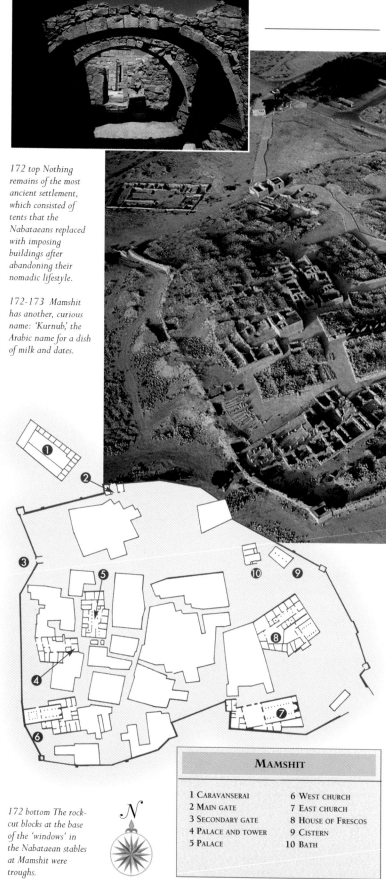

*172 bottom The rock-
cut blocks at the base
of the 'windows' in
the Nabataean stables
at Mamshit are
troughs.*

MAMSHIT	
1 CARAVANSERAI	6 WEST CHURCH
2 MAIN GATE	7 EAST CHURCH
3 SECONDARY GATE	8 HOUSE OF FRESCOS
4 PALACE AND TOWER	9 CISTERN
5 PALACE	10 BATH

winged beings and the mythological story of Leda and the swan.

The southeast corner of the site has the ruins of the so-called 'East Church,' or 'cathedral,' a Byzantine construction with a nave and two lateral aisles which still has a mosaic pavement with floral motifs and a baptistery. On the opposite, southwest side of Mamshit are the remains of the contemporaneous West Church, whose mosaic pavement is considered the most beautiful in the Negev region. Here the rendering is naturalistic—with birds, baskets of fruit, and wine amphorae—as well as geometric, with swastikas and other motifs. There is also a medallion bearing the name of the founder of the church, a certain Nilus.

173 top right The angular lines of late-Nabataean architecture date from the period when the kingdom became part of the Province of Arabia in 106 AD.

173 bottom left North of the baldachin over the baptistery of the East Church was a door used by the newly baptized to enter the basilica.

173 bottom right The white marble columns in the West Church contrast with the color of the sandstone, so typical of the Negev.

functions arranged around an asymmetrical central court. This edifice also had an area used to shelter livestock, which is recognizable because of the stone troughs at the base of the arched windows along the dividing wall, as well as a residential area that was originally two storys high. This latter section was lavishly decorated. There are mosaics on the floors of the first story rooms and some beautiful frescos on the walls of a room on the ground floor have been preserved; the most interesting panels depict Eros and Psyche in the guise of

SHIVTA, THE CITY OF PEACE

174-175 *Shivta, ancient Sobata, reached its maximum magnitude in the Byzantine period, when it became* Christian and a pilgrimage site. Yet it remained a basically Nabataean city even after the annexation of the kingdom.

Like Mamshit, Nessana and Avdat, Shivta was founded by the Nabataeans in the Negev desert and flourished in the 1st century AD, when these ingenious trader-caravaneers began to settle down to devote their energy to agriculture and livestock raising. Ancient Sobata ('Subeita' in Arabic), situated about 30 miles west-southwest of Mamshit, was founded either during the reign of Obodas II (30-9 BC) or at the beginning of Aretas IV's reign (9-40 AD) in an area more suited for agriculture than the territory around Mamshit, and because of this the population doubled in the space of a few decades, with perhaps 3,000 inhabitants. The Nabataeans were quite skillful in collecting and channelling the little water available in these desert areas, and built a

large reservoir north of the city that was fed by rainfall and the seasonal flooding of a nearby *wadi*.

Nothing is known of the early history of Shivta, but it seems that the city benfitted from the *Pax Romana*: unlike Nessana, Avdat and Mamshit, which were fortified and, in the case of Mamshit, had walls during Diocletian's rule (late 3rd century AD), it seems that the town plan of Shivta underwent no substantial changes. This prosperous and peaceful city maintained its 'civil' character even during the Byzantine age, when it became a major monastic center and attraction for Christian pilgrims. The period between the 4th and 6th centuries witnessed the construction of the three local churches, which were distinguished by their location in the

city. Just east of the large cistern in the middle of town is the South Church, with an almost square plan, two side aisles and three apses. The plaster on these latter still have sacred wall paintings, among which one can recognize a depiction of the Transfiguration of Christ. The area north of this edifice contains a cruciform

baptistery hewn out of a large monolith that was probably used to baptize adults, and a more accessible baptismal font for children.

Northward is the small Central Church, which was built in the 6th-7th century and is on one of the main streets in Shivta. This too has three apses, a rare feature indeed in the religious

174 left
A semicircular apse in the North Church (left) housed the massive cruciform baptistery.

174 below left Two simple Byzantine crosses flank the more complex 'Jerusalem cross.'

174 bottom right Peace-loving Shivta was respected by the Muslims and was destroyed only by time.

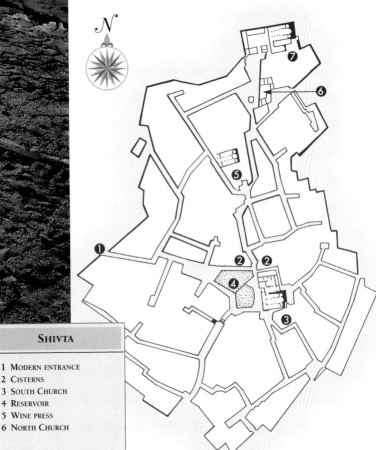

SHIVTA

1 MODERN ENTRANCE
2 CISTERNS
3 SOUTH CHURCH
4 RESERVOIR
5 WINE PRESS
6 NORTH CHURCH

architecture of the Negev. At the northern end of the site is the North Church, the home of a pillar saint upon whose death the church became a pilgrimage site. It was founded in the 4th century, probably with only one apse, to which two lateral ones were added in the 6th century. This church is really the center of a complex that comprises a baptistery, a mortuary chapel and a monastery annex consisting of dozens of rooms arranged around several inner courtyards. Unlike the other Nabataean cities in the Negev region, Shivta did not decline under the Omayyad conquerors. Quite the contrary, the mosque next to the South Church was built so as not to damage the baptistery, eloquent testimony of the peaceful co-existence that lasted for at least two centuries.

175 top The base of the column used by a stylite stood in a square in the middle of the atrium of the South Church.

175 bottom The Central Church is the smallest and most recent of the three in Shivta.

AVDAT, THE DESERT ACROPOLIS

Avdat, ancient Oboda, rose up in the 4th-3rd century BC from a camp that the Nabataeans had set up a few miles south of Shivta, in the Negev desert. There are no architectural remains of the original settlement, but we know for certain that it defended an important stopping point along the caravan route that linked Petra with Eilat and Gaza. At the end of the first century BC the military function of Avdat was complemented by ceramics production in a vast industrial complex east of the rise, and by sheep and dromedary raising, which

flourished thanks to the development of agriculture, which made giant strides thanks to the Natabaeans' extraordinary irrigation techniques. However, in 106 AD the city was destroyed by emperor Hadrian, who made the Nabataean kingdom part of the Province of Arabia. Avdat was rebuilt in the 3rd century and once again flourished during Byzantine rule with the cultivation of grapes and wine production. In the 7th century, the Omayyad invasion coincided with the decline of the city, which was abandoned in the 10th century. It was then covered by sand, which is the reason it is in such a fine state of preservation.

Most of the ruins of Avdat date back

176 left This pair of crudely sculpted facing lions is part of the Byzantine decoration.

is attested to by the numerous enclosures on the slopes of the hill and in the surrounding area. The robust dromedaries were used not only for commercial purposes, but for military ones as well: northeast of the site are traces of the camp for the Nabataean 'camel troops,' a 328 square foot area. Toward the end of the 1st century AD the economy of Avdat

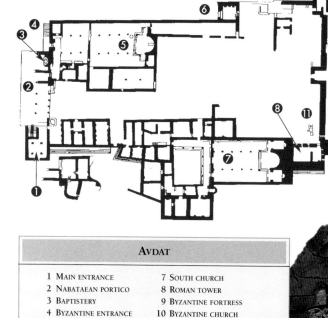

AVDAT	
1 MAIN ENTRANCE	7 SOUTH CHURCH
2 NABATAEAN PORTICO	8 ROMAN TOWER
3 BAPTISTERY	9 BYZANTINE FORTRESS
4 BYZANTINE ENTRANCE	10 BYZANTINE CHURCH
5 NORTH CHURCH	11 CISTERN
6 NABATAEAN EXIT	

to the Byzantine period. The Nabataean ruins consist only of the temple founded during the reign of Obodas (30-9 BC) at the southwestern end of the acropolis. The remains of the latter comprise part of the colonnade and two gates giving access to the upper city: the main gate, situated in the southern corner of the precinct, consisting of a large courtyard with the plinths of four pillars, and the northern access gate, which is a square tower made of large blocks of stone whose ceiling was supported by three arches.

During the Byzantine epoch the acropolis housed two basilicas which for the most part were built at the expense of the Nabataean edifices. The north church was built in the early 4th century and lies north of the Nabataean temple. It still has its apse, the bishop's cathedra, and the remains of a cruciform baptistery built over the ruins of the temple. An epigraph on the site identifies the south church, east of the first basilica, as the Martyrion of St. Theodore, the interior of which consists of a nave with two aisles ending in a semicircular apse flanked by two square rooms that housed the relics of the martyrs.

Just east of the acropolis, in the vicinity of the parking lot, are the remains of the Byzantine-age bath-house. Probably used up to the Arab period and quite well preserved, these baths were modeled after the traditional Roman *thermae*. A short distance south of the site are some rock-cut loculi, perhaps of Nabataean origin, that were used up to the mid 3rd century AD.

EN AVDAT, THE ANIMAL OASIS

A few miles north of Avdat, the harsh desert terrain unexpectedly becomes soft in one of the most beautiful localities in the Negev region. However, at En Avdat–literally, 'the spring of Avdat'–the main attraction is not the work of man: hidden at the bottom of a complex and extremely fascinating network of craggy gorges,that create an incredibly beautiful setting, is a natural pool fed by the crystal-clear and surprisingly cool (even in the torrid summer) water of an underground spring. The enchanting geological and hydrological nature in this site is enhanced by its absolutely unique flora and fauna which are protected from the scorching desert heat by the awesome walls of the gorges. At En Avdat the luxuriant tropical vegetation is an ideal environment for animals which could not live outside an oasis like this. The rocks are inhabited by ibexes, gazelles and badgers, as well as a large number of different species of birds.

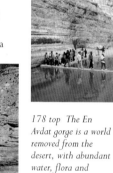

178 top The En Avdat gorge is a world removed from the desert, with abundant water, flora and fauna.

178 top right The water here is a welcome relief in the torrid Negev region, but it is also deep, so it is advisable not to venture into the gorge alone.

TIMNA AND THE MOST ANCIENT MINES IN THE WORLD

A legend for centuries that became a myth in literature, King Solomon's Mines are in fact real. They were brought to light in 1951 in the locality of Timna, at the end of the barren Arava Valley toward the Gulf of Aqaba. This is an erosional amphitheater of about 23 square miles surrounded by hills that on an average are 984 feet high and were known since the 3rd millennium BC for their rich copper deposits, which means that Timna is the oldest mining complex in the world. As far back as the 15th century BC the 18th dynasty Egyptian pharaohs made these mines one of their sources of wealth by building a network of tunnels and shafts as well as providing all the necessary mining structures and equipment needed to extract the metal, including smelting furnaces, an air vent system, lodgings for the miners and even temples. Lastly, they built walls around the area so that the copper could not be taken out and laborers could not escape.

With time, the Egyptians had the metal extracted by the local populations, the Midianites and Amalekites, who continued to exploit the mines when the pharaohs abandoned the region at the beginning of the 11th century, after the Ramessid age and at the end of the New Kingdom. A century later the mines earned the legendary name related to King Solomon, since much of the wealth and opulence that characterized his reign originated in Timna. The mines were again exploited by the Romans in the 2nd century AD and were then abandoned for centuries until they were reopened and studied by the Israelis in 1951. The location of the mines was known already in the late 19th century, but it was only in the 1930s that the mining activity was dated precisely at King Solomon's time (10th century BC).

Today, the area around Timna is a national park rich in archaeological and

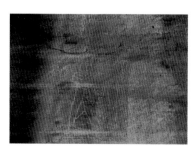

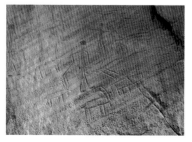

natural attractions. In the middle of this reserve are 'Solomon's Pillars,' majestic rock formations about 164 feet high created by a violent earthquake that raised the land in prehistoric times and then modeled it by wind and water erosion. Close by is a small temple dedicated to the Egyptian goddess Hathor, the 'mistress of turquoise' and protectress of the mines. This was built during the reign of Sethos I (1318-1304 BC) and was used until 1150 BC. It consisted of a courtyard (29.5 x 19.5 feet) facing the *adytum*, the rock-cut niche that housed the statue of the goddess. The temple was damaged by a quake and rebuilt under Ramses II (1304-1237 BC): the courtyard, where a casting furnace for making votive statues was found, was enlarged (32 x 29.5 feet); a new white stone pavement was added; and the façade was beautified with white stone from the mines. The temple was later used by the Midianites, who added a bench for offerings in the entrance and a chamber, perhaps for the priest, outside the east wall. They also removed the heads of Hathor that had decorated the two

pillars flanking the naos.

Along the walls of the temple enclosure archaeologists found some wool, which proves that the Midianites had changed the temple into a desert tent sanctuary. Among the finds from this period are votive gifts and a copper statuette in the shape of a serpent with a gilded head that is similar to the head of the brass serpent described in the Bible. Finds from the Midianite period have demonstrated that this was a sophisticated civilization, and they are also extremely important in illustrating the biblical account of the meeting between Moses and Jethro, the Midianite priest. A stairway goes from the temple to a viewpoint where, with the help of a spyglass, you can see a hieroglyphic inscription illustrating a sacrifice to Hathor officiated by Ramses III. This is one of the many inscriptions that decorated this site during the Egyptian period, most of which were later defaced.

178-179 The spectacular products of a prehistoric earthquake, 'Solomon's Pillars' dominate the most ancient mines in the world.

178 bottom left The pharaoh making offerings and the goddess—the owner and patron of the mines—are carved on 'Solomon's Pillars.'

178 bottom right The memory of the ancient inhabitants of Timna— shepherds and the world's first miners—emerges from the terrain.

179 center The friendly countenance of Hathor on the temple of the mining facilities protected the ancient Egyptians.

180-181 Natural bastions and man-made walls—more suitable for a fort than a holy site—have made the monastery an oasis of peace since the 6th century AD.

180 bottom left The monastery lies in a narrow valley that to the west opens out into the 'camp plain,' where the Israelites set up camp when Moses ascended Mount Sinai.

180 bottom right The tower on the northeast corner of the wall and the fortification west of it were built in 1800 at the behest of one of Napoleon's generals, Jean Baptiste Kléber.

ST. CATHERINE'S MONASTERY, STRONGHOLD OF FAITH

The earliest documentation regarding this monastery on the floor of a valley north of Jebel Musa–'Moses' mountain,' better known as Mount Sinai (7,500 feet)–dates from the 9th century and was written by Eustychios, the patriarch of Alexandria. The monastery was named after another Alexandrian, Dorothea (later made a saint with the name of Catherine), an extraordinarily cultured girl of noble extraction who was decapitated in the 4th century for opposing Maxentius's persecution of the Christians and who, according to legend, was placed on the top of Mount Sinai by angels. The patriarch relates that in 327 Queen Helena, who had identified the rugged valley as the place where Moses spoke with the Burning Bush before receiving the tablets of the Ten Commandments, decided to build a church there and dedicate it to the Virgin Mary. The edifice soon received generous ecclesiastic donations, and was raided so often by the Bedouin that three years later the hermits who had settled in this harsh land persuaded the emperor Justinian to fortify the original church with red granite walls, part of which are still intact. Protected by the express will of the prophet Mohammed himself–written in a document a copy of which is still on display–and by the isolation of the site, the monastery was untouched by the Arab invasion of 640, the iconoclastic fury of Leo III, who in 726 ordered the destruction of all sacred images, and the bloody conflicts caused by the Crusades, becoming the only Christian cenobitic community

181 Immediately northwest of the monastery, the harsh Sinai terrain becomes soft thanks to the monks' centuries-old terraced gardens.

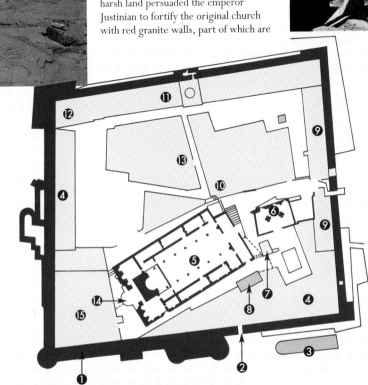

PLAN OF THE MONASTERY

1 Justinian's wall
2 Present-day entrance
3 Underground cistern
4 Monks' living quarters
5 Basilica
6 Mosque
7 Minaret
8 Moses' Fountain
9 Guest rooms
10 Archive
11 Library
12 Icon museum
13 Chapel of St. Anthony
14 Chapel of the Burning Bush
15 Service buildings

N

administered uninterruptedly from the 6th century to the present. And it is precisely this combination of favorable conditions that saved the monastery's invaluable treasures, from the hundreds of religious and philosophical manuscripts in Arabic, Greek, Syrian, Georgian, Coptic, Old Slavic and Armenian that are kept in the library (not open to the public) to the precious icons on display in the adjoining museum and in the basilica, the most beautiful of which are encaustic (i.e. executed with hot wax colors).

An oasis of peace that is rare in such turbulent centuries, St. Catherine's Monastery became even more distinctive in 1527 when Constantinople recognized the autonomy of the monastic complex, which since that time has been the smallest Greek Orthodox diocese in the world. Today the monastery counts about forty monks–including those who work in other places, especially in Syria and Egypt–who are flanked by a certain number of laymen involved in the maintenance of the community, such as the Bedouin who for centuries have defended the site, and the fishermen of el-Tur on the distant shores of the Red Sea.

The Justinian enclosure (roughly 279 x 250 feet), which is decorated with the Maltese crosses that were carved during the construction of the complex, is now accessible via a 19th-century entranceway

with three iron gates. But for centuries, when the original entrance was bricked up for security reasons, access to the monastery was gained by means of a pulley in the bartizan on the northern side of the wall, about 32 feet above the ground, next to the massive double 'Klébler' tower. Along the inner side of the enclosure wall are the different living quarters: the reception rooms along the northeastern side are followed by the guest rooms to the northwest, and the library in the southern corner of the walls, which in turn is flanked to the southeast by the monks' dormitories, the refectory and the treasurer's office.

The areas and buildings inside the walls remind one of a medieval village, with their series of small courtyards, stairways, balconies, vaulted passageways and narrow corridors that go to make up a fascinating mixture of different styles

182 top In the heart of the monastery the 19th-century bell-tower, a gift from Czar Alexander II, and the minaret on the medieval mosque symbolize peaceful coexistence.

182 bottom The Scotsman David Roberts, a fine artist and brave explorer, visited St. Catherine's Monastery in 1839 and executed some splendid views: the one reproduced here depicts the abbot, the archbishop of Sinai, the only one dressed in black.

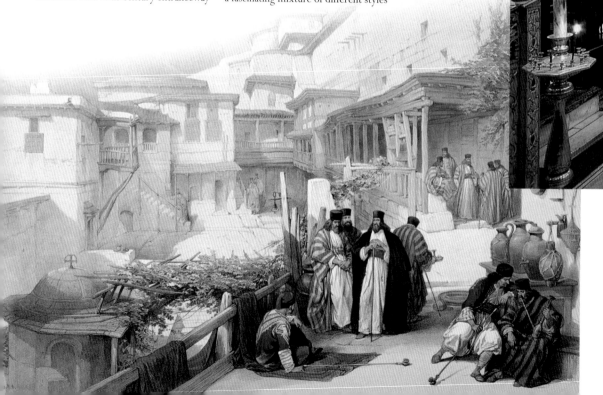

183 top right Peter is half-asleep at his Master's feet, surrounded by the prophets and saints in this mosaic in the Basilica of the Transfiguration.

183 bottom The Chapel of the Burning Bush altar is the holiest place in the monastery; one must go there barefoot, as Moses did before God.

182-183 Rebuilt only thanks to the donations made over the centuries, the interior of the Basilica of the Transfiguration has remained virtually intact since Justinian's time.

183 top left The Chapel of the Skulls (or of St. Triphonius) lies among the kitchen gardens northwest of the wall. It houses the skulls of the monks who lived here through the centuries. The most ancient one belongs to a 6th-century hermit.

and proportions. In this regard, it is quite surprising to find a mosque here. It was built in the 12th century immediately west of the basilica in homage to the protection Muslims have always afforded the monastery and is still used by the worshippers of Islam who work in the monastery, helping the Greek Orthodox monks with the maintenance.

Various wells provide water for the monastic community; the most important of these, Bir Musa, or 'Moses' well,' is situated just to the right of the entrance. Another well faces the guest quarters, and an underground cistern lies just outside the northern corner of the wall.

The heart of the monastery, opposite Moses' well, is the Basilica of the Transfiguration, one of the most ancient that is still virtually intact. Once past the four wooden wings of the portal, a magnificent 6th-century Byzantine work, the nave is separated from the two aisles by twelve monolithic granite columns, each having a capital with a different shape. Halfway down the nave, to the left, is the tall marble pulpit (1787), which faces the cathedra and a representation of the monastery in the 18th century. Behind the wooden panels of iconostasis and the crucifix that crowns it—17th-century works by Jeremiah of Crete depicting Christ, the Virgin Mary, St. Catherine and St. John the Baptist—is the choir, which houses the marble sarcophagus and two silver reliquaries with the mortal remains of the martyr Catherine, which were taken to the monastery from the site of the mystic

185 center The portraits generically called 'icons' are of Byzantine origin and date from the foundation of the monastery.

185 bottom left The fiery gold and red hues of the robe illuminate St. Paul's somber face.

185 bottom right The title page of an 11th-century Greek manuscript. Hundreds of works found accidentally by monks in the monastery in 1975 were added to the thousands of invaluable manuscripts and books already kept in the library.

184 bottom The Virgin Mary and the Holy Child are the most frequently represented motifs in the icons, the most typical manifestation of Eastern Christian art.

185 top Bright panels painted with lines of persons around the figure of Christ decorate each column in the Basilica of the Transfiguration.

184-185 A monk shows one of the precious codices kept in the monastery library. The Codex Sinaiticus, once here, is now in the British Museum, London.

deposition in the 9th century mentioned above.

At the end of the nave is the high altar, dominated by the stupendous, refulgent mosaic (565 AD) in the conch of the apse, in which the transfigured Christ is surrounded by the figures of the prophet Elijah, Moses and the apostles John, James and the sleeping Peter. Behind the apse, on a lower level, is the Chapel of the Burning Bush, the oldest part of the monastery and also the holiest, because it lies over the exact spot where the biblical episode took place. The chapel is lined with white and blue damescening and precious rugs; the altar lies on the roots of the only specimen of this species of bramble in the Sinai.

MOUNT SINAI, THE MOUNTAIN OF THE LAW

Because of the uncertainty regarding the route followed by the Israelites from Egypt to Canaan and the fact that the Scriptures indicate two names for the site where Moses received the Ten Commandments–Mount Sinai, or 'Mountain of the Lord,' and Mount Horeb–it is impossible to establish where the biblical Sinai really is. However, the most deep-rooted tradition, which is

186 left The view from the top of Mount Sinai (7,500 feet) more than compensates for the long hike: it takes in the peaks of Sinai from Suez to Aqaba. Below is the Chapel of Elijah.

186 top right Only the faithful who had been absolved of their sins could continue past the Gate of the Confessions to the top of Moses' mountain, Sinai.

corroborated by Jews, Christians and Muslims alike, has no doubts about it: Mount Sinai is Jebel Musa, which stands 7,500 feet above St. Catherine Monastery, while Horeb is the name of the massif crowned by the Sinai peak.

The climb to the top of Mount Sinai is by no means easy and takes two to three hours, because the path is quite exposed and some of it is steep. One can follow the path that starts off east of the monastery walls, or take the hundreds of steps on the spectacular Moses' Stairway. The latter, which was reputedly hewn by only one monk, leads to the Gate of the Confessions, an arch under which pilgrims came to confess to one of the monks at the St. Catherine Monastery before going to the top of the mountain barefoot, exactly like Moses.

After passing through the arch, there is a col whose rugged terrain is relieved somewhat by the presence of cypress trees. Here, with the peak in view, a rock covered with inscriptions commemorates an ancient Muslim pilgrimage, and a small construction, the Chapel of Elijah, affords access to the cave where the prophet supposedly took refuge to escape from his idolatrous persecutors. This viewpoint has a panorama that takes in the 8,649 feet of the nearby Jebel Katherina, to the east, which towers over the stretch of Sinai mountains and wadis as well as the monastery and the el-Rahah plain below. A short hike leads to the porphyry and red granite summit, which is occupied by a small building dating back to 363, and by an equally small mosque that indicates the place where the prophet Nabi Saleh ascended to heaven.

186 bottom right Already in the 4th century there was a chapel on the summit of Jebel Musa. It was isolated until the Muslims also made it a holy site and built a mosque opposite the Byzantine edifice, which has been replaced by a 20th-century chapel.

187 Often those who hike up the mountain choose to spend the night there to admire the view at dawn, when the scorched earth of the Sinai peninsula seems to glow from within.

FROM PETRA TO PELLA, AN ARCHAEOLOGICAL TOUR OF JORDAN

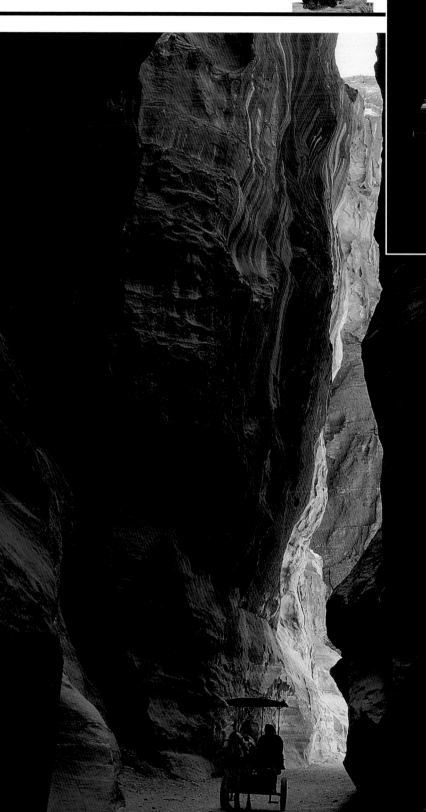

188 top right The Siq—the main accessway to Petra— is a deep gorge created by an earthquake and then made smooth by the raging waters of the Wadi Musa.

188 Upon entering Petra from the Siq, the unexpected sight of the Khazna is an unforgettable moment: the façade of this mortuary temple is 131 feet high.

189 top left The function of the Djinn Blocks is still uncertain, but they were probably tombs.

189 bottom right Although the Tomb of the Obelisks and the Bab el-Siq Triclinium underneath seem to be a single edifice, the two monuments really date from different periods.

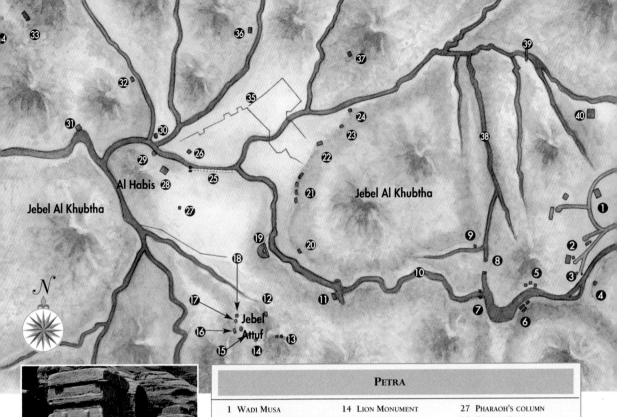

PETRA,
THE ROCK-CUT CITY

Petra is one of the most extraordinary ancient monumental complexes in the world, both because of its unique edifices, which were cut out of the rock, and for its enthralling position among steep, multicolored sandstone cliffs. Located in southern Jordan, this unique site is often mentioned in the Bible as 'Sela,' which means 'rock' in Hebrew, while it is called Wadi Musa (Valley of Moses) by the Arabs. The indigenous name of the city was Reqem, and Petra is nothing but the Greek translation of the biblical placename. Although the most ancient known settlement dates back to the Iron Age, the importance of the site is connected to the Nabataean occupation, which took place in the second half of the 4th century BC but most probably began long before that by means of a long process of penetration in the region.

190 top left and center The delicate decoration on the façade of the Khazna is eloquent proof of the high level of workmanship achieved by the Nabataean craftsmen.

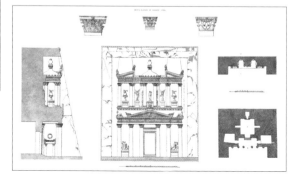

190 bottom right This accurate relief map of the Khazna is the work of Léon de Laborde, a French artist and traveller who visited Petra in 1828. It was he who executed the first illustrations of the Nabataean city. This drawing is from Voyage de l'Arabie Pétrée, published in Paris in 1830.

191 Sublime, spectacular, and well preserved, the Khazna is the symbol of Petra. Scholars think it was a king's tomb.

190 bottom left The interior of the Khazna consists of a large cubic hall forty feet square.

190-191 The Khazna faces an expanse of alluvium. Recent surveys have shown that the ancient pavement in this area lies about 12 feet below the ground: the Khazna was therefore accessible via a stairway.

In the 3rd century BC Petra developed into a true rock-cut city at the junction of three canyons, becoming in a short span of time the center for the assembly and defense of the neighboring tribes. The decision to make it their capital was dictated by its position: hidden among the mountains, with few accessways that were easily guarded and controlled, Petra was an ideal shelter that ensured safety. Its proximity to the Red Sea allowed for rapid and fruitful communication with Arabia and Mesopotamia, while the caravan route through the Negev desert toward Gaza guaranteed an outlet in the Mediterranean and access to the busy Syrian ports. The city's constant relations with the major trade movements and its ever growing prosperity brought about a high degree of Hellenization, which can be seen above all in the many monuments the Nabataean rulers had cut out of the faces of the cliffs from the

Nomads from the Arabian peninsula, the Nabataeans were sheep-farmers: tough, determined and ingenious, they survived in the desert because of the cisterns they cut out of the rock, where the rare rainwater remained during the driest months. They owed their prosperity to their control of the caravan routes between Arabia and the Mediterranean, and between Egypt and Mesopotamia, which they maintained even after they had occupied Petra.

Having taken refuge on one of the rocky spurs in the area, the Nabataeans succeeded in resisting the attempted conquest of Antigonus I (312 BC), one of the successors of Alexander the Great, thus establishing their independence and giving rise to a period of great splendor.

1st century BC to the 1st century AD.

In this veritable golden age, the Nabataean kingdom expanded to Hegra, in the Saudi Arabian desert, to the cities in the Negev region (modern-day Avdat, Mamshit and Shivta, in Israel) and as far as Damascus. In the meantime, the urban population was most probably 30,000-40,000, most of which was engaged in commerce. In 64 BC, Rome began its conquest of Palestine and Syria; in a short time the Hellenistic cities east of the Jordan River (Amman, Gerasa, Pella, Gadara, etc.) fell under Roman

Empire was chosen as the capital of the province of *Palaestina Taertia*.

After the Arab conquest of the region and some disastrous earthquakes, Petra declined definitively, even though the Crusaders fortified and defended it for a brief period. After the 13th century the city was totally abandoned and the Western world completely forgot it until 1812, when it was rediscovered by the Swiss traveller and Orientalist Johann Ludwig Burckhardt. From that moment on, the fame of the Pink City grew by leaps and

dominion and became part of the *Decapolis*, a confederacy of ten cities. Formally, the Nabataean kingdom remained independent until 106 AD, when Trajan annexed it to the Province of Arabia.

The Roman occupation hindered the development of Petra, but it did not stop it, so that the city went through another long period of prosperity partly thanks to the road that Trajan had built from Aqaba to Damascus to favour trade. However, the growing importance of other caravan cities, especially Gerasa and Palmyra, and the creation of the new capital at Bosra in the 3rd century AD, led to the decline of Petra.

For a few centuries the rock-cut city stubbornly continued to be a major metropolis, became a diocese, and after Diocletian's reorganization of the Roman

192 top The theater
pulpitum, the low
wall of the
proscenium, is
decorated with a series
of niches.

192 center Léon de
Laborde's rendering of
the enormous cavea
in the theater,
entirely cut out of the
side of the mountain.

192 bottom This
majestic tomb near the
theater affords a
magnificent example
of a 'double cornice'
façade.

192-193 The cavea
of the theater still
boasts exceptional
acoustics. Built during
the reign of King
Aretas IV (9-40 AD),
the theater was
enlarged by the
Romans.

193 top The façade
of the Tomb of
Uneishu also belongs
to the 'double cornice'
category. The
sepulchre was named
after Queen
Shaquilat's devoted
minister, who was
buried there around
70 or 76 AD.

193 bottom In the
area around the
theater, along the
walls of the Siq one
can see many large
rock-cut structures,
some of which were
probably used as
houses.

bounds and the capital of the Nabataean
kingdom is now one of the most famous and
popular archaeological sites in the world.

All this fame, however, is nothing new,
because already in antiquity Petra had
aroused astonishment and great admiration
for its highly unusual appearance. The place
where the city rose up and prospered is
shaped like an amphitheater enclosed by
tall, steep cliffs and is a little over half a
mile long from east to west and half that
length from north to south. The usually dry
bed of a torrent, the Wadi Musa, crosses
the spacious valley where the true

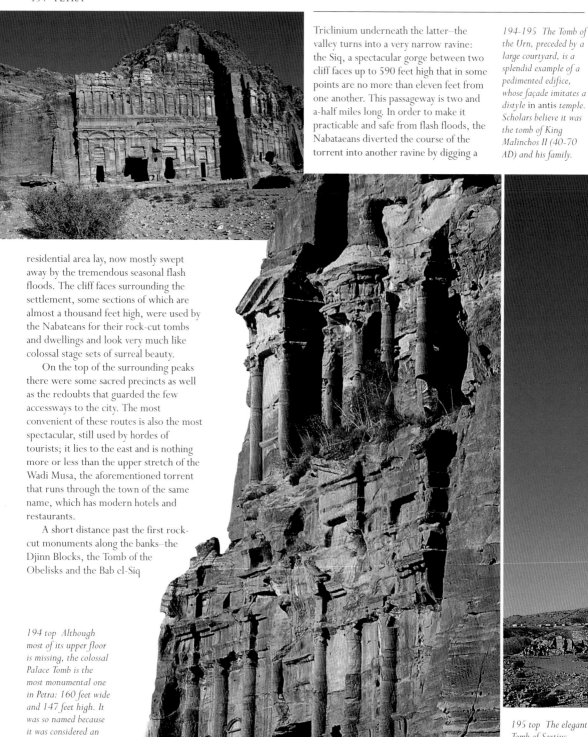

Triclinium underneath the latter—the valley turns into a very narrow ravine: the Siq, a spectacular gorge between two cliff faces up to 590 feet high that in some points are no more than eleven feet from one another. This passageway is two and a-half miles long. In order to make it practicable and safe from flash floods, the Nabataeans diverted the course of the torrent into another ravine by digging a

194-195 The Tomb of the Urn, preceded by a large courtyard, is a splendid example of a pedimented edifice, whose façade imitates a distyle in antis temple. Scholars believe it was the tomb of King Malinchos II (40-70 AD) and his family.

residential area lay, now mostly swept away by the tremendous seasonal flash floods. The cliff faces surrounding the settlement, some sections of which are almost a thousand feet high, were used by the Nabateans for their rock-cut tombs and dwellings and look very much like colossal stage sets of surreal beauty.

On the top of the surrounding peaks there were some sacred precincts as well as the redoubts that guarded the few accessways to the city. The most convenient of these routes is also the most spectacular, still used by hordes of tourists; it lies to the east and is nothing more or less than the upper stretch of the Wadi Musa, the aforementioned torrent that runs through the town of the same name, which has modern hotels and restaurants.

A short distance past the first rock-cut monuments along the banks—the Djinn Blocks, the Tomb of the Obelisks and the Bab el-Siq

194 top Although most of its upper floor is missing, the colossal Palace Tomb is the most monumental one in Petra: 160 feet wide and 147 feet high. It was so named because it was considered an imitation of the façade of a Hellenistic palace.

194 bottom The Corinthian Tomb, similar to the Khazna but not so well preserved, owes its name to the style of the capitals.

195 top The elegant Tomb of Sextius Florentinus, propraetor of the Province of Arabia in 126-129, reveals the persistence of the Hellenistic architectural style even after the Roman conquest.

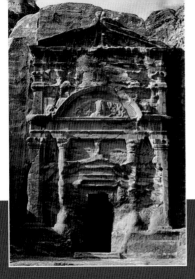

tunnel that is 282 feet long and still serves this purpose. Two aqueducts used for the city water supply ran along both cliff faces; they were made of terracotta pipes placed in the deep crevices hewn out of the rock, which can be seen for the entire length of the Siq.

This gorge, with its mysterious, disturbing fascination, is always in the half-light: everywhere, the multicolored rock appears to have been sculpted by continuous erosion. In various points the slit of the Siq opens out and forms caves and areas that were once used exclusively as *caravanserai* and camps for the arriving caravans. About halfway along the Siq, at a spot where it abruptly changes direction, is the towering el-Khazna, a mortuary temple hewn out of the mountain that has no equal in the entire world.

195 bottom left The interior of the Tomb of the Urn consists of an enormous hall 62 x 55 feet.

195 bottom right The Tomb of Silk is famous for its striking multicolored façade.

196 top The interior of the Temple of the Winged Lions, dating from the first half of the 1st century BC, is characterized by a multitude of columns.

196-197 This panoramic photograph shows the Colonnaded Street in its entirety. In the foreground is Temenos Gate.

196 bottom left The columns flanking the main street in Petra date back to the Roman period town-planning activity.

The contrast between the dim precipice and the delicately pink stone of the monument is quite impressive, to say the least, as are its perfect symmetry and exquisitely refined proportions. The façade is 131 feet high and 82 feet wide and is divided into two registers, the lower one consisting of a pedimented portico with six Corinthian columns 41 feet high. Between the two pairs of outer columns there are two colossal equestrian groups in bas-relief, now quite deteriorated, depicting the Dioscures. The frieze decoration comprises a series of facing griffons, while the tympanum, in the middle of which there was a Gorgon's head (which some scholars believe is an eagle with outspread wings), is decorated with volutes. In the corners of the architrave, two lions serve as acroteria. The upper register,

characterized by ethereal elegance, is divided into three elements: in the middle is a *tholos*–a small round temple, on a reduced scale, a typical feature of the local architecture–with a conical roof surmounted by an urn. The Arab name of the edifice, 'Treasury,' derives from this last-mentioned element. Indeed, the Bedouin believed that great riches lay hidden in the interior and in their attempt to find it they shot at the monument with their rifles in order to break it open.

The *tholos* is flanked by two semi-pediments, each supported by four corner columns. The niches contain reliefs of female figures that are unfortunately badly eroded: Amazons brandishing axes, Nike, the goddess of victory and, in the central section of the *tholos*, the goddess of fortune Tyche, who here looks like Isis. Lastly, four gigantic eagles served as the acroteria of the semi-pediments.

The interior of the Khazna is preceded by a large vestibule with eight steps leading into the central chamber, a large hall forty feet square, flanked on three sides by smaller chambers. The layout of the inner chambers and the lack of an altar, as well as the position of the monument in the narrow ravine which certainly would not have facilitated religious ceremonies–all lead to the conclusion that the Khazna was the monumental tomb of a local monarch

196 bottom right The west end of the Colonnaded Street had a monumental arch with three openings that was destroyed by a quake and partly reconstructed by archaeologists. This Roman structure served as the gate of the temenos (sacred precinct), on which stood the Qasr al-Bint temple.

rather than a temple, as was believed in the past.

Just past the Khazna, the Siq becomes wider and wider. To the left is the theater, which was entirely hewn out of the rock and whose tiers have a seating capacity of 6,000. Along the opposite cliff face, in a row, are the so-called Royal Tombs (the Tomb of Uneishu, the Tomb of the Urn, the multicolored Tomb of Silk, the elegant Corinthian Tomb, and the gigantic Palace Tomb), all built in the 1st century AD. The point where the Siq widens in the alluvial plain enclosed in the large

197 top Temenos gate was richly decorated with bas-relief panels with alternating busts of gods and floral motifs.

197 bottom The Temple of the Winged Lions was surrounded by several buildings, including artisans' workshops.

amphitheater of rock, marked the beginning of the residential area proper. Its main street, which was completely paved and colonnaded, ran parallel to the present-day route of the Wadi Musa, which at that time flowed between thick stonework embankments that were connected at several points. This spectacular artery was lined with various workshops and, to the south, with three complexes built on sloping terraces; these were commonly known as 'markets' (recently, one was identified as a ceremonial precinct that had

gardens and a pond). These edifices were followed by the Great Temple, which can be dated at the first half of the 1st century AD. On the opposite side of the Wadi Musa was a series of different constructions whose function is still an open question, what was perhaps a sumptuous royal palace, and the so-called Temple of the Winged Lions. The Colonnaded Street, whose present appearance is probably the result of the rebuilding work ordered by Trajan after 106 AD, ended in a monumental arch with three openings that

served as the gate of the *temenos*, the sacred precinct at the end of which stood the gigantic temple known as Qasr al-Bint, the only surviving free-standing edifice in Petra. A short distance from the temple is the new Archaeological Museum, near which is a path leading into a gorge that soon turns into a steep series of steps. After climbing up these for more than 1,150 feet one arrives at the Deir, or Monastery, which was built in the late 1st century AD and is undoubtedly the most grandiose monument in the Nabataean

198 top right Again
on the slopes of the al-
Habis massif, the
acropolis of Petra, is
the mysterious
hypogeum known as
the Columbarium.

198-199 Of all the
free-standing edifices
that constituted the
urban fabric of Petra,
the Qasr-al Bint
temple is the only
surviving one.

capital. The completely rock-cut façade of
the mortuary temple is 160 feet wide and
128 feet high. The lower register of the
façade, with pilasters at either end, has
eight half-columns that frame the two side
niches and the pedimented portal in the
middle. This entrance leads to a large
square hall, in the back wall of which is the
niche that housed the altar. On the upper
register, the façade has a central *tholos*, two
massive semi-pediments on either side,
and two projecting square antae. The
various architectural elements on the
second register are linked by a lovely
Doric frieze in which the metopes are
replaced by smooth disks.

The hill opposite the Deir offers a fine
view of the valley of Petra; however, the
best viewpoint to admire the Pink City is
without a doubt the summit of Jebel Attuf
mountain, where there is an open-air

199 top and bottom
right The Qasr al-
Bint, dating from the
second half of the 1st
century BC, was a
temple that was perhaps
dedicated to the two
chief local gods,
Dushara and Al Uzza.

199 bottom left The
purpose of the
Columbarium has
not yet been
ascertained; it may
have been a common
tomb, a rock-cut
temple, or a
columbarium.

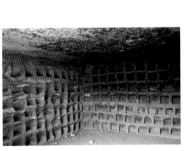

200-201 The rock-cut Deir—created in the 1st century AD— is perhaps the most grandiose, spectacular and impressive creation of Nabataean architecture. Situated in a col of the Jebel el-Deir, this cenotaph of Obodas I is 160 feet wide and 128 feet high.

200 bottom The size of the Deir is simply extraordinary: the cone-shaped top of the tholos alone, surmounted by an urn on a Nabataean capital, is 30 feet high.

201 top Along the ascent to the Deir is the Triclinium of the Lions. Structures of this kind, used for funerary banquets, were part of the most important tombs.

sanctuary, the High Place of Sacrifices, which can be reached by means of a steep path that begins near the theater. From here, Petra truly seems a fantasy instead of the splendid reality it is. The path that descends west from the Jebel Attuf to the Wadi Farasa gorge allows visitors to see some other interesting monuments such as the Garden Tomb, the Tomb of the Roman Soldier and the annexed Triclinium (whose interior, articulated into niches and pilaster strips, is certainly the most sumptuous of the over 800 hypogea in Petra), the Tomb of the Renaissance, and the Tomb of the Broken Pediment.

There is an age-old debate concerning the function of the rock-cut monuments

that make Petra so unique. Accurate studies have determined that they were used for the most part for funerary purposes, but some of them were actual residences consisting of several rooms connected to one another and with windows in the façade. These houses are decorated with frescos of vine shoots, floral motifs and polychromatic backgrounds.

201 center The Mughar an Nasara necropolis, situated northeast of the central section of Petra. The Tomb of Armor can be seen at the far left.

201 bottom The Triclinium of the Lions was named after the animal sacred to the local goddess, Al Uzza.

The architectural types at Petra are quite heterogeneous, each one a testimony of a different historical period as well as of a different cultural influence. Although not all scholars agree on the dating, and some actually believe that the various types of façades do not correspond to a specific chronological sequence, for reasons of convenience the various Nabataean architectural styles are usually divided in keeping with the following classification. The first tombs used by the Nabataeans–dating back to the 4th-3rd century BC–were the 'common graves,' which were for the most part rectangular, cut out of the rock and scattered everywhere in the area. The 'shaft tombs' must date from a later period. These are underground funerary chambers–which could be reached via a sort of chimney–where the corpses were laid inside graves covered with stone slabs. The 'dromos tombs' are quite similar; here the shaft is replaced by a horizontal corridor and the façade is smooth, with the

202 top left Facing the Tomb of the Roman Soldier is a large hall, the Triclinium, the polychrome walls of which have alternating niches and pilaster strips.

202 center left The austere Tomb of the Broken Pediment stands at the end of a steep stepped ramp on one side of the Wadi Farasa.

202 bottom The so-called Garden Tomb is an enigmatic monument: most scholars think it was a temple instead of a tomb.

door framed by simple pilaster strips and just a hint of a lintel. In the second century BC much more complex mortuary monuments, the 'Assyrian style tombs,' made their appearance. It is probable that the earliest had a very simple, smooth façade surmounted by only one row of stepped 'merlons,' the door of which was sometimes framed by half-columns. This type of sepulchre was a Nabataean adaptation of models that were widespread in nearby Syria.

202 top right A short way from the Tomb of the Broken Pediment is the singular Tomb of the Renaissance with its elegant portal.

202-203 The Tomb of the Roman Soldier, also in the Wadi Farasa, is a fine example of the 'classical Roman style.'

203 bottom left On the summit of Jebel Attuf are two monolithic obelisks about 22 feet high that were perhaps symbols of the gods Dushara and Al Uzza.

Later on a second row of merlons was placed above the first one.

The following two centuries witnessed the development of more sophisticated models that incorporated Egyptian influences. In the meantime a special type of capital, known as 'Nabataean,' had been created. The result of this evolution were the 'cavetto tombs,' in which the façade is crowned by a rather showy curved cornice similar to the so-called Egyptian *cyma*, on which lie only two large stepped merlons (these tombs are also known as 'stepped tombs'). The front often stands among pilaster strips with Nabataean capitals, and the door is surmounted by rather complex lintels. An elegant transformation of the preceding type is the 'double cornice tomb,' in which there is a second, classical-style cornice under the cavetto molding cornice. The attic story between the two cornices may be occupied by short antae with

203 bottom right Three high-ranking figures–perhaps an official and his sons–are portrayed in the niches on the façade of the Tomb of the Roman Soldier.

Nabataean capitals, and the façade usually has two or four pilaster strips framing an elaborate portal that is often surmounted by a tympanum pediment with acroteria. In the second half of the 1st century BC Petra began to use, on a large scale, certain architectural motifs from the Hellenized West (for example, the Doric frieze and the floral Corinthian capital) that may have been introduced by Alexandrian architects. The Khazna or Treasury belongs to this category and is the first example of the so-called classical Nabataean style. From this time on structural elements were employed more and more for purely decorative purposes, and it was not uncommon for them to be superposed, which naturally produced a chaotic effect. However, the provincial nature of Nabataean art, which developed in a region in the middle of the desert that was rather isolated from the Mediterranean hub, justified the persistence of autochthonous and obsolete decorative elements such as rosettes and animals facing one another in heraldic fashion. After the mid 1st century AD, the remarkable wealth of the architectural figurative motifs at Petra was flanked by a marked interest in theatrical grandiosity, and the rock-cut façades attained colossal proportions, with orders of columns superimposed to imitate temple façades and theater wings. The Corinthian Tomb and the Palace Tomb belong to this period, while the Deir seems to be the result of an isolated attempt to assert the achievement of a truly independent Nabataean style vis-à-vis the formal Hellenistic artistic vocabulary. Lastly, certain pediment tombs–that is, those with a temple-like façade–such as the Tomb of the Roman Soldier, belong to the so-called classic Roman style, sebsequent to 106 AD.

205 top left The Old Museum lies in a hypogeum cut out of the slopes of al-Habis that was probably a temple.

205 top right In a modern building constructed for this purpose, the New Museum houses works of art and everyday objects found during the digs at Petra.

205 bottom left The two side aisles of the Byzantine basilica have magnificent mosaic floors, which include this portrait of Oceanus. The mosaics at Petra were the work of highly specialized craftsmen and also reveal the persistence of pagan motifs in Early Christian culture.

205 right The male figure portrayed in this bust above the door of the Old Museum may be Serapis. It is a Roman copy of a Hellenistic original.

THE CRUSADER CASTLES, TESTIMONY OF A SANGUINARY PAST

Scattered amid the arid stretches of land north of Petra along the splendid Kings' Road, in the direction of Amman, are the remains of castles and forts, towers and *thermae*, caravanserais and palaces, that are known as the 'desert castles.' These monuments date back to different periods in the history of Jordan, from Roman dominion to the Omayyad dynasty and, lastly, the period of the Crusaders, who played such a fundamental role in one of the most epic and bloodthirsty chapters in the history of the Holy Land.

Situated a few miles north of Petra, As-Shawbak is perched on a rise that dominates the Kings' Road. Despite the ravages of both Man and time, this castle is particularly fascinating, partly thanks to its totally isolated position in the middle of a timeless land. It was built in 1115 at the behest of Baldwin I, Latin king of Jerusalem, and was originally called *Mons Regalis* because of its grandiosity. The castle was strategically extremely important because, together with the one at Kerak, it was part of a defensive system that was established to control the routes between Syria and Aqaba. However, its very importance proved to be the cause of its ruin: in 1189 As-Shawbak was besieged and then conquered by Saladin. It was then

abandoned in ruins until the 13th century, when the Mamluks restored it, making it one of their strongholds, a transformation that can be noted in the many inscriptions there. During the Ottoman period the castle was no longer useful in controlling the Kings' Road and was therefore abandoned for good. Today the remains comprise the massive wall with its towers, the ruins of a Crusader church and chapel, as well as part of the Mamluk structures. The extremely long stairway built by the Crusaders, which descends into the depths of the hill as far as the aquifer that supplied the garrison with its water supply, is very interesting but also extremely difficult and dangerous.

206 top A museum occupies some of the halls of Kerak castle, with finds ranging from the Bronze Age to the Mamluk period.

206 center Kerak castle lies in a strategic position about 3,116 feet above the sea level along the Kings' Road, which runs from Amman to Aqaba.

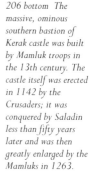

206 bottom The massive, ominous southern bastion of Kerak castle was built by Mamluk troops in the 13th century. The castle itself was erected in 1142 by the Crusaders; it was conquered by Saladin less than fifty years later and was then greatly enlarged by the Mamluks in 1263.

The most famous citadel in Jordan is without a doubt the one at Kerak, a city about 80 miles south of Amman that is also located along the enchanting Kings' Road. The modern-day city occupies the site of Kharak Muba, the ancient capital of the biblical kingdom of Moab. It was conquered by the Assyrians, the Nabataeans and the

206-207 The As-Shawbak castle stands on the top of a hill, dominating the Kings' Road. Its majestic appearance justifies its ancient name—Mons Regalis.

207 top These pointed arches are all that remains of the Crusader church inside the walls of As-Shawbak. The castle was captured by Saladin's troops in 1189.

207 bottom left Inside As-Shawbak castle is a small exhibition of various medieval artifacts, including several catapult missiles.

207 bottom right Many inscriptions in Arabic testify to the transformation the Crusader castle underwent in the 13th century at the hands of the Mamluks.

Romans, and flourished during the Byzantine period, when it became the archbishop's residence. The enormous citadel that to this day dominates the town was built in 1142 for the Crusader king Baldwin I in order to defend communications between Aqaba, Jerusalem and Syria from the Arabs. The last ruler of Kerak was the cruel Renauld de Chatillon, who made himself notorious by having his prisoners thrown from the bulwarks of the castle. Besieged by Saladin in 1183 and conquered in 1189, the citadel was later occupied by a Mamluk garrison, which effected many architectural changes. It was then taken over by the Ottomans and again restored and rebuilt, until it was finally abandoned during the 16th century.

Despite the repeated destruction it has suffered, the fortress is still quite impressive:

it has a roughly trapezoidal plan, is surrounded by very steep escarpments, with massive towers along the entire length of the wall, which on the west side is a double curtain wall. The north side, originally built by the Crusaders, has preserved its entrance portal and some halls with vaulted stonework ceilings. The massive south tower, rebuilt by the Mamluks

in the 13th century, is remarkable. Inside the wall are several rooms used for different purposes (stables, workshops, kitchens, dormitories), bread-making ovens, a large cistern and a good archaeological museum. Interestingly enough, the Crusader period walls are made of dark balsaltic stone, while the Mamluk ones consist of light-colored limestone.

MADABA,
THE HOLY LAND REVEALED

his very ancient city situated 20 miles from Amman on the Kings' Road is famous above all for the splendid Byzantine mosaic pavements that once decorated the many Christian churches as well as the public buildings and private houses. The most celebrated mosaic of all is without a doubt the one kept in the Greek-Orthodox St. George's Cathedral, a rather recent and somewhat nondescript edifice that is the result of reconstruction work effected in 1880: this is the Map of Palestine (or Madaba Map), which represents a large geographic area between the coast of Lebanon and the Nile river Delta, and from the Mediterranean to the desert. Although many parts of the map were destroyed when the church was rebuilt over and over again, the sections that have been preserved include no fewer than 157 localities with their Greek names, the salient architectural features of the chief cities and many orographical features as well. The

208 top Madaba is famous for the spectacular mosaic pavements in the Byzantine churches. The 6th-century mosaics seen here are in the Hall of Hippolytus.

208 bottom The present-day Church of St. George, which houses the Map of Palestine, was rebuilt in 1880.

mosaic–which dates from the second half of the 6th century AD and originally must have consisted of over two million polychrome tesserae–is of fundamental importance for the study of the Holy Land in the Byzantine period. Besides the Jordan River, the Dead Sea and the mountain chains, the map contains the most important biblical localities, such as Jericho and Bethlehem; the largest city, Jerusalem, is immediately recognizable and scholars have identified 38 streets and monuments, including the Holy Sepulchre and the Nea Basilica, which is now in ruins.

Among the other edifices in Madaba that have fine mosaics, mention should be made of the 8th-century Church of the Virgin Mary and the adjacent Hall of Hippolytus, in which a mosaic dating from the mid 6th century AD drew inspiration from the Greek tragedy by Euripides; the Church of the Apostles, with a mosaic dated at 578, in the middle of which is the female personification of the sea; the Cathedral, with the chapels of the martyr Theodore (the pavement of which dates back to 562) and the Baptistery. Other mosaic fragments are kept in the local Archaeological Museum, which is extremely interesting.

209 bottom This amphora among plant motifs in the Madaba Archaeological Museum is part of the mosaic decoration in the Church of the Acropolis of Ma'in.

208-209 150 localities can be identified in the famous mosaic known as the Map of Palestine. In the middle is the Dead Sea; just below it is 'the holy city of Jerusalem,' rendered in detail.

209 top A detail from the Hall of Hippolytus that is the personification of one of the four seasons.

209 center A few miles west of Madaba is the locality of Ma'in. Among the ruins of the Church of the Acropolis archaeologists found a mosaic that depicts some Jordanian cities, among other things. This detail is of Gadara.

MOUNT NEBO AND THE PROMISED LAND

Situated six miles from Madaba and about twenty-five from Amman, Mount Nebo (or Jebel Naba, 2,637 feet above the sea level) is famous because according to biblical tradition Moses climbed up this mountain at God's behest to contemplate the Promised Land before dying. And indeed, when the sky is clear the view is simply superb, ranging from the low Jordan River valley to the Dead Sea, and even taking in Jerusalem. On the western summit of the mountain, known as Jebel al-Siyagha, archaeological excavations carried out by Franciscan friars from the 1930s on have brought to light the foundation of a large basilica that was built in the 6th century over what was reputedly Moses' tomb; it is now covered by a modern structure. The apsidal section consists of the original church with a trefoiled cruciform plan that dates back to the mid 4th century. The Byzantine complex comprised a room known as the *diaconicón* (a sort of sacristy where the holy objects were kept), a baptistery, and the Chapel of the Virgin (the *Theotokos*). Next to the

church–which was originally preceded by a large square courtyard–was a large monastery whose foundation was unearthed by archaeologists. Besides the noteworthy 6th-century decorated capitals inside the basilica, there are some extraordinary mosaic floors, the most beautiful of which (at right, in the *diaconicón*) was executed in 531 by three artists whose names have been found (Kaiomos, Soelos and Elias). The central section has a remarkably lively representation of hunting and sheep-farming scenes that are divided into four registers framed by braid motifs. The lower register depicts two figures–a white man and a black man–holding a zebra, a dromedary and an ostrich by their reins. The mosaics in the baptistery and the *Theotokos* (to the left) are also quite lovely. The basilica also has splendid mosaic pavements from other buildings and churches in the area that are mounted on vertical panels so they can be distinguished from those found *in situ*. A fragment from St. George's Church, depicting two gazelles, contains the oldest archaic Arabic inscription in Jordan.

210 left These two pictures show the apse and interior of the Byzantine basilica of Mount Nebo, built in two phases from 350 to 550 and then abandoned in the 9th century.

210 bottom left The basilica at Mount Nebo contains many mosaics from other churches in the region.

210 top right This mosaic has a word (at left) that many scholars think was written in archaic Arabic: bisalameh, 'in peace.'

210-211 The splendid mosaic pavement in the diaconicón (sacristy) was discovered in 1976. The sheep-farming and hunting scenes are obvious references to the Classic age. The diaconicón was the baptistery of the original church and took on its new function in the second half of the 6th century.

211 A common motif in Early Christian art, the peacock was the symbol of immortality. This detail is from the mosaic pavement in the Byzantine church of St. George, in the nearby village of Khirbet el-Mukhayyat, which has also been reconstructed in the Mount Nebo basilica.

AMMAN, ANCIENT PHILADELPHIA

The capital of Jordan is a metropolis with a long and troubled history going back to ancient times that is reflected in its present-day appearance. The singular contrast between the ancient and recent buildings, with no traces of intermediate phases, is in fact one of the most evident features of the city. Amman was founded during the late Bronze Age (around 1300 BC) by the Ammonites, who called it 'Rabbath Ammon.' Its builders were part of a population of Syrians that had settled east of the Jordan River and were in constant conflict with the Israelites. It is therefore no accident that the settlement was besieged and finally conquered by King David around 985 BC, was retaken shortly afterwards by the Ammonites, who were subdued by the Assyrians, who in turn were replaced by the Babylonians.

In the first half of the 3rd century BC the city was named Philadelphia in honor of the Hellenistic ruler Ptolemy II Philadelphus, who had annexed the city. In 218 BC it fell under the yoke of the Seleucids of Syria and later on was conquered by the Nabataeans. In 30 BC the Roman general Pompey took the city,

212-213 Built in 169-177 during the reign of Marcus Aurelius, the Roman theater is still used as a venue for shows.

212 left The three surviving columns in the Temple of Hercules, built by Marcus Aurelius, are on the acropolis.

enjoyed another 'golden age.' During the Abbasid and Fatimid periods the city declined and was finally abandoned under the Mamluks, remaining virtually deserted until 1868, when it was repopulated by Circassian colonists.

After the fall of the Ottoman Empire Amman underwent large-scale rebuilding. Chosen as the capital of Transjordan in 1921 and of the Kingdom of Jordan in 1950, the city is now a young capital that boasts extremely interesting ancient monuments. Scattered among the modern buildings are grandiose Imperial-Age ruins, such as the Roman theater and nearby odeon. The theater, which is in the lower part of the city center, in the Wadi Amman valley, has preserved its spectacular tiers built on the slope of a hill that are divided into three horizontal sections (*ima, media* and *summa cavea*) with a seating capacity of over 6,000. In the middle of the upper section there is

212 right The odeon at Amman, with its serene elegance, was superbly restored quite recently. The tiers, which originally could seat 500 spectators, was divided into two horizontal sections.

213 right The National Archaeological Museum, housed in a modern building on the acropolis, boasts finds from all of Jordan, with large Hellenistic, Nabataean and Roman collections.

213 bottom left The so-called Audience Hall is the best preserved part of the al-Qasr, the Ommayad

palace built between 720 and 750 on the acropolis. This area, where the most ancient district in Amman rose up, also has the remains of a Roman street and the ruins of a one-apse Byzantine basilica.

which became part of the *Decapolis* confederation. Amman flourished because of its strategic position along the caravan route from Bosra (in Syria) to Petra and the Gulf of Aqaba, reaching its apogee in the 2nd-3rd century BC. In 106 AD it became part of the Roman province of Arabia and was a diocese in the Byzantine age. In 635 it was conquered by the Arabs and during the Ommayad period (661-750)

an exedra flanked by two apsidal niches. What remains of the stage and the skene is the fruit of meticulous restoration work and anastylosis. Similar reconstruction was effected in the adjacent odeon, which like the theater was built in the 2nd century AD: besides the cavea, which was restored to its original state, the orchestra and lower part of the skene are in a good state of preservation. Between the odeon and the theater there once lay the Forum of Amman, one of the largest in the entire Roman Empire: the remains comprise the spectacular southern Corinthian order colonnade and part of the western one. Curiously enough, the Forum had a trapezoidal shape.

On the hill of the citadel, which was the ancient acropolis, there are three Corinthian columns from a Roman temple dedicated to Hercules that was built in 161-169. Not far away are the ruins of a 6th-century Byzantine church and a sumptuous Umayyad palace known as al-Qasr, with the well-preserved Audience Hall, which has a Greek cross layout and a wealth of sculpted decoration.

ARAQ AL-AMIR,
HYRCANUS' PALACE

214 top The long western side and the southern façade of the Qasr el-Abd, also known as Hyrcanus' Palace.

214 bottom In the west side of the monument is a fountain consisting of a huge monolith with high-relief sculpture of a lioness and her cub.

The locality of Araq al-Amir, eleven miles west of Amman, is famous for the majestic ruins of a 'fortress' (known as Qasr el-Abd), which was built in the early 2nd century BC. It seems that the construction, situated in a striking position in the middle of a cirque, stood in the middle of a small artificial lake, which no longer exists, that was fed by an aqueduct some remains of which can still be seen. This extraordinary edifice

is one of best examples of a Hellenistic palace that has survived to our time, and much of its original structure was carefully restored in the 1990s. It has a rectangular layout, with four massive towers at the corners (only the lower section of which remains), and was built with enormous blocks of stone, some of which weigh as much as 20 tons. Scholars seem to agree that the entire structure—covered with flat roofs—was two storys high and had large cisterns to collect water. The ground floor housed the storerooms for provisions, while the upper level, which can be reached by means of a stairway in the northeast tower, was the residence proper. The north side has a two-column portico surmounted by a frieze with reliefs of lions and lionesses that runs onto the outer sides of the corner towers as well. Over the frieze was a loggia with six

pilasters, with a corresponding number of large windows in the towers, each one divided by two columns. The long sides of the palace each have seven windows, while on the south side there is a portico similar to the one on the north side which, however, is lacking the part above the trabeation. Scholars today feel that rather than a fortress, the Qasr al-Abd was a residential palace built at the behest of Tobias Hyrcanus, who belonged to the powerful Tobiad family, which had created a small buffer state for itself in this region that was a bone of contention between the Ptolemies of Egypt and the Seleucids of Syria. Some elements of the structure have led scholars to presume that the palace was never finished but was used all the same. It was then transformed into a monastery by the Byzantine rulers.

214-215 The interior of Qasr el-Abd shows that the palace was not finished and was then used for different purposes in Byzantine times. It was then destroyed by an earthquake, perhaps in the mid 8th century.

215 bottom The attribution of Qasr el-Abd to King Hyrcanus is substantiated by the description given by Flavius Josephus. This photo shows the eastern side of the edifice, along which is another fountain decorated with a lion.

GERASA, THE CITY OF APHRODITE

216-217 The cardo maximus from the oval Forum to the propylaea of the Temple of Artemis. Halfway down the street are the ruins of the southern tetrapylon.

216 bottom left From the Forum to the northern tetrapylon the cardo maximus was lined with elegant Corinthian-order colonnades.

216 bottom right The ruins of the north tetrapylon—a large arch with four façades—stand at the junction of the cardo *and the north* decumanus.

The ancient city of Gerasa, now called Jerash, lies about 22 miles north of Amman in a broad valley with a small river, the Chrysorhoas (now known as the Wadi Gerasa). The city was founded in the 4th century BC by a population of Semitic extraction in a site that had already been settled during the Neolithic era. During the Hellenistic period Gerasa was populated by the Macedonian veterans of Alexander the Great's troops and became a flourishing commercial city. When it fell under the Roman sphere of influence in the late 1st century BC, it became one of the metropolises of the *Decapolis*, the confederation of ten cities of which Gerasa is the best preserved. In the second half of the 1st century AD the city enjoyed great prosperity thanks to the caravan trade, achieving its 'golden age' during the reign of emperor Antoninus Pius. After a period of decadence in the years bridging the 3rd and 4th centuries, Gerasa—which had become Christian—went through another, brief phase of prosperity under Justinian (527-566), when many churches with fine mosaic pavements were constructed. The city was razed to the ground in the Crusader period and was abandoned, being repopulated only in 1878. And it was precisely these centuries of oblivion

217 The elaborate portal of the Gerasa cathedral, which was founded around 400 AD, is on the cardo maximus *a few yards south of the* nymphaeum. *The church was built over an ancient temple.*

218-219 *The unique oval Roman Forum at Gerasa was surrounded by a colonnade with 160 Ionic columns. It was built in the 1st century AD, perhaps on the site of a more ancient marketplace.*

218 bottom left *The triumphal arch with three openings, built in 130 AD in honor of* Emperor Hadrian, *lies about 420 yards south of the south gate.*

218 bottom right *A view of the Temple of Zeus (161-166 AD) on a hill southwest of the Roman Forum. Its columns are 46 feet high.*

that kept the ruins of the Roman and Byzantine monuments in such a good state of preservation.

The ancient city (whose eastern sector is now mostly a modern residential area) has a Roman grid plan, with a long street running from North to South, the *cardo maximus*, that is intersected at right angles by two other streets, the *decumani*, which in the center of town crosses the river via two bridges. About 1,300 feet outside the South Gate is a grandiose triumphal arch with three openings that was built in 130 AD on the occasion of the visit of Emperor Hadrian. Next to this is the hippodrome, which dates back to the mid 2nd century AD; it is 803 feet long and has a seating capacity of 15,000. Near the south gate of the city is Jerash Rest House, which also comprises the local information bureau and a restaurant. Upon entering the city proper, to the left is the Temple of Zeus, with its eight-column façade, built in 161-166 AD on the top of a hillock, and the South Theater,

sacred precinct (365,972 square feet), access to which is afforded by a monumental staircase that begins at the *cardo maximus*. The temple courtyard, 528 x 397 feet, was originally surrounded by a peristyle with a host of columns. The temple itself had two rows of six columns on the façade and one six-column row on the other three sides, and stood on a podium 131 feet long, 74 feet wide and slightly more than 13 feet high. Its

whose tiers can seat 3,000 spectators.

Just opposite the Temple of Zeus was the extremely original Forum, which is the only one of its kind: instead of the usual rectangular plan, it is like an oval plaza, 298 x 262 feet, surrounded by an arcade with Ionic columns that housed a long line of shops. Some scholars claim that the Forum of Gerasa, built in a natural depression, played an economic rather than political or religious role in the life of the city, a hypothesis also supported by its clearly decentralized position. According to this theory, the Romans made the large sanctuary of Artemis, located in the very heart of the city, the hub of Gerasa's social and spiritual life.

The temple dedicated to the tutelary goddess of Gerasa–one of the most splendid and best preserved Hellenistic-Roman monuments in the entire Near East–stands in the middle of an enormous

219 The inner façade of the south gate of Gerasa. The impressive city walls, with their 101 towers, had four gates (one to the south, one to the north and two to the west) and two passageways through which the Chrysorhoas River flowed.

surviving Corinthian columns are 43.2 feet high. The Temple of Artemis complex faces the *cardo maximus* through a large *propylaeum*, which is counter-balanced by a similar structure on the opposite side of the street; the east *propylaeum* in turn gave access to a processional road that crossed the river by means of a massive bridge and connected the town center with the eastern sector. Near the west *propylaeum* is a large *nymphaeum*, the exedra of which was occupied by a large ornamental pool.

At the intersection of the *cardo maximus* and the two *decumani* there are two *tetrapyla*, south and east of the Temple of Artemis. The south *tetrapylon*, the more grandiose one, consisted of four pedestals, each of which supported four columns. This monument stands in the center of a circular plaza bounded by arcades with columns lined with shops. The north *tetrapylon* is smaller and lies in the center of the quadrivial crossroads of the *cardo* and second *decumanus*. Along the latter, between the *tetrapylon* and the Chrysorhoas River, lie the remains of a large bathing establishment known as the West Thermae, built in the 2nd century AD, which has the usual *calidarium*, *tepidarium* and *frigidarium*. On the opposite side of the *cardo maximus*, in the northwestern sector of the city, are the ruins of a theater built in 162-166 AD that is smaller than the South Theater. Among the other Roman monuments there is a second public bath complex that was discovered on the east bank of the river. Outside the north gate (115 AD), the *cardo maximus* is flanked by a long line of monumental tombs that continues as far as the ruins of a small Antonine period theater, in the vicinity of which there was

220 top This extremely elaborate niche decorates the façade of the grandiose western propylaeum *of the Temple of Artemis.*

220-221 The South Theater at Gerasa was built during the rule of emperor Domitian (81-96 AD).

220 bottom left Built in 191 AD along the cardo maximus, *the* nymphaeum *is one of the most splendid and best preserved monuments in ancient Gerasa.*

220 bottom right A singular view of the two rows of columns standing in front of the majestic Temple of Artemis.

221 top The Temple of Artemis façade had two parallel rows of six columns each, with Corinthian capitals. The impressive temple stood out in the middle of a large rectangular precinct that had peristyles on all four sides. Access to the sacred precinct was gained via the cardo maximus *by going up a monumental staircase preceded by a* propylaeum.

221 bottom Another view of the magnificent South Theater. Archaeologists have reconstructed the lower register of the skene, which is animated by columns and niches. This large construction had a seating capacity of 3,000.

a large pool that may have been used for aquatic spectacles connected with the feast of a local divinity.

Other noteworthy monuments in Gerasa are the numerous Christian churches–built from the early 5th century on–and the ruins of a synagogue with a fragmentary floor mosaic depicting pairs of animals ready to go on board Noah's Ark. There are also beautiful mosaic pavements in St. Theodore Church and in the monumental complex consisting of three adjoining churches dedicated respectively to St. John the Baptist, St. George, and Saints Cosmas and Damian. Lastly, the modern Archaeological Museum, a few yards east of the Forum, is well worth a visit.

PELLA, THE CITY OF BASILICAS

The city named after the ancient capital of Macedonia lies about 60 miles north of Amman. The ancient ruins, which were brought to light from 1979 on, lie in the vicinity of the humble village of Tabaqat al-Fahl and have been a windfall for the local economy. Founded by officers of Alexander the Great around 310 BC in a locality already inhabited in the Neolithic age and rich in springs, Pella was quite prosperous thanks to commerce and to its favorable position in the Jordan Valley.

222 top The large basilica, several columns of which were raised, was built in the late 4th century, when Pella was a diocese. It was destroyed by a quake in 747.

222 bottom At left we can see the large stairway added in the 6th century as a monumental entrance to the basilica. Nearby are the remains of the Roman odeon.

During the period of Roman dominion it was part of the *Decapolis* and, according to Eusebius of Caesarea, in 70 AD offered refuge to Christians who had fled from Jerusalem, which was being attacked by Titus. Pella reached its maximum splendor between the 1st and 2nd century AD, the period of the construction of the small theater–or better, odeon (now in ruins) –in an enchanting position in the Wadi Jirm al Moz, a short distance from a perennial spring. Next to this edifice are the contemporary city *thermae*, whose water certainly came from the spring. Pella declined slowly from the 3rd century to the Byzantine period (5th-6th century), when a grandiose basilica and at least three other churches were built in the city. In 635 the Muslim armies defeated the Christians near the city and Pella took on the name of 'Fahl.' During the Omayyad dynasty building activity continued uninterruptedly, and an impressive mosque was added to the older monuments. In 747 a violent earthquake totally destroyed the center of town, which was abandoned until the 10th century, when it was reoccupied by the Abbasids. Under the Mamluks another mosque was built in the 15th-16th century; it is still being used as a place of worship.

The most interesting monument in Pella–besides the ruins of the Temple of Zeus Areios, the foundations of some Roman-Byzantine houses, and the above-mentioned odeon and *thermae*–is undoubtedly the adjacent basilica, built around 400 AD. A large court with a peristyle led to the nave with two aisles marked off by columns with Corinthian capitals. In the 6th century three apses were added, and about a century later, a monumental stairway, traces of which can still be seen, was built on the west side. In the nave, sections of the lavish mosaic pavement are still visible.

222-223 Another inspiring view of the basilica of Pella. There are ruins of three other churches, dating from the 4th-5th century, which demonstrate the rapid rise of Christianity in the city.

APSE: a semicircular, vaulted architectural structure usually at the east end of a chancel or chapel.

ADYTON: inner sanctuary of a temple.

AMBULATORY: passageway stretched between inner columnades and perimetral walls of a church.

ANASTYLOSIS: rebuilding of ancient structures.

ANTA (-AE): a pier produced by thickening a wall at its termination.

ARK OF THE COVENANT: mythical container of the Tablets of the Law; according to tradition, in the First Temple it was placed on the foundation stone, on which the world was created.

ARON HAKODESH: in Hebrew, "holy ark"; the cabinet in synagogues used to house the scrolls of the Torah, either set against or into the wall facing Jerusalem.

BASILICA: oblongated rectangular building shared in naves by two columnades or more, and ending in one or more apses.

BAMAH: cultic elevated platform, originally cananean, later found in churches and synagogues

BET HA-KENESET: synagogue; literally, 'meeting house.'

CALIDARIUM: hall in a Roman public bath with warm water.

CARDO MAXIMUS: street that crosses Roman camps and cities in a North-South direction, perpendicular to the *decumanus*.

CASEMATE WALL: fortification wall composed by two parallel walls filled with debris in case of danger.

CASTRUM: fortified roman camp, shared in quarters by the Cardo and the Decumanus.

CAVEA: the tiers for spectators in an ancient theater.

CELLA: central chamber of temples and sanctuaries, often containing the statue of the god.

DECUMANUS: streets that cross Roman camps and cities in an East-West direction, at right angles with the *cardo*.

DIADOCHOI: everyone of the immediate successors of Alexander the Great.

DISTYLE, TETRASTYLE etc.: indicates the number of columns erected along the front of a temple.

EN (Heb.) EIN, AIN (Arab.): spring.

ENCAUSTIC PAINTING: ancient pictorial tecnique in which the colors are melted with hot wax.

FRIGIDARIUM: hall in a Roman public bath with cold water.

ETHROG: cedar used in the Jewish feast day of the Sukkot.

HEGIRA: the flight of Muhammad from Mecca to Medina, marks the beginning of the Muslim era.

HYPOCAUST: ancient Roman heating system with underground furnace and tile flues to distribute the heat.

HYPOGEUM: underground room or channel.

HYPETRAL: building with a roofless central space.

ICONOCLAST: member of the byzantine heretical movement pursuing the destruction of religious images in order to stop idolatry.

INTERCOLUMIATION: the distance between two adiacent columns.

IN ANTIS: columns set between two *anta* (see *anta*).

KABBALAH: mystic Jewish doctrine based on the interpetation of the esoteric passages in the Old Testament.

KEEP: the most fortified stronghold of medieval and Renaissance castles.

KHAN/CARAVANSERAI: typical Islamic commercial building laid out around a central courtyard; the ground floor had storerooms, and on the first floor were lodgings for the merchants.

LAURA: a Greek Orthodox monastery typical of desert areas, organized to house hermits who dwell in local caves or cells.

LOCULUS: a rock-cut recess in an ancient tomb or catacomb that houses the body or funerary urn of the deceased. An arched cell or niche used to house a sarcophagus is called an *arcosolium*.

LULAV: palm, myrtle or willow branches used together with cedar in the Jewish feast day of the Sukkot.

MADRASA: an Islamic theological school.

MARTYRION: basilica dedicated to the Martyrs.

MENORAH: the seven-branched Jewish candelabrum used in synagogues.

MIDRASH: research and commentaries on a biblical text.

MIHRAB: nich in the mosques that indicates the direction of Mecca, which the faithful must face while praying.

MIKVEH: Jewish ritual bath.

MINARET: tower adjacent to the mosque from which the *muezzin* calls the faithful to prayer.

MINBAR: pulpit in the mosques.

MISHNAH: systematic codification of the Judaic oral tradition compiled at the end of the 2nd century AD.

NAHAL: seasonal waterstream.

NAOS: the innermost chamber (or stone or wooden tabernacle) in a pagan temple containing the statue of the god.

NARTHEX: vestibule leading to the nave of the early Christian church.

NECROPOLIS: cemetery, usually ancient, of archaeological importance.

NEFESH: literally meaning "Soul", indicates a funerary stela typical of the Semitic cultures.

OSTRAKON: inscribed fragment of pottery vessel.

PERIPTERAL: building, usually a temple, enclosed with and held up by one continuous colonnade.

PERISTYLE: open courtyard surrounded by columns.

PRONAOS: vestibule in temples and tombs giving access to the *naos*.

PROPYLAEUM (-EA): structure containing the grand gateway to a sacred or other particularly important place.

SANHENDRIN: the Jewish Supreme Council in Palestine during the Graeco-Roman period.

SHOFAR: musical instrument made of a ram's horn used during the Jewish New Year and other holy holidays.

TALMUD: compilation of rabbinical discussions and interpretations of the Mishnah (3rd-5th century AD).

TEL, TELL: artificial hill consisting of the accumulated layers of successive ancient settlements.

TEMENOS: sacred precinct of a sanctuary encircled by a wall.

TEPIDARIUM: warm room in the Roman baths used for massages after a hot bath and sauna.

TETRAPYLON: structure built at the intersection of the streets in the roman cities, composed by four piers bearing columns.

TORAH: the Jewish Scriptures, or Pentateuch, and the corresponding oral tradition.

VESTIBULE: the colonnaded entrance court of the temple sanctuary.

VOMITORIUM: entrance to the *cavea* (see *cavea*) of a theater or amphitheater.

WADI: typical desert ravine torrent that is usually arid but often floods during the rainy season.

ESSENTIAL BIBLIOGRAPHY

A.A.V.V. *The New Encyclopedia of Archaeological Excavations in the Holy Land*, Jerusalem 1993.

Aharoni Y., *The Land of the Bible: A Historical Geography*, London-Philadelphia, 1979.

Barnavi, E. (a cura di), *Atlante storico del popolo ebraico*, Bologna 1995.

Bem-Arieh Y., *The Rediscovery of the Holy Land in the Nineteenth Century*, Jerusalem 1979.

Benvenisti M., *The Crusaders in the Holy Land*, Jerusalem 1970.

Grant M., *L'antica civiltà d'Israele - Il popolo della Bibbia alla luce della storia*, Milano 1984.

Kochav S., *Israele - Viaggio nell'arte e nella storia della Terra Santa*, Vercelli 1995.

Murphy-O'Connor J., *La Terra Santa, Guida storico archeologica*, Bologna 1996.

Shanks H., *Judaism in Stone, the Archaeology of Ancient Synagogues*, Jerusalem 1979.

Dichter B.,*The Orders and Churches of Crusader Acre*, Akko 1979.

Raban A., *The Harbors of Caesarea Maritima*, Oxford 1989.

Negev A., *Personal Names in the Nabatean Realm*, Jerusalem 1991.

Rostovtzeff M., *Città carovaniere*, Bari 1971.

Avigad N., *Discovering Jerusalem*, Oxford 1984.

Bahat D.,*Carta's Historical Atlas of Jerusalem*, Jerusalem 1986.

Brunelli R., *Storia di Gerusalemme*, Milano 1990.

Dehan E., *The Jewish Quarter in the Old City of Jerusalem*, Jerusalem 1984.

Kroyanker D., *Jerusalem Architecture*, New York 1994.

Yadin Y., *Jerusalem Revealed - Archaeology in the Holy City 1968-1974*, Jerusalem 1976.

Wager E., Illustrated Guide to Jerusalem, Jerusalem1988.

Corbo V., *Herodium I, gli edifici della reggia-fortezza*, Gerusalemme 1989.

Netzer E., *Herodium: An Archaeological Guide*, Jerusalem 1987.

Davies G.I., *Megiddo*, Cambridge 1986.

Bourbon F., *Petra, Guida archeologica alla città scolpita nella roccia*, Vercelli 1999.

Vermes G., *The Dead Sea Scrolls: Qumran in Perspective*, London 1977.
Papaioannou E., *The Monastery of St. Catherine - Sinai*, St Catherine, s.a.
Dothan M., *Hammath Tiberias: Early Synagogues and the Hellenistic and Roman Remains*, Jerusalem 1983.

PERIODICALS
Biblical Archaelogical Review, Biblical Archaelogical Society, Washington DC.
Eretz, The Geographic Magazin from Israel, Givatayim.
Palestine Exploration Quaterly, Palestine Exploration Fund, London.

INDEX

Picture credits

228 The artists who created the Zodiac mosaic at Hammat Tiberias have succeeded in stopping time in their sublime work: for seventeen centuries Leo has made his celestial leap and Autumn offers the fruit of its grape harvest to the Sun.

Cover

The Dome of the Rock, in Jerusalem.
© Itamar Grinberg

Top left
Cesarea's fortifications.
© Antonio Attini /
Archivio White Star

Back cover

Top
The ruins of Herodium.
© Itamar Grinberg

Center
The Deir, in Petra.
© Massimo Borchi /
Archivio White Star

Bottom
Masada Rock.
© Itamar Grinberg